STRANGERS

ON THE

WATER

ONE FAMILY'S INCREDIBLE JOURNEY TO AMERICA

JOHN DOAN

STEVEN E. JUSTICE

With all the love and admiration,
I dedicate this book to my Mom and Dad,
who gave birth, raised, and loved their children unconditionally.

John Doan would like to thank: my brother Doat, my sister Thi Tuyen, and my younger siblings: Kim Tuyen, Joe, and Tom for helping one another through the Vietnam War and assisting Mom and Dad by taking care of the younger siblings, my partner Luke Jones for being patient and giving support throughout the years, my friend Dan Maloney for his support and encouragement in this project, my friend Laurie Volkmar, who introduced me to Steven E. Justice who brought my stories to life. Lastly, I would like to thank everyone who has touched my life and volunteered their time to make the world a better place.

Steven E. Justice would like to thank: my lovely and supportive wife Vicki for tolerating my grumpiness for two years, Caroline Justice for her marketing and social media expertise, Anita Damian for her legal guidance, Margaret Howell and her excellent editing skills, Barry Justice for his help with U.S. Navy history, Phyllis Owens, who is still teaching me grammar after 40 years, John Doan, the entire Doan family, and Luke Jones for letting me be a part of your lives, and Laurie Volkmar, who put me in touch with John and gave me this wonderful journey.

Prologue

I t was an unusual place for war, but war chose it anyway. Tucked into an inconspicuous corner of Asia, the land we call Vietnam was cursed to be an object of imperial desire. Despite its minimal strategic value and modest natural resources, it was coveted by emperors in search of colonies. For more than 2,000 years, the great powers of the world came to conquer. But the people of this watery stretch of land on the western edge of the South China Sea treasured their independence and learned to fight for it - until fighting became a part of their identity. They never backed down, never quit, no matter the size of the opponent. More than once they failed. But the people of Vietnam never forgot who they were.

For a thousand years China possessed it, burning its culture—and a growing defiance—into the hearts of the people. Finally, in 938 A.D., the Vietnamese destroyed the Chinese navy and established their independent kingdom. The Chinese didn't go away. They attempted to recapture Dai Viet for hundreds more years before the emperor to the north accepted that the fierce people of the Red River Delta could not be effectively subjugated. War had become a way of life for the

Vietnamese. They could be defeated, but they could never be enslaved.

The lessons China learned the hard way would not be heeded by other countries. When the Industrial Revolution turned Western Europe into a giant factory, it created an insatiable appetite for manpower and raw materials. Britain and France, powerful and bitter rivals, joined the game, carving the world into possessions to be owned and exploited. With their advanced technology and weaponry, conquest came easily over poor, agrarian societies with obsolete weapons.

In the mid-nineteenth century, countries available for the taking were rapidly disappearing. Britain was the clear winner of the imperial game, having captured Australia, India, and much of Africa. Its jealous rival France was looking to make a play and turned its gaze to Vietnam. Vietnam had rice, rubber, and the muddy Mekong River, which was a direct water route to the riches of interior China.

In the summer of 1858, French troops landed at Da Nang on the central Vietnam coast. Resistance crumbled in days and the French had their colony. For the next 20 years, France would expand and consolidate its holdings until it owned all of Vietnam, as well as neighboring Laos and Cambodia. The colony was named French Indochina.

Instead of trying to win the loyalty of their new subjects, the French invaders chose to exploit and abuse them. They were cruel masters, conscripting natives for construction projects and taxing the already impoverished citizens. What these westerners did not know was that the people they meant to rule had been resisting invaders since a time when France was called Gaul and living under their own occupiers, the

Romans. The arrogant colonials viewed the Vietnamese merely as capital to be expended, ignoring their humanity and their history. Their brutality created a growing resentment that would be the seed of rebellion. It would be a rebellion that would tear the country apart and inflict decade upon decade of misery.

Every uprising has a leader. In 1890, that leader was born in an inconspicuous village in the province of Nghe An, a rugged land rich in scenic beauty, with green mountains that tumble into a placid sea. The boy's name was Nguyen Sinh Cung. As he grew, Cung's thirst for learning became apparent. He nearly always had a book in his hands.

When a Vietnamese boy entered adolescence in those days, it was customary for parents to give the child a new name. Cung's father gave him the name Nguyen Tat Thanh, meaning "he who will succeed," and sent the newly christened Thanh to a village school. The teacher was a clandestine radical who agitated against the puppet government installed by France. He indoctrinated his students to do the same. It was here that the fire of patriotism was first ignited in Thanh, who became possessed by a desire to see Vietnam free of the colonial yoke.

In 1907, Thanh's father received an appointment to a government position in Hue, the imperial capital. Both Thanh and his brother were accepted into the city's prestigious National Academy, a European-style school founded and governed by the French. Thanh's understanding of the French language improved dramatically at the academy. While he was a student, demonstrations against French rule spread ominously through the country.

In 1908, a large protest erupted in Hue. Farmers streamed into the city to voice their demands for lower taxes and an end to conscripted labor. Thanh and a few other students decided to join the protest to serve as translators between the angry peasants and the French-speaking authorities. The day ended in horror as police attacked the agitated crowd. Several people were killed. Because he was so close to the front to help translate, Thanh was beaten by the police. Worse still, he was recognized as a student at the Academy.

Thanh was expelled from school. In addition to his expulsion, his name had been blacklisted by the government, making it impossible for him to find work. He made his way south, to the port of Saigon, and boarded a steamer bound for France. He told a friend that if he was going to help defeat the French and liberate his country, he had to go to the source of their success and see it for himself. As his ship glided out of the Mekong into the South China Sea, Thanh had no idea that 30 years would pass before he would see his country again. He began his journey as a lowly cook's assistant on a ship bound for Marseilles. He would return a conqueror.

In France, Thanh entered a boiling cauldron of political unrest that would soon explode into a horrific world war that would begin dismantling the old imperial order of Europe and reconfigure the balance of power in the entire world. This coming world war, and the worse one that would follow, would touch every habitable continent on earth and come to define the twentieth century.

Over the next 20 years, Thanh turned to communism and became a leader in the movement. The corrupt brand of crony capitalism he had seen in Vietnam, with its exploitation and abuse of power, undoubtedly influenced his thoughts. Communism, on the other hand, was as yet untested on the state level, having just been instituted in the newly formed Soviet Union. Its seductive promises of a cooperative system and fairness for those living at the bottom of the socioeconomic scale fit more naturally with the Vietnamese village mindset, which valued community effort over individual achievement. Mostly, though, Thanh's primary objective was liberation from colonial bondage. The economic model that would follow was of secondary concern to him.

As the 1920s and 30s unfolded, Thanh's abilities multiplied. The fires of social upheaval worked like a forge on his character, purifying and hardening him, erasing his reticence, and transforming him into a passionate advocate for his country. He was a small man, unimposing in every way except for his eyes, which burned with the intensity of the possessed.

Thanh had to change his name to throw off the French authorities who had taken notice of this increasingly troublesome agitator. The self-styled Nguyen Ai Quoc (Nguyen the Patriot) became the primary leader of the Vietnamese liberation movement and a rising star of the communist party.

As the 1930s ended, another war started. This war would forever alter the balance of power in the world. Few nations would be changed as much as Vietnam. France quickly succumbed to German conquest and became powerless to administer their far-flung colony on the other side of the world. Japan, sensing an opportunity, sent troops to occupy Vietnam and appropriate its rice and rubber. Nguyen Ai Quoc sensed an opportunity too. He reentered his country at last and built an army of peasants called the Viet Minh.

STRANGERS ON THE WATER

The boy born Nguyen Sinh Cung, who had gone by two other official names and multiple pen names and aliases, changed his name one last time just before his return home in 1941. It would be a name that would resonate throughout the world for the rest of the century. The name was Ho Chi Minh.

Part 1

Luong Dien, Thai Binh, North Vietnam

1

Dung, wake up, it is time to go get Phu."

Vu Thi Dung rolled over on her thatched sleeping mat. Her face was obscured by tangles of jet-black hair.

"Dung, get up," her mother called again. "Hurry, child, you can't be late."

The groggy girl scratched and yawned. She had a few more seasons before puberty hit, but the sleep-craving had already arrived. Gone was her mother's bright-eyed morning bird. A woman would take her place soon enough. Dung's mother sighed at the thought of fleeting childhood as she watched her lanky girl stretch as she walked across the room, astonished that her child seemed to grow overnight.

Dung grabbed a handful of cooked rice and a small piece of fish and started to walk out the door. Her mother cleared her throat. Dung stopped in her tracks. Her mother motioned to the handmade wooden cross beside the door. Dung crossed herself three times as the priest had instructed when she was taking the catechism.

"Hail Mary, full of grace," Dung mumbled as she disappeared out the door.

As she reached Phu's house, she could see him peering around the corner. Dung didn't always enjoy talking to people. The stultifying back-and-forth of conversation didn't appeal to her introverted nature. Animals, on the other hand, were delightful conversationalists. They

3

neither demanded response nor judged long silences. Dung brightened at the prospect of spending the day free of forced communication.

"There you are, Phu! Are you ready to go to the beach?"

Phu flapped his ears and swished his tail. The great buffalo ambled towards Dung with easy familiarity. She climbed aboard his broad gray back and patted the coarse hair of his shoulder. His thick coat was designed to shed the tremendous amounts of rain that fell during monsoon season. His imposing size and sharp, sweeping horns would be intimidating to most grown men, much less a skinny child, but to Dung, Phu was a baby and she was his babysitter.

The swamp buffalo of Vietnam were often called "tractors of the east," do-it-all animals that made life immeasurably easier for the hard-toiling farmers. Buffalo plowed the rice field, carried supplies, and served as family pets. Ownership of a single buffalo conferred status and provided income potential, as the owner could rent out the animal to neighbors who didn't have one. To own more than one buffalo meant a higher living standard and even more status.

The Vu family of Luong Dien village did not own a buffalo. They were at the bottom of the economic ladder. The precarious position of the family manifested itself in the tattered clothes that Dung had to wear and the rumbling that was often present in her stomach. Nearly every rice farmer in Luong Dien lived uncomfortably close to the margin of starvation. Dung and her family lived closer than most, which was especially dangerous since the great famine was now in its second year. Dung's parents never told her of the famine or its political origins, they just quietly ate less themselves so their children could eat and grow.

Vietnamese girls could not go to school, so Dung had time to supplement her family's income by taking care of Phu, who belonged to the elderly farmer, Nguyen. Nguyen had no children of his own to look after Phu, so Dung was assigned by her father to be the buffalo's caretaker. Every day, she had to feed him and keep him ready to plow. If there was no plowing to be done, Dung would take him to a pasture to graze all day.

Dung didn't mind. She loved Phu and treated him like a baby. She rode contentedly along the dirt road that served as Luong Dien's main street, swaying with Phu's lazy gait. The flat plain of Thai Binh province had few roads but was crisscrossed with canals that served the rice farms which patterned the land in neat green squares. Dung would ride south on this road to the Catholic Church and then turn left towards the sea.

"Hey, Dung, wait up," called a voice from behind. It was her friend Mai riding her family's buffalo. Mai was the same age as Dung and an unstoppable chatterbox, made even worse by the fact that she had recently become boy crazy. Dung rolled her eyes. Her quiet day was about to be buried by an avalanche of words.

"You know who the cutest boy in town is?" Mai asked.

Dung rolled her eyes again. She was not interested but she answered anyway.

"Who?"

"Dinh Doan," said Mai.

"I don't know him," said Dung, trying to manufacture some interest.

"He's older, but he's so cute," Mai said. "He is so serious. Acts like a grown-up. He will be a good husband to someone."

5

"Whatever," replied Dung.

As Mai continued reciting her list of Luong Dien's most eligible teenage boys, Dung was distracted by something going on in front of the church. In addition to the half dozen beggars—emaciated adults and children who had mysteriously started showing up about a year ago—a group of men, maybe five or six, huddled on the steps of the church in a tight circle. Dung's father was one of the men. Father Tran Thieu, the local priest, was talking to them. Dung could not hear what he was saying, but judging from his dramatic gestures, it must have been important.

After a few minutes of wondering what the priest could have been talking about, Dung dismissed it as probably boring adult stuff. She returned her attention to Mai, who had not stopped talking and had not noticed that Dung had stopped listening as they passed the church.

The girls made their way to the coast. The four-kilometer trip took almost two hours at the pace of an unhurried buffalo. Dung noticed more beggars along the road than usual, gaunt skeletons shuffling pitifully in search of food.

Dung interrupted Mai.

"Have you noticed more sick-looking people on the road today?"

Mai, clueless to anything beyond her awakening libido, shrugged her shoulders.

"They look like they are starving. So skinny," Dung said.

Mai shrugged her shoulders again. She was just about to change the subject when she let out a gasp.

Ahead of them, just off the road in a ditch, was a body. Dung followed Mai's gaze and her mouth dropped open. Gray and fly-

6

covered, the small corpse lay just as it had fallen. The girls stopped their animals and stared at it. The smell of rotting flesh was sickening.

"What should we do?" asked Dung.

Mai didn't answer. She just stared at it in horror.

After a few seconds more of staring, the girls gently nudged their buffaloes and rode on in silence. Neither girl had the capacity to process what they had just seen, except to know it was awful. Each worked independently to erase the memory. Because of her obsession with boys, Mai didn't really have room in her brain to dwell on the dead body, and was able to easily minimize the horrific scene. By the time the girls reached their destination, she was back to her old self again. Dung was not so lucky. The sight of the corpse, and all the ones to follow, would remain with her for a long, long time.

Just west of the beach dunes, a large pasture spread out before the girls. It was buffalo paradise, with acres upon acres of grass to eat. Dung and Mai were not alone. Dozens of girls and boys from nearby villages had brought their buffaloes to the field as well. After depositing their animals at the pasture, the girls crossed the dunes to play on the beach. Dung was still shaken from the sight on the road, but she felt a bit revived as she burrowed her feet into the cool sand. She loved the salty smell and the views of the endless sea, but she had no explorer's discontent. She loved her little village, her peaceful seashore, and her quiet life. When she was old enough, she figured she would be married to a rice farmer, have children, and spend the rest of her life in Luong Dien, just as her ancestors had done since creation.

"Hey, Dung, do you want to go out on the sandbar?" Mai asked.

7

Dung shook her head no. The large sandbar stretched more than two kilometers into the dark, deep water. Something about it looked haunted and gave her cold feelings of dread, as if death itself waited for someone foolish enough to trespass on that devil's beach. Her fear was born of a tale she once heard about children who had been stranded on the bar and drowned when the tide came in. That fear was compounded by what she had just seen on the road.

"Come on," Mai persisted, "the tide won't come in for hours."

"No," Dung said.

"Suit yourself, I see some cute boys out there," Mai said.

Dung watched as Mai waded through knee-high water to the sandbar. Anxiety welled up in her as she imagined her friend being swept out to sea by merciless waves, becoming a corpse like she had seen on the road. Dung held her breath, paralyzed.

After a few more seconds, Dung shook herself from the dream and began to breathe. She focused on Mai as she made her way around the bar, surveying each group of children as she passed. Eventually, Mai waded back across the water. When she reached Dung, she couldn't contain her excitement.

"There are so many boys out there I have never seen before! And they are all so cute! I wonder what villages they come from?"

Dung sighed, realizing that this would be the topic of conversation for the rest of the day. When the sun began to sink behind them, the girls returned to the pasture to find their animals who were still happily munching.

"Phu, did you get enough to eat? It's time to go home," Dung cooed at him.

Phu kept eating, but when Dung mounted his back, Phu turned and walked to the edge of the pasture. Dung steered him with her feet. The girls turned west for Luong Dien. Mai talked the whole way until they passed the body again. It was still there, frozen in its grotesque pose. The girls did not look at it this time. They held their breath as long as they could and nudged their buffaloes to go a little faster.

After returning Phu to his pen, Dung walked to her house. She had not eaten since leaving home that morning and she was famished. Her mother had a small bowl of rice and vegetables waiting for her.

As Dung ate, she decided to hazard a question to her father about what she had seen at the church and on the road. Her father was generally brooding and silent, so Dung worried that her attempt might be met with a harsh rebuke. She tried anyway.

"Papa, I saw you and the other men talking to Father Thieu this morning. What was he talking about?"

Dung's father had been sitting absentmindedly, lost in thought, but he bolted upright at the question and pierced the girl with his sharp black eyes. Dung braced for the worst. Instead, he drew a deep breath and began to speak.

"The Japanese have surrendered and are leaving. Ho Chi Minh gave a speech in Hanoi, declaring the country to be independent."

"Is that good?" Dung asked.

"It is good that the Japanese are leaving," her father answered, "the Japanese army caused this famine…"

Dung had never heard the word famine before, but decided to hold her question so as to not derail her father. He continued.

9

"…but Ho Chi Minh is a communist. The communists in Russia and China do not allow people to worship God. If he is successful, Vietnam will be communist."

Communist. Dung had not heard that word before, either. She turned it over in her mind. She wondered why anyone would want to prevent people from attending church.

"Can't somebody stop Ho Chi Minh?" Dung asked.

Her father answered, "The French were greatly damaged in their war with the Germans. They may not be strong enough to withstand the Viet Minh. Regardless of who wins, another war is coming." With these words, he let out a weary sigh.

"What can we do, Papa?"

"Pray," he said. "And work."

2

It was the Year of the Rooster, 1945. With a flash of light and cloud of fire, the Japanese were beaten. The Americans had unlocked the terrible power of the atom and built the most fearsome and destructive weapon in history. In an instant, an entire city and 100,000 souls were blown into dust.

In the wake of the departing Japanese, Death crept quietly through the rice fields of northern Vietnam preparing a different kind of harvest. The pressures of a military occupation throughout the war years had reduced the people's food supplies. Then the Americans bombed roads out of commission to weaken the supply lines to Japan's army. If that weren't enough to inflict misery on the people, a lingering drought in 1944, followed by storm damage and flooding in 1945, wrecked the harvest. Starvation soon followed. Death would claim between 500 thousand and 2 million lives, many times more than were lost in the bombings of Hiroshima and Nagasaki.

Into this maelstrom walked the native son, Ho Chi Minh, promising deliverance. Eight days after the Japanese army left Vietnam, he stood in the center of Hanoi and proclaimed independence for his country. He began his speech by audaciously quoting Thomas Jefferson, saying, "All men are created equal; they are endowed by their creator with certain unalienable rights; among these are life, liberty, and the pursuit of happiness." It was an electrifying, yet puzzling moment; a communist had quoted one of the forefathers of individual liberty. Jefferson was the very antithesis of Marx. To many in the communist party, the borrowed line bordered on heresy. To westerners, it was a shocking appropriation of hallowed words by the enemy.

To the Christians in Vietnam, like Dung Vu's father and the other farmers of Luong Dien, the ascendancy of Ho Chi Minh was not a rhetorical outrage, but an existential threat. It was bad enough that the French and Japanese had occupied their land and wrecked the fine balance of the village economy for their imperial needs. It was worse that mighty America had bombed their transportation routes to cripple the Japanese army. It was catastrophic when a typhoon slammed into the low-lying delta, tearing the northern farms to shreds and creating famine. But through all the hardships inflicted upon innocents by warring men and indiscriminate nature, hope remained. Hope was one of the essential teachings of Jesus. Just as his words found fertile soil in the hearts of men and women oppressed by the great Roman empire 2,000 years ago, they also found receptive souls half a world away among the Vietnamese who had strained for millennia under the thumb of great empires.

The communists, on the other hand, threatened even hope. Their hostility to religion and the persecution that followed terrified the Catholics far more than war or famine. Worst of all, the atrocities of Marxism were committed by their own countrymen. Stalin had killed 25 million of his own people in Russia. Mao killed untold millions of Chinese. The Vietnamese Christians wondered how many of the faithful would be killed by their leaders if communists came to power.

"Dinh, the rice is ready," said his mother.

Dinh Doan, temporary object of Mai's fickle affections, was dressing in the small bedroom he shared with his brothers, inspecting his clothes for stains or dirt. He was a fastidious boy, unusually concerned about his appearance at all times, but especially so on this day.

"I'm coming, mother," Dinh said.

When he walked into the room, impeccably pressed, coiffed, and oiled, she smirked.

"You look nice enough to meet the emperor," she said with a hint of a laugh.

Dinh frowned at her gentle mockery.

I will probably see Father Thieu there," Dinh said, "I want to look good."

As always, she thought, noting her oldest son's peculiarities. He wasn't earthy and raw like the other boys his age. He was refined, serious, and so anxious to grow up. Not that any of Dinh's affectation would matter in Luong Dien. A child born to the rice farm would live out his days as a rice farmer. His mother decided to leave his youthful naivete intact and said nothing. He would get a dose of reality soon enough.

Dinh loaded a pot full of rice and headed for the door. The Doans were one of the wealthier families of Luong Dien. They owned a large tract of land and many buffaloes, thus were able to withstand the famine better than most. They regularly gave surplus rice to the church which then distributed it to the needy.

"Hey Dinh," she called to him as the smile drained from her face.

"Yes, mother," he answered.

"It's..."

She searched for a word that would describe the grisly scene Dinh was about to encounter. She couldn't come up with an adequate descriptor.

"It's...bad out there today. Be strong."

Dinh nodded and walked out.

As he carried his pot of rice toward the church in the center of town, the moment of levity he shared with his mom was replaced by awful reality. It was a walk through Hell. Dead bodies slumped along the roadside like carelessly dropped litter. The smell of decaying flesh filled the air. There were no emergency services in Luong Dien, so the corpses lay where they fell until a few brave neighbors dug shallow mass graves and dragged the bodies to be buried. One such grave on Dinh's route was not deep enough for all the bodies. Arms, legs, and hands protruded gruesomely from the dirt. The horror that surrounded Dinh seeped deep into his consciousness as he struggled to shake off his mounting fear. He kept walking until he got to the church.

The church looked like many other Christian churches in the world with one exception. Where the steeples of western churches were solid spires piercing the sky like daggers, Luong Dien's church had a group of three multi-level pagodas. The corners of each pagoda roof were turned upward and ornamented, making the church look like a kite that might just lift off in a strong breeze. Its airy, happy architecture was sorely out of place with the events on the ground.

Draped across the steps of the church were a few emaciated wretches, barely alive. Dinh felt foolish. He had let his ego be inflated so much by the contrived honor of carrying rice to the church, he dressed himself as if he were going to Easter Mass. The sunken eyes watched impassively as Dinh approached, their graying skin thinly stretched over bones, and mouths frozen open in a look of eternal misery. Dinh did not meet their gaze.

Over the last few weeks, as the famine entered its most deadly phase, a dead body on the church steps was becoming a daily occurrence. Dinh saw a body splayed in an awkward position on the steps, face down in the dirt. Another victim who didn't make it through the night. Starvation was a particularly awful way to die. Slow and excruciating, the body deprived of calories begins to eat itself. First, the stores of sugars are consumed, then fats, and finally protein that make up muscle and tissue are catabolized as the body fights to stay alive. Weight drops. Skin dries and cracks. Vitamin deficiencies prevent normal organ function. Infection and cardiac arrest most commonly deliver the final blow, bringing a merciful end to suffering.

Dinh was a boy in a hurry to be a man. He felt ashamed to feel fear of the dead, so he fought himself until he suppressed his childish emotions and went about the business of being responsible. He stepped up to the corpse and forced himself to look closely at it to make sure the person wasn't still alive. Dinh placed the back of his hand near the open mouth to see if he could feel a breath. When satisfied that no life remained, he went inside to find Father Thieu. He found him in his cramped office, lost in thought, holding a cup so tightly in his hand his knuckles were white.

15

Dinh knocked softly. Father Thieu looked over his glasses and motioned Dinh to come in as he loosened his grip on the cup. He noticed Dinh was overdressed but said nothing. Like Mrs. Doan, the priest knew the boy's personality. Though he was a bit of a peacock, Dinh reminded him of himself. Father Thieu couldn't help but like him.

Father Thieu, like most men in Luong Dien, was small. He was a tightly wound, intense man with boundless energy. Unlike most of the villagers, he was not a native of the town, but sent by the bishop from his home in the big port city of Haiphong. He was a young man, full of a young man's idealism and righteous self-assurance. Dinh admired his decisiveness, his education, and his relative worldliness. Dinh had been pulled from school just a year before by his father, and the embarrassment still stung him. He was a smart boy, maybe smart enough to attend university, but it was not to be. Education was a luxury, and though Dinh's family was solidly middle class by Vietnam's standards, farms didn't run on luxuries, but by hands, legs, and backs.

"What can I do for you, Dinh?" Father Thieu asked.

"There's another one out there," Dinh answered.

Father Thieu removed his glasses and pinched the bridge of his nose. He sighed and replaced the glasses.

"I'll see to it," he said. "Do you have some rice for me today?"

Dinh nodded solemnly, "Yes Father, right here."

"Very good. Thank you. You can leave it here and I will see to it."

"Yes, Father. I will be back tomorrow." Dinh turned to leave.

"Dinh, wait. I have something to ask you."

"Yes, Father?"

"Do you enjoy singing in the choir?"

16

"Yes, Father."

"I need someone to direct the choir. I have been told that you are proficient on drums, guitar, and flute. I know you are young...how old are you again?"

"Fifteen, Father."

Thieu paused for a moment as he wrestled with second thoughts about the boy's age. He decided to plunge ahead.

"Well, no matter, I can tell you are a natural leader. What do you think?"

Dinh felt woozy from the words of his idol. He had been recognized and was being offered a real, important position. Dinh didn't take time to consider the responsibilities of the offer, he just swelled with pride and blurted an enthusiastic, "Yes!"

For a moment, Dinh forgot about the horror on the steps. He floated out of Father Thieu's office and across the sanctuary toward the front door. The triumph didn't last long. As Dinh opened the heavy wooden door, the putrid smell of rotting bodies was waiting for him.

Dinh ran home, holding his breath at intervals to avoid the foul odor. He burst into the house and nearly shouted at his mother.

"Mom! You won't believe it! Father Thieu asked me to lead the choir!"

His mother acted excited and surprised. She was excited for her son, but she was not surprised. Father Thieu had approached her days before about the subject. After another torrent of words, Dinh rushed to his room where he pulled out his beaten, scuffed flute. He practiced the old French Catholic Hymn, *A Revoir Camarade.* As he played the sad notes, he recalled the lyrics and thought about the body he found on the steps.

Au Revoir, Camarade
May the Lord watch over you
On the road where your angel will protect you
May the Virgin show you the path of the stars
Where we will meet tomorrow

3

The power vacuum created by the departing Japanese army was brilliantly seized by Ho Chi Minh, but he wasn't alone. Seemingly overnight, the great powers of the world descended on the tiny country, determined to either rule it or exploit it. The Chinese sent an army to manage the evacuation of the Japanese army. A British contingent accompanied the French army as they sought to reassert their claim. The Americans and Soviets, now atop the world political order, moved cautiously; advising, collecting information, and waiting. Ho was aware of the complexity of the situation and acted shrewdly. He solicited all the nations for their support, even France and the U.S. He built his power base with a careful appeal to nationalism rather than communism in order to convince his countrymen and placate the capitalists who were watching. By the thousands the Vietnamese joined. Things were going well except for one thing. The French were having none of it. They wanted their property back.

Mauled and conquered by Germany, France was reconstituted after World War II. Weakened, but still proud, Paris soon made it clear they had no intention of giving up their colony. So, while most of the world was taking a break from bloodshed, Vietnam was at the threshold of a war that would go on and on.

World War II had been easy to understand. All the combatants had declared themselves on one side or the other, started fighting, and stuck with those allegiances throughout the war. But this war, called the First Indochina War by the French and the Anti-French Resistance War by the Vietnamese, started as a hazy, tangled web of divided loyalties, confusing sides, and shadowy power brokers. The great conundrum for the Americans, British, and even some French citizens was the conflict between their ideological support of Vietnamese independence and their absolute rejection of communism. Even the Vietnamese were divided amongst themselves.

By 1950 though, the big players had all chosen sides. China's civil war had been won by the communists. In the west, the Soviet Union had placed all of Eastern Europe under its iron thumb, sentencing millions to oppression that would last nearly half a century. The growing strength and expansionist appetite of communism terrified the capitalist countries, so in the end, the fear of communism outweighed the desire to liberate. The Americans, worried that all of Asia would fall if Vietnam turned communist, joined the French. The Chinese and the Soviets poured resources, weapons, and advisors into the Viet Minh forces.

The Cold War had begun. In Vietnam, though, the Cold War would become hot and stay that way for more than 20 years. The Vietnamese may have been simply struggling for independence, but to the rest of the world it was the dueling ground of two incompatible ideologies. The little country on the shore of the South China Sea, fighting to be free, was about to be crushed between giants fighting to rule the world.

Even with a fresh supply of guns from China and the Soviet Union, the Viet Minh generals knew that they could not fight toe-to-toe with the more advanced weapons of the French, so they waged a guerilla war designed to exhaust their opponents. From 1946 to 1953, they hid in the jungles and mountains, coming out only to slash and disappear. Their patience was long, their commitment unwavering. Ho Chi Minh warned prophetically, "You will kill ten of our men for every one of yours we kill. But even at those odds, you will tire of it first, and we will win."

The year was 1953, the Year of the Snake. In the northern village of Luong Dien, Ho Chi Minh's struggle was far away. Isolated without radio or phone, the people of the village got their news at the speed of a water buffalo pulling a cart of letters. The Catholic rice farmers of the area had been greatly concerned when the communists first seized power in 1945, but years had passed without any change and the French seemed to be repelling the advances of the communist armies. Slowly, the Catholics let down their guard and returned attention to their primary concern—growing food. The residents of Luong Dien had seen starvation up close and never wanted to see it again, so they poured themselves into cultivating their crops. Mother Nature rewarded their industriousness with years of bounty. Harvests had been good for many seasons by the mid-50s, reducing the famine of 1944-45 to a hazy memory, disturbing only the dreams of those who had seen the cold face of death firsthand. With full bellies, the people of Luong Dien turned their thoughts to the sweet rhythm of the seasons; the faith, family, and friends that made enduring a hard life worthwhile.

Dinh Doan and Dung Vu had been adolescents during the famine. Both of them carried the psychological scars of it, but otherwise grew up strong and healthy. Dinh, now 23, had transformed from a serious boy into a serious young man. He still led Father Thieu's choir and it had grown to some 50 voices. Leadership was but one of his gifts.

Dung, now 19 and the oldest child in her family, had grown up taking care of her younger siblings in addition to Phu, the neighbor's water buffalo. Dung was kindhearted, reliable, and hard-working. She was well liked in the village. As she had grown, a shy grin had blossomed into a dazzling white smile. Over the past few years, that smile had gotten her noticed by the church committee which was in charge of the Marian parade.

The Virgin Mary was celebrated every May, called the 'month of flowers' by Catholics. Each festival culminated in a parade through town. A large statue of Mary was carried by eight men dressed in white. Walking in front of the statue, several young women, also dressed in white with attached angel wings, threw flower petals in the air. Dung was selected to be one of the angels. It was the highest honor a girl could get in Luong Dien. Dung was not the type who sought notoriety, but she enjoyed her role immensely. She was picked to be an angel year after year.

"Dung, isn't this so much fun!" her friend Mai shouted as she threw a handful of petals.

Mai was also selected to be a parade girl though she wasn't known for her Christian virtue. Shapely and sultry, Mai looked more like a temptress than an angel. Village women were scandalized by her inclusion in the parade. Village men didn't seem to mind.

"Yes!" Dung replied, as she smiled broadly at the cheering crowd which included Dinh, and more importantly, his mother.

"Dinh," his mother said, pointing at the girls. "How would you like that one for your wife?"

Dinh looked in the direction of her outstretched finger and raised his eyebrows.

"You mean Mai? Mother, I don't think…"

"Not that hussy," she interrupted. "The one beside her with the big smile. Dung Vu."

"Oh, her," he said. "She seems okay, but I don't know her."

"Leave that to me," his mother said.

Arranged marriages were once common throughout the world, but fell out of favor in most cultures during the 20th century. They were still the custom in small town Vietnam in the 1950s, with a complex set of rules that underscored an unspoken but very real hierarchy. Niceties were observed on the surface of this society, but underneath was a tooth and nail battle for status. Mrs. Doan, blessed with both wealth and shrewdness, excelled at the game. She set her sights on Dung.

A few days before the monsoon season began its months-long dominance, Dung awakened before first light to get started on her day. She would take Phu to the big pasture near the beach with her childhood friend Mai. In the dim candlelight, she cooked a bowl of rice for her journey. Coal was too expensive and wood was scarce, so Dung had to use straw and husks from last season's harvest for the fire. She ate quietly then packed her things and walked toward the door. As she exited the house, she crossed herself and mumbled her prayers.

"Hail Mary, full of Grace, The Lord is with thee…," she whispered as her bare feet patted out a rhythm on the dirt road.

While Dung was gone with Phu, Dinh's parents paid a call on the Vu household. They carried a small vase of homemade rice wine, betel leaves, and areca nuts. Inside the house, they shared a few pleasantries. Dinh's father went through the motions with barely disguised impatience. Like his son, he was intense and anxious. He shifted uneasily on his seat until they came to the point of the visit. At last they began *le dam ngo,* or the wedding proposal.

"Your daughter Dung is beautiful, compassionate, and responsible."

"Your son is handsome, talented, and a natural leader."

"We think they would be a good match for each other."

"Yes, they would."

With all the caution and measured words of a diplomatic mission, the elaborate dance of compliments and agreements continued. A Vietnamese wedding was once a highly ritualized affair, drawing on traditions from many faiths and thousands of years of cultural practice. Marriage was as much an alliance between two families as it was the union of two people. As a result, the proposal and engagement period had a structure and schedule which probed the compatibility of the couple and strengthened the bond between the families.

The *le dam ngo* was completed to the satisfaction of the two families. They all stood up from the floor mats upon which they had been sitting. With a bow toward the Vu's ancestral altar and another to their hosts, the Doans left the house. For several minutes, Dung's parents remained motionless, contemplating what had just happened. Dung's mother shed a tear and spoke.

"She is such a sweet girl."

"It is time," her father answered.

"Yes, I know, but why did it have to come so soon?"

4

D ung closed the gate of Phu's enclosure and sauntered home. It had been a nice day. The oppressive humidity and endless rain of the monsoon was just around the corner which made the final days of the dry season precious.

The salty air of the sea had been cleansing to Dung. Though she was technically at work, a day at the beach was more like a holiday. Dung had been working since her parents took her out of school at the age of eight. She took care of Phu and her younger brothers, cooked, cleaned, and farmed. Her hands were calloused and cracked, her body sinewed and supple. She remembered nothing about school, but the days and years of toil that followed left deep tracks in her soul. She had grown in devotion to her Catholic faith, attending Mass daily, praying the rosary diligently, taking spiritual sustenance from the hardships of the suffering saints who carried burdens much like the ones that poverty had inflicted on her young body and mind. She could not read the passages in the Bible, but had memorized her favorites and recited them when she became weary.

Come to me, all who labor and are heavy laden, and I will give you rest.

Dung walked through the door of her house and could sense the tension. Her parents were standing by the ancestral altar, praying. A single tear left its track on her mother's cheek.

"What's wrong?" Dung asked.

"Come sit down," her father said as he motioned to the jute mats on the floor. The three hastily sat down and shifted uncomfortably. Dung's father searched for the right combination of words to soften the blow. After a few moments of frustration he gave up and decided to be direct.

"You have been betrothed."

The words punched Dung's chest.

"What?" she breathed.

"The parents of Doan Van Dinh came today. They asked permission for their son to marry you."

Dung looked on in stunned silence. Finally she spoke.

"What did you say?"

"He is an honorable man. Hard working and bright. He will make an excellent husband and will provide for you."

The positive descriptors her father used—*honorable, hard-working,* and *bright*—felt awkward in his mouth, as if he was trying too hard to make a sale to a customer who was slipping away. Dung didn't pay attention. She was consumed by feelings of abandonment. Hot tears burst from her eyes.

"Don't you want me anymore?" she wailed.

"Of course we do," her father answered. "But that is not the way of the world. You are a woman now. It is time for you to be married."

Dung's mother reached out to touch her daughter, but she jerked away.

"I don't even know him," Dung feebly protested.

She knew enough about arranged marriage to realize familiarity with one's groom was hardly a prerequisite. She felt the cold dread of inevitability closing around her.

"You will," her mother said. "Your father and I barely knew each other when we were married. It has turned out fine."

Dung was shocked by this news. She had assumed that her parents had known each other since birth. Still, the revelation from her mother did little to put out the fire of outrage, betrayal, and fear that burned within her. Dung was too respectful to explode in rage at her parents, so after a few more words of restrained protest, she ran to her bed and sobbed for hours.

Dung's mother returned to the ancestral altar to pray for her daughter. She also begged The Virgin for the success of the decision they just made for their child. Along with her petitions, a feeling of lost time permeated her thoughts and she lamented the things that she had planned yet failed to do.

Dung's father sighed and picked up the vase of wine the Doans brought. He walked outside to ponder what had just happened. His days had been so routine, so similar, it was sometimes hard to measure the passage of time. A sudden event like this was a jolting reminder that his time was indeed slipping away. It seemed only yesterday that he was holding his baby girl in his arms. In a few months, she would be gone. He took a swig of the wine. It was strong and made him grimace as he swallowed. He leaned against the wall made of bamboo beams and clay, wrapped in coconut leaves. He had recently replaced the sheathing with fresh leaves to weatherproof the clay exterior. They still smelled fresh. He breathed in the pungent odor and looked at the stars which would soon be obscured for months by the clouds of the monsoon.

Across town, Dinh and his friends gathered in the backyard of his house. The weekly ritual included wine and music. Someone usually brought snails dug from the riverbank to boil and eat. Dinh played his guitar and directed the impromptu choir.

"I have something to tell you," Dinh said as he sat a flickering lamp in the middle of the circle of friends.

The friends took turns calling out derisive answers.

"You're really a woman," one said.

"You are Ho Chi Minh," said another.

"You have conquered your fear of snakes," said a third.

At this, they all laughed. Dinh was not fond of hunting for snails in the river, which entailed sticking a hand in a hole and pulling out the creature inside. Snails and crabs were usually extracted, but sometimes a snake resided in the hole. Anytime Dinh pulled out a snake, he squealed and jumped, sending his friends into fits of laughter.

Dinh enjoyed the jokes at his expense and laughed along. When the roasting died down, he told them his news.

"I am going to be married."

The broad grins of the men faded to open-mouthed disbelief. A pall was cast over the party and everyone remained silent for several moments as if a death had just been announced.

"Who is it?" asked one of them after what he considered to be a respectful amount of silence.

"Dung Vu," Dinh answered.

More silence followed.

"The one with the pretty smile, yeah I know her," one answered, warming to the idea.

The others chimed in as well, hoping to regain the momentum of the party and set their friend at ease. Mostly, though, they wanted to put the uncomfortable subject behind them.

"She's nice."

"She will make a very good wife."

"She looks pretty in the angel costume."

When everyone murmured their approval, the party returned to its normal arc. But everyone knew it wasn't the same. It would never be the same again.

"What are we going to sing tonight, Dinh?"

Dinh started strumming the chords to a beloved folk song and voices filled the night air.

Who is going to the Tuong river wharf?
Message the charming person I love
Many days I have yearned for that passionate love
Months with dim days, tinged with grief
My soul dreams of you.

5

Word traveled with astonishing speed in the tiny village. Dung's friend Mai heard the news before the sun came up and made a beeline for her house. She burst in, expecting Dung to be alone.

"Dinh Doan?" she screamed. "I can't believe it!"

The words ricocheted off the walls before she realized that Dung's parents were there. They had been silently eating a bowl of rice, but stopped and stared in surprise at the explosion of energy that had just ripped into their quiet morning.

"Oh, I'm so sorry, Mr. and Mrs. Vu, I beg your pardon. Please forgive me."

Mai could've crawled under a rock in shame. Mrs. Vu was well aware of Mai's brash personality, and although Mai's incessant talking could sometimes be tiring, she brought some lively balance to Dung's natural reticence. Besides, she was a good source of information about the goings-on in Luong Dien. Dung's mother rescued her from her impetuousness.

"It's okay, Mai, we are aware of the news of Dung's engagement," she said with a smirk.

Mai didn't say anything, but stood there in shock over her faux pas. She considered herself the pinnacle of demure grace, unaware of her reputation as one of the town's incorrigible gossips.

"Dung's in her bed," her mother said as she pointed at the bamboo screen that separated Dung's space from the rest of the house. She nodded at Mai to let her know it was okay to go to her friend. Dung tiptoed over and peeked around the corner.

"Dung, are you awake?" Mai whispered.

Dung sat in the corner of her bed with her arms wrapped around her legs, pulling her knees into her chest. Her eyes were red and swollen. She didn't speak or look at Mai.

"Do you want me to come back later?" she asked. Dung shook her head.

Mai sat down on the mattress, a lumpy burlap bag stuffed with rice straw. She didn't speak, but sat there waiting for Dung to say something. Dung didn't speak.

Mai hated silence. She had always taken it upon herself to fill the void for her less talkative friend. Mai believed that every problem could be solved with words. If talking failed to produce a remedy, that only meant she hadn't talked enough. She furiously expended her energy on action and words with nothing left over for introspection. Mai happily led an unexamined life. To her, life wasn't to be thought about. It was to be lived thoroughly and loudly.

On this morning, however, for the first time in her life, Mai didn't try to fill the silence, mostly because she couldn't find words from her limited experience. She was unmoored and in uncharted waters. She sat with her friend and allowed the uneasiness to wash over her. It was unnatural, uncomfortable. The longer Dung remained quiet, the more Mai realized that this was something different than the usual teenage drama. The world as they knew it really was about to end. Mai felt more despondent with each passing minute. A sense of claustrophobia closed in. She was just about to fake an excuse and escape when Dung scooted out of her corner and sat beside her friend. She wrapped her arms around Mai, buried her head in Mai's shoulder and cried some more.

Mai was now trapped. To her credit, she stayed put and let her friend hold onto her. Finally, Dung stopped crying and wiped her eyes with her sleeve. She stood up.

"What are you doing?" Mai asked.

"It's late. I have to start my chores," Dung said.

"Don't you want to talk about it?" Mai asked.

"Talk about what?"

Mai was floored. She strained to lower her voice to a whisper, knowing that Dung's parents were just a few feet away.

"Dinh Doan! You're getting married!"

Dung sighed in exasperation at her friend's persistence.

"I don't want to talk about it. My parents have made their decision and I have to respect it. I'm going to Mass if you want to go."

Mai didn't want to go. Her commitment to Jesus was much more casual than her consuming interest in boys and gossip. She watched as Dung took a deep breath, marched across the house, and stormed out the door without speaking to her parents.

A few days later, Dinh Doan got dressed in his house across the village. His hands shook nervously as he prepared himself. Outside, he could hear the catcalls of the friends who had gathered to escort him to Dung's house for the *Dam Hoi*, or engagement ceremony. Usually self-assured and decisive, Dinh was surprised to discover he was frightened. He hadn't been this scared since the famine of 1945. The taunts of his friends, full of sexual innuendo, did not help. In his haste to be an achiever, Dinh had ignored girls. Now the time had come to address the subject, and he felt like a student being given a test for which he had not studied.

Dinh emerged from the house to more jeers from his friends. Dinh's mother scolded them, which only slightly diminished the insults. Good natured punches and back slaps rained down on him and a broad smile crept across his mouth. The teasing from his friends had finally broken the tension, yet that lighthearted moment only highlighted the change that was being thrust upon him. Things and people never stop changing, but with just enough routine and youthful inexperience, Dinh had been lulled into an illusion that life was static.

All his assumptions had been shattered as he walked through town at the head of a small procession of family and friends. A thin sheet of clouds stretched across the sky, portending the heavier, rain-bearing clouds to come. The dry season was nearly over. The coming monsoon would soon put an end to such displays of pomp and circumstance as everyone would be busy in the rice paddies. The procession made its way along the main street of Luong Dien, past dozens of hand-built houses with corrugated tin roofs, a couple of shops that stocked a few

36

food items and supplies, and the big Catholic Church where Dinh was the choir director.

At the Vu's house, Dinh and his party waited outside until Dung's father invited them into the house. Everyone stood quietly except for two of Dinh's young cousins who had been assigned to carry a large platter containing a roast pig. They had argued the whole way about the proper way to transport it, and continued to whisper insults about the competence of each other until their mother threatened them.

Five of Dinh's cousins and friends carried small boxes wrapped in red paper. Odd numbers and the color red were signs of good luck to the Vietnamese. In an arranged marriage where the bride and groom were strangers, luck would be an essential ingredient to success and its favor would be called upon many times during the ceremony.

Dung's grandfather emerged from the house and invited the Doan party inside. The five gifts carried by the Doan males were presented to five females of the Vu family. The gifts of mango, betel leaves, tobacco, tea, and areca nuts were symbolic representations of the groom's financial stability. According to custom, the Vus had to approve the gifts before the ceremony could continue. They nodded solemnly and the gifts were placed on the ancestral altar.

When the gift presentation was complete, it was time to introduce the families. This honor was reserved for respected elders. Dinh's grandfather introduced his family and Dung's grandfather did the same for hers. Then, Grandfather Doan stated the purpose for the visit.

"We are honored by your hospitality. We have come to join our families, and request the hand of your lovely daughter, Dung, in marriage to our son, Dinh. May God and the ancestors look upon their union with favor and bless them."

A reverent hush fell over the house. The only sound was a soft sniffling from behind the bamboo screen. It was time to present the bride-to-be. Dung's father stood up and walked across the room to the screen and stretched his hand out behind it. It lingered in midair for a few moments too long. He narrowed his eyes at the hesitating figure.

Dung stepped out. Her father escorted her to face the Doan family. She was dressed simply in a borrowed *ao dai*, the national costume of Vietnam. The basic *ao dai* is a form-fitting top with long panels that hang nearly to the floor over billowy trousers. The rich had many *ao dai* in bright colors, made of silk and embossed with dragons or phoenix. The poor did not usually own one, but had to canvas the neighborhood to borrow one of a suitable size. Dung's *ao dai* was old, handed down year after year. It was plain black cotton, not ornamented silk.

Despite the obvious age of her outfit, Dung cut a striking figure. Her shiny black hair flowed over the black shoulders of her *ao dai*, making her look like a warrior goddess from a fairy tale. Half expecting her to unsheathe a sword, everyone in the room straightened their spines at the sight. Dung's silence only added to the mystique. She did not deploy the smile that had gotten her noticed. Dinh was both attracted to and terrified by this stranger.

Dung did not feel like a warrior or a goddess. She was miserable and scared. Her only wish was for the awful ceremony to end quickly. Time, the cruel trickster, slowed to a crawl in response to her wishes.

A pot of tea was brought out. According to custom, the future bride and groom had to serve tea to their future in-laws. Dung completed this task robotically, without betraying any emotion. Dinh's mother looked at her with pity, perhaps remembering her own arranged marriage years earlier. Once Dung was finished, she handed the teapot to Dinh, who poured tea for Dung's family.

When the tea ceremony was complete, the new couple went to the altar. In addition to the red gift boxes, pictures of Dung's deceased ancestors crowded the table. Catholic orthodoxy prohibited the ancient practice of ancestor worship, but most Christian families in Luong Dien continued the tradition anyway. Dung and Dinh lit incense sticks and offered silent prayers to all the deities and spirits present for the success of their marriage.

When the *Dam Hoi* was complete, it was time to party. The pig was carved and served. The Vu women brought out steaming pots of rice, cabbage, cauliflower and broccoli. Trays of rambutan, mangosteen, and lychee added color to the feast. A festive mood replaced the solemnity of the ceremony. Everyone relaxed and chatted happily, except one person. Still dressed in her black *ao dai*, she stood with her back to a wall, wondering how everyone could be so happy when she, the object of this farce, was in misery.

Dinh's mother noticed this and called her son over. He had been sharing a laugh with the men of Dung's family. She whispered in his ear.

"Go to your bride. She is scared and unhappy."

"What do I say?" Dinh asked.

"Acknowledge her feelings. Tell her you are frightened too," she said.

Dinh's pride was insulted. He stiffened at the accusation.

39

"I'm not scared," he said.

His mother raised her eyebrows at him.

"Don't lie to your mother. I know you better than you know yourself. Now, go talk to her."

Dinh apologized and shuffled over to Dung.

"Hi," he said.

Dung nodded but did not speak. Dinh searched for words. Best to start slowly, he thought.

"This is a nice party," he said.

Dung did not acknowledge him. He tried again.

"I hope you like the pig, I helped my father roast it."

Dung remained speechless. Nervous energy lit a fire in Dinh's heart as he realized he was sinking fast. He made one last flailing attempt to get her to respond.

"How many children do you think we will have?"

It was a disastrous attempt. Dung frowned and a single tear leaked from her left eye. She looked away from Dinh to prevent an embarrassing outburst. Dinh looked at his mother who had been watching the exchange. He shrugged helplessly and walked away.

The party eventually lost steam and the guests went home. Dung changed out of her *ao dai* and back into her regular clothes. She slipped out of the house while her parents were talking to the last few guests. She walked to farmer Nguyen's house and crept around back to where Phu was penned. She petted his face and wept. A song her mother had taught her came back to her and she sang softly through her tears.

Buffalo, let me tell you something

Go out and plow with me
Out in the field, me and you
As long as the rice stalks are blooming
There will be blades of grass for you to eat

The clouds thickened, accelerating the coming of dusk. Dung hugged Phu's great neck and started back home. As she walked, rain started to fall in lazy, fat drops. By the time she made it to her house, the rain had grown angry, pounding the dirt into mud that would last for months.

The water dragon was upon the land. The monsoon had arrived.

6

ong before men started fighting over Vietnam, the land was a battleground. Long before people crossed the vast Asian continent and discovered the place where the land sinks into the blue abyss, great forces clashed here in an epic struggle that continues to this day. Though this clash takes place beyond the reach of humans, it has had a profound effect on all the billions of people that have ever lived in this part of the world.

Far north of China, past the haunting steppes of Mongolia, lies an ancient and mysterious lake in the forested heart of Siberia. The lake, named Baikal, is the deepest in the world and is said to hold more than 20 percent of the planet's fresh water. As the sun's grip on the northern hemisphere weakens each autumn, the coldest air on Earth rises from the depths of Lake Baikal and spills southward. It bounces off the Tibetan plateau and spreads across Southeast Asia, bringing low temperatures and dry blue skies to Vietnam. The pattern holds for months, preserving innocuous weather through winter and into spring.

But the dry season is only a pause, a desiccated facsimile of life as the land takes its rest, turning brown like death. The people rest too, taking time to repair their fields, tools, and houses. They plan weddings and celebrate holidays. They breathe the rejuvenating Siberian air and relax the taut muscles honed in the rice fields. But in the back of their minds, they know that *it* is coming back. They understand all their dry season activity is just preparation for the real business of living. When the rain comes, it brings life to the fallow paddies as well as the souls of the Vietnamese, infusing their days with purpose. The monsoon knits hardness into their bones even as it softens the land.

Spring comes and the dragon awakens in its watery bed. In Chinese mythology, the dragon descends from the sky. In Vietnam, the dragon rises from the sea, the four-fold deity of cloud, rain, thunder, and lightning. The northern hemisphere turns its face toward the sun and the dragon grows strong. Warm air from the south smashes into the cold Siberian flow, pushing it back north and pumping moisture up from the Bay of Bengal and the South China Sea. The farmers tense in anticipation. Violence is upon them. The dragon sends great armies of water-thickened clouds, black and menacing, from the oceans. They drop their ordnance with frightening intensity, inundating the land, dumping as much as 12 inches of rain per month. By comparison, the rainiest city in the United States—Mobile, Alabama—gets barely half that amount in its wettest months.

The people of the temperate world are bullied by rain. They shield themselves with umbrellas and dash to shelter in even the mildest shower. The Vietnamese don't run inside when it rains. They run outside to face the raging dragon as it thrashes before them, bending a hundred palm trees with its hands, wielding them like leafy swords. The wind shrieks through the jungle and the gray sheets of rain lash them. Afraid but determined, they don their conical hat, the *non la,* and let the rain roll off their backs like black-clad ducks as they return to their muddy fields to dance with the dragon. The enigmatic beast has the power of life and death, fierce enough to destroy everything in its path, but benevolent enough to generate and preserve life. The monsoon grows rice and feeds the people, but only in exchange for work; backbreaking, seemingly interminable, toil. It is the price of living.

When the monsoon came in 1953, the betrothed Dung Vu returned to the fields, relieved to have a diversion from her upcoming wedding. The wedding would take place in January of 1954, when the cold Siberian giant would once again push the dragon back into the southern seas.

For the moment, Dung would busy herself and try to forget about marriage. She walked the rows and flung seeds. She cooked rice, cleaned the house, and cared for her younger brothers. She lovingly tended Phu with a wistful realization that this would be their last season together. And when the rain stopped and the rice stalks turned a riotous yellow, she returned to the paddy; chopping, gathering, drying, and then pounding the sustaining grain out of the plant.

Life was work.

Life was rice.

Life was the monsoon.

As Dung, Dinh, and their fellow farmers immersed themselves in the watery earth during the rainy season of 1953, Ho Chi Minh and his generals occupied themselves by battering the French army. Systematically, the Viet Minh forces wore down the French, forcing them into a defensive posture, as the Vietnamese guerillas swarmed all around them.

In the spring of 1953, a French general named Navarre was assigned to lead an effort to subdue the rebellious colony. After viewing the situation up close, he ominously reported back to Paris that there was no possibility of winning the war in Indochina. The best they could hope for was a stalemate. In November, Navarre chose to concentrate his forces in a small valley near the town of Dien Bien Phu to block the Viet Minh push into neighboring Laos. It was a sound tactical decision, but it marked the beginning of the end for the French. Ho Chi Minh had warned that he would lose ten Viet Minh for every French soldier killed yet still win. His prophecy was coming true. France was getting tired.

On a clear January night, in the village of Luong Dien in 1954, Dung sat in her parents' house. The dragon was temporarily locked in its underwater prison. Cool, dry, air wafted in through the open doorway. A single lamp lit the small interior. Flickering shadows danced across the walls. Dung's mother stood behind her, brushing her luxurious black hair for the last time. The next day, her daughter would be married. The hair brushing was a touching and sad Vietnamese tradition, marking the end of the mother/daughter bond.

"Mama, do I have to do this?" the young woman asked.

"It is our way, Dung. It is how it has always been," her mother answered.

"But why? I don't know him. I don't think I even like him," she said weakly, with a hint of shame and resignation in her voice. A tear ran down her cheek.

Dung's mother remembered her own wedding years earlier. She had asked the same question, felt the same fear. For a moment, she wondered why the hurtful system of arranged marriage had evolved and persisted for so long. But this was not the time to air her own misgivings to her daughter. A celebration was already planned and paid for. Everyone in town was expecting it. The Vus, already poor, had emptied their meager savings to host the event.

Earlier in the day, a small number of Dinh's family had traveled to Dung's house to ask permission "to receive the bride." This tradition was a polite way of ensuring the bride had not run away in protest, and confirming the wedding would take place as scheduled. Dung's father presented her briefly and assured the Doans that the wedding was still on. Allowing their daughter to back out now would be an unthinkable breach of contract. She decided to take a different tack in answering Dung's question.

"Do you remember the famine in 1945?" her mother asked.

Dung's recollection had become fuzzy over the nine years since that awful time, but she remembered the corpses on the road, gray and leathery, flies buzzing around the bodies like they did the roast pigs that Dung ate on special occasions. Dung had never thought of people as being made of meat. It was a gruesome revelation, a disturbing picture burned painfully into the deepest place in Dung's memory.

"Yes," Dung answered.

"We barely made it through. Your father and I ate one small bowl of rice every two or three days so that we could feed you and your brothers. Starvation is a horrible way to die, and a worse way to live. We were right on the edge of it. I could feel my own body consuming itself. It was like death lived inside me. I don't ever want to go through that again, and I don't want you to experience it either."

"I'm sorry," Dung said. "Why didn't you tell me?"

"Parents do many things they never tell their children. But everything we do is for you. It is how God made us."

"Doan's family has many buffaloes. They are rich," Dung said, beginning to realize her parents' rationale.

"Yes," her mother said. "I can't promise you will never experience hunger, but you stand a better chance of avoiding it with them."

Dung grew quiet as she considered her mother's confession. Her mother was nearly bursting with things she wanted to say, but could not find the words. For a long time, the only sound was that of the coarse brush sweeping through Dung's thick hair. Finally, Dung spoke.

"Mama."

"Yes, Dung," her mother replied.

"It's going to be okay."

"Yes, it is," her mother said as she leaned over and kissed her baby on the head.

7

The Vietnamese are a study in simplicity. The Buddhist tradition of relinquishing attachment laid deep tracks in the culture. Several centuries after Buddhism arrived, exploring Portuguese traders found a sea route to Asia around the Horn of Africa. Along with merchants came Christian missionaries who established churches in Vietnam and converted some of the Buddhists to this 'new' religion. The teachings of Jesus urged the newly converted Catholics to avoid placing their faith in worldly things; to be in the world, but not of it. The austerity of the message resonated in Asia. Unlike the gilded excesses of the European church, the rigors of rice farming did not permit a flowering of superfluous frivolity. The people were practical, tied to the rhythms and immutable laws of earth, sun, and monsoon.

However, there was one exception to their subsistence lifestyle: the wedding ceremony. It was as if the pent-up creative energy forced by hard living found its outlet in this singularly extravagant event. The wedding of Doan Van Dinh and Vu Thi Dung was no different.

Mid-morning, Dinh's entourage lined up outside the Doan house for the procession to Dung's house. The order of participants was highly scripted according to tradition. The head of the group was chosen by the family, usually a man of status. Dinh's loquacious uncle was chosen for this honor, mostly because his booming voice and his eagerness to share his opinion made him something of a leader in town. Behind him followed Dinh's father, then Dinh and the rest of the wedding party. Dinh was flanked by two friends carrying ceremonial umbrellas. The cylindrical-shaped contraptions looked more like lampshades. They would have been utterly useless against the monsoon— flimsy, adorned with ruffles and dyed an outrageous shade of pink. Umbrellas were a luxury in Vietnam, expensive and hard to obtain. They were coveted status symbols. Even non-functional facsimiles were valued.

As it was in the *Dam Hoi*, an odd number of gifts were carried to give to the family of the bride. Dinh's rowdy friends carried the red wrapped gift boxes and whispered the same bawdy jokes to him. A roast pig was carried by the same cousins who disagreed about the last pig they carried together. They still did not see eye-to-eye about the task, arguing vigorously as they walked down the road and shifting positions wildly, each trying to get primacy over the other. Miraculously, the pig did not go sliding off the platter into the dirt.

Dinh's mother was not available this time to be a regulating presence over the shenanigans. It was custom for the groom's mother to be absent from the procession as a sign that she would not interfere with the new couple. She stayed at home and readied the house for the arrival of the wedding party. The groomsmen were free to roast the groom, while the pig carriers nearly came to blows over their disagreement.

When Dinh's group arrived at the Vu's house, firecrackers were lit to announce their presence. In return, representatives of the Vu family lit their own firecrackers in acknowledgement. Firecrackers, like umbrellas, were luxuries in a poor village like Luong Dien. The participants lit them with gusto and tremendously enjoyed the racket.

Once inside the house, the ceremony unfolded much like the *Dam Hoi*. The gifts were presented from groomsmen to bridesmaids. Mai smiled coquettishly at Dinh's friend Tuan as he handed her the red box of betel leaves. A spark of interest ignited in Tuan. He smiled back.

Dung was then presented. Her father had splurged for a new *ao dai*. Even though it was cotton, not silk, it was new and it made Dung feel like a princess. Unlike the fearful girl who cried during the engagement ceremony, a confident woman walked to Dinh's side.

"You look very nice," Dinh whispered.

"Thank you," Dung replied.

The bride and groom lit incense and bowed before the ancestral altar to make their petitions to the deceased. The tea ceremony was completed just as it had been in the *Dam Hoi,* and then it was time for the wedding party to make the kilometer journey to Dinh's house. Along the way, they would stop at the church to fulfill the obligation of a Christian ceremony, which had been wedged in amongst the older traditions.

As Dung left her house, she took one last look at the only home she had ever known. She allowed herself a moment of sadness, but no more. It was a busy day and there was a lot left to do.

As they neared the church, they could see some kind of gathering on the wide steps in front where Dinh found the corpse many years before. Dozens upon dozens of people clustered in groups spilled out into the road. Frilly umbrellas hung in the air like balloons.

"What is happening?" Dung asked Dinh.

They were the first voluntary words she had spoken to him. A shudder of panic rose through her as she imagined all those people looking at her as she walked down the aisle.

"We are one of twenty couples getting married today," he said.

"Is this normal?" she asked, figuring Dinh's position as choir director gave him some access to the inner workings of the church.

"Father Thieu is the priest for three other villages, so group weddings are common. Our church is the biggest so the ceremonies are held here. I've never seen one this big, though."

"Why so many?" Dung asked.

"Father Thieu thinks he may have to go south. Many of these couples are headed to Saigon soon and wanted to be married before they left."

Saigon was a thousand miles from Luong Dien. It might as well have been on the moon to Dung, who had never been more than five miles from her home.

"Why are they leaving?"

"The Viet Minh are growing strong. They have been harassing Catholics in Hai Phong and Thai Binh. Communists are hostile to Christians. If they take over and Father Thieu leaves, the people are afraid we won't get another priest. These couples will be making the journey on foot. It will take them weeks and weeks, but it will be safe in the south if they make it."

Dung's mind exploded with countless questions. Just when she was about to make peace with her marriage, another blow landed. Fear swirled inside her like a spinning typhoon. She could feel her heart rate rising and she breathed in shallow gasps. She couldn't imagine life without Mass. She couldn't imagine traveling to Saigon. She couldn't imagine leaving Luong Dien. She blurted out the question that rose to the top of her mind.

"Am I going to have to move, too?"

She still referred to herself in the singular, not yet accustomed to the new reality that she was no longer an *I*, but a *we*. Dinh noticed her exclusion of him and corrected her gently.

"No," he answered. "I am sure *we* will not have to leave."

Dung wondered how he was so sure. The couples around them had been convinced to take a journey that would be long, miserable, and dangerous. What did they know that Dinh didn't? On the other hand, she was so relieved to hear the answer she desired, she dared not ask any more questions that might change his answer or cast doubt into her mind. She locked this new anxiety into the same box where she kept all the other fears that had found fertile soil in her mind during the last six months. Soon she would need a bigger box.

The wedding would've been an odd sight to western eyes. Twenty couples walked down the aisle and formed themselves into two perfect lines like an army platoon. Each bride was on the left and each groom on the right. The church was overflowing with relatives and friends. Each of the 20 marriages had been arranged. None of the brides or grooms were awash with the glow of love that infuses a voluntary wedding. They were grim-faced, determined to comply with their parents' wishes.

Still, the sheer size of the gathering gave the ceremony a sense of divine authority. Surely the Lord was working in the room. Surely He had a plan to preserve and protect His children. Surely they would survive to multiply themselves and fulfill His good plan. Surely God would not allow them to be destroyed by the communists.

As the ceremony continued, the novelty of the group's size became awe, awe became reverence, and reverence sparked joy. Father Thieu capitalized on the collective emotion and guided it expertly, weaving wisdom and even a bit of humor into the proceedings. He joked that he expected a vigorous business in baptisms in nine months. After the rings were exchanged and the final vows uttered, he concluded with a lovely benediction.

Lord bless these beautiful couples with love and hope, we pray

Keep alive forevermore the vows they've pledged today

May You bless their dreams and visions

And always keep them safe

May peace and joy be with them now

On their blessed wedding day

Amen

Dung and Dinh, along with the other couples, made the sign of the cross at the end of the prayermor. One by one, 20 new pairs of husbands and wives filed back up the aisle and into the sunshine. Outside the church, each wedding party reformed. Ruffled umbrellas were raised and carried in all directions toward the house of each groom.

As the new Doan couple approached Dinh's house, more firecrackers were lit. Neighbors and friends gathered out front and welcomed them with cheers and applause. Dung smiled despite her fear.

The couple was shown inside for the concluding ritual. They bowed before the Doan altar to ask the ancestor's blessing. Then Dinh escorted Dung to show her the marriage bed. The bedroom was a new addition to the house, far removed from the other sleeping areas to give the newlyweds some privacy. Dung looked impassively at the bed, which was much larger than her previous bed. She shuddered in distaste to think what she would have to do there later that night.

At the end of the ceremony, the party started. Trays of pork, lobster, rice, vegetables, and fruit were presented and devoured. Wine flowed as well as the sweet beverage *che dau den*, which was a concoction of black beans, tapioca, light brown sugar and coconut milk.

Dinh's church choir sang to the new couple. Neighbors and family members made speeches giving advice and well wishes. Mai and the groomsman Tuan hit it off, staying close to one another throughout the reception until they left together early in the evening. The party went on well into the crisp night. Sometime near midnight, the last few guests filtered out and just the family was left in the house. It was time for Dung to go to bed with her husband.

She shook with fear as she got undressed. The words the priest had said in the benediction, *always keep them safe,* echoed inside her and gave her a moment of respite from her anxiety. She hung onto those words like a lifebuoy in a tumultuous sea. Then she remembered a verse from the Book of Job that ripped at her lifebuoy, renewing her doubt, making her wonder if the waters of her life would ever grow calm again.

For man is born for trouble as sure as sparks fly upward.

Dung lay on the bed, closed her eyes, and became Dinh's wife.

8

Ho Chi Minh's top general, Vo Nguyen Giap, had been beaten time after time by the experienced and well-armed French. In the process, Giap had lost thousands of men and several years but gained invaluable insights about the conduct of war. As Giap learned his lessons, the French became fatigued. The Viet Minh had often been easy to beat due to their primitive weapons and tactics, but they kept coming with an inexhaustible supply of lives to launch against the French battlements. They did not stop. They would never stop.

When General Navarre delivered his sobering report, calling the war unwinnable, Paris tasked Navarre to look for a political solution to the conflict. The people of France had long wanted to relinquish their colony in Indochina, but politicians, ever prideful and covetous, delayed admitting defeat until they could no longer justify the cost of lives and treasure.

However, the Vietnamese troops gave the French an exit they did not expect. Giap methodically moved his 50,000 troops to surround French fighters in Dien Bien Phu. He placed his new Soviet artillery on the high ground above town and concealed it in tunnels dug into the mountainside. He took care to stockpile ammunition. When he was satisfied that he had all his chess pieces on the board, Giap unleashed hell.

Viet Minh artillery rained fire on French positions. Because they were encased in the mountain, the big guns were impervious to French artillery attempts to knock them out. The airfield which resupplied the French was bombed out of service. Once his enemy's supply lines were cut, Giap threw his whole army at them. The Viet Minh dug trenches ever closer to their enemy, tightening the noose by degrees. They attacked incessantly.

The French fought back valiantly. Their tenacity and desperation inflicted heavy losses on the Vietnamese. Soldiers on both sides referred to the battle as "fifty-seven days of hell," reminiscent of the butchery of trench warfare in World War I. In less than two months, nearly 3,000 French were killed. The Viet Minh lost between 4,000 and 8,000 men.

In the end, the sheer numbers of Viet Minh soldiers plus Giap's hard-won expertise overwhelmed the French defenses. One by one, the seven strongholds of Dien Bien Phu were overrun and defeated. The French commanders were humiliated and distraught. One of them committed suicide rather than face certain death at the hands of the Vietnamese.

The captured soldiers did not fare much better. Forced to march 500 miles to prison camps, more than half of them perished. Fewer than three in ten made it back to France.

France's defeat at Dien Bien Phu reverberated throughout Vietnam and around the world. Post World War II, countries had been sorting themselves into one of two teams: capitalist or communist. To the horror of western capitalists, Asia seemed to be slipping away. China, the giant dragon of the east, had recently adopted Marxism. Korea halved itself and its north followed China. Now, Ho Chi Minh and the communists in Vietnam had defeated France. More ominously, they had won a war with capitalism itself, for France hadn't been the only country beaten by Ho Chi Minh at Dien Bien Phu.

In the economic rubble of World War II, France could not afford to take on the Viet Minh alone. The United States, clear winners of WWII in every aspect, had risen to become the political leader of the free world, the standard bearer of global commerce, and the primary defender against expansive communism. The Americans had secretly funded 80% of France's war with the Viet Minh and watched with sick stomachs as their investment vaporized at Dien Bien Phu. Still, the prospect of losing all of Asia, and its massive markets, to an ideology of oppressive statism was unacceptable. While France bore the public shame of defeat, the Americans privately licked their wounds and retreated to the shadows. Washington waited to see what happened at the Geneva Conference before making their next move, but Uncle Sam was far from exhausted.

The Geneva Conference had been convened by the world's most powerful countries (USA, USSR, China, UK, and France) to solve the problems of war in Asia, particularly in Korea and Vietnam. Coincidentally, the conference opened on May 8, 1954, the day after the fall of Dien Bien Phu. The Geneva Conference reached an agreement that would split the country into a communist north under Ho Chi Minh, and capitalist south headed by the former French (then Japanese, then American) puppet emperor Bao Dai and prime minister Ngo Dinh Diem, who was Catholic.

The country was divided at the 17th parallel with plans to hold reunification elections in two years. The Americans had no intention of supporting the election, which they saw as a sure win for Ho and his communists. They poured money and advisors into the southern capital of Saigon to solidify the southern government. They sent CIA spies to sow chaos and fear in the north with a many-tentacled propaganda campaign. The United States, the richest and most powerful country in the history of the Earth, made their stand; first privately, then publicly. First with treasure, then with blood. They pledged that the tide of communism would be stopped at the 17th.

The Geneva agreements allowed a period of 300 days of free movement between north and south. The Americans saw this as a golden opportunity to weaken the north. They began by targeting the Catholics to relocate to the south where their freedom of religion would be protected.

God Has Gone South

Pamphlets and posters with this slogan were produced by the CIA and plastered all over Hanoi and Haiphong, warning Catholics of the dangers of communism. The propaganda warned that private property would be seized, the Chinese army would be allowed to occupy North Vietnam, and American nuclear weapons would be used against Hanoi. It was suggested that even God had left the north. To ensure their own salvation, Christians were urged to follow God to the promised land of the South.

The propaganda had the desired effect. The French and South Vietnamese authorities had predicted between 10,000 and 30,000 refugees would make the move, but by August, at least 200,000 people crammed the port of Haiphong looking to escape the coming horror. Conditions at makeshift refugee centers rapidly deteriorated. Starvation, dehydration, disease, and violence turned the camps into barbarous hellscapes of filth and despair. Something would have to be done.

The French authorities were ill-equipped to handle the unfolding disaster. They were occupied with the effort to get their defeated army out of the country and had little capacity for fleeing citizens. They turned to the United States for help. The American Navy pressed several of their wartime transport ships into action, retrofitting them for humanitarian service as they steamed north from the Philippines to Haiphong.

The codename for the evacuation was *Operation Passage to Freedom.*

9

F) ather) Tran Thieu was born in the seaport town of Haiphong, which sits on the southern bank of the Song Cam, a few miles upstream from the place where it empties into the Gulf of Tonkin. The second son, Tran was afforded none of the hereditary benefits of his older brother. His father was an angry man who worked in the shipyard in town and owned a small rice plot on its outskirts. Tran's mother worked long hours sewing clothing in a French colonialist's factory. She was seldom home. Despite their dual incomes, there never seemed to be enough money to make ends meet. Worse, their house was devoid of love, barren and broken. Failure and estrangement incubated bitterness and frustration, which begat abuse as Tran's father slapped and punched his children for the slightest offense.

Life was no kinder on the streets of the rough port town. Gangs of bullies tormented the bookish Tran, beating him any chance they got. Tran survived by learning when to fight and when to run. His bruising childhood forged a character of steely determination and unsentimental urgency. Intensity that bordered on rage radiated from his compact frame.

Tran found a safe place for both body and spirit in the church. He identified with the suffering of Paul, and nurtured secret joy in the promises of glory to the afflicted. The Psalms particularly comforted him when the rest of his world showed him only violence and neglect.

> *I keep my eyes always on the Lord.*
> *With Him at my right hand, I will not be shaken.*
> *He makes known to me the path of life.*

Tran started as an altar boy. He swelled with pride when he wore the simple servant dress of alb and cincture. The uniform satisfied his unfulfilled need to belong and stirred a powerful attraction to status. He eyed the cassock and surplice of the senior altar boys with longing.

Someday, I will wear one of those, he promised himself.

Eventually he did wear the cassock and surplice. Tran then set his sights on the white collar of the priesthood. With the financial backing of his mother, who had hoarded her clothing factory earnings from her rapacious husband, Tran was admitted to the seminary. He was not academically gifted, but he sailed through school by sheer will and bottomless energy.

The newly ordained Father Thieu was sent to the diocese of Thai Binh to serve as the parish priest for Luong Dien, a backwater rice farming town wedged between two watery arms of the Red River Delta. Father Thieu was secretly dissatisfied not to be given a parish in a more visible and upwardly-mobile urban area, but he swallowed his disappointment and accepted his assignment with gratitude. Whatever the disadvantages of sleepy Luong Dien, it would be better than the life of a Haiphong dockworker.

In Luong Dien, Father Thieu found what he expected—acre after acre of rice fields dotted by thatch huts, bordered by tall palms. Along with the unfamiliar landscape, the people also were different from what he had experienced in the city. The population was more docile, sober, and serious than the drunken, pugnacious reprobates in Haiphong. That alone was a refreshing change from the brawling chaos of his childhood.

Tran arrived fresh-faced and naïve. He had ample ego and a city-slicker's natural condescension toward country folk, yet he was eager to learn the bucolic rhythms of farming life so he could connect with, and then direct, his parishioners. He needn't have tried. The townspeople treated him with a reverent solicitude usually reserved for an emperor. As was common in Vietnam, a priest in a predominantly Catholic village carried the authority of a king. In some towns, priests even used their position to build private armies with which they fought the Viet Minh.

Father Thieu did not form a militia like some others, but once he figured out how to use his influence, he wielded near absolute authority. He did not become utterly degenerate, but power suited his ambition and corrupted him nonetheless. His great sin was the same one that severs many a soul from grace, the one that separated Lucifer from God, the one that plagues most who rise from nothing to a position of power. He was proud. Until 1945.

The Great Famine that had affected Dung and Dinh throughout their lives also left deep scars in Father Thieu's psyche. He was a young man when he arrived in the village, with a young man's hubris. He imagined himself the spiritual, as well as intellectual, superior to everyone in the province, and therefore able to direct the lives of thousands with his righteous mandate.

When bodies started falling along the road, and then on the steps of his church, Thieu's confidence left him. It was one thing to bloviate on innocuous theory, but when the stench of rotting human flesh filled the air, he had no answers. There were so many corpses. The sight of gray, sunken bodies of people he had known horrified him.

He retreated into shocked silence, preferring to hide in his office for most of the day rather than ministering to his hungry, disaster-stricken flock. Throughout the day he drank *ruou cuoc lui*, the local wine made from rice or corn, trying to numb the psychological torture of the sight. And the smell.

One day, a local teenager came to alert him that yet another life had ended on the church steps. The boy, Doan Van Dinh, seemed so poised, so courageous, it shamed Tran out of his stupor. Dinh had impressed Tran as a gifted boy, a talented musician, and leader. Tran asked Dinh to be the director of the church choir so he could keep him close and draw inspiration from him. Dinh accepted the offer. Then Tran lifted himself from his chair and returned to lead the town in its darkest hour, organizing farmers into teams for the gruesome task of collecting the bodies and burying them.

That had been nine years ago. The famine ended and life returned to normal. The residents of Luong Dien never publicly spoke of it again. They practiced a collective amnesia, smothering their grief and binding their cracked souls with silence.

Father Thieu rebounded, too. The people of the village hadn't witnessed his personal crisis, only his strength. He emerged from the disaster venerated by parishioners who would walk through fire for him. His choir director, Dinh, remained with him and became a friend and confidant, a valuable adjutant with significant leadership skills of his own.

The bishop in Thai Binh, Tran's boss, kept him informed of the worsening situation throughout the eight years of war with France. Vietnam's Catholic hierarchy was unabashedly pro-French, unflinching in their preference for the indignity of colonialism to the threat of extermination under communism. This bias filtered down through the church and heavily influenced nearly every Christian in the country.

The bishop's letters had grown more dire through the monsoon of 1953, and then around Christmastime, he made a visit to Father Thieu's parish. After Mass, the priest and the bishop talked privately.

"Father, I'm going to get right to the point, things are going badly in the war. According to our sources, the armies are converging on some hill town in the west...Dien Bien Phu is its name, I think. A large battle will occur soon, but regardless of the outcome, things don't look good long term. The French people no longer support the war. It seems to be just a matter of time before France surrenders the north," the bishop said.

"Just the north?" Father Thieu asked.

"Yes, for now, the communists are much stronger in the north than the south. The rumor I have heard is that there may be two Vietnams. If so, the south will be a safe place for us to worship our Lord. We are advising our priests to prepare to move at a moment's notice, and convince as many parishioners as they can to make the move as well. You have a great deal of influence here, it should not be hard for you."

Thieu was shocked. He held his breath while his mind exploded with questions. *Leave home? Convince people to leave the only place they have known for generations? How? When? Where?*

"Bishop, this is…so much to think about. Where do I start?"

"Begin by planting seeds," said the Bishop. "We do not want a panic, so start small. Let the people know what you have heard about the war. Tell them that you fear persecution, and may have to leave. That will make them think."

Father Thieu stood there open-mouthed, dumbstruck. The bishop continued.

"I will send you as much information as I can, but our couriers increasingly come under attack. If you think the time is right, don't wait on word from me, just go."

Just go. A vaguer command was never uttered.

"Go? Where?"

"South," said the bishop.

Tran didn't sleep much that night, or any night after that for many months. He hadn't felt so inadequate to a task since the Great Famine.

10

The fall of Dien Bien Phu sent shockwaves throughout the country. In the months leading up to May 8, 1954, a slow trickle of refugees set out on foot to escape south. Carrying only what their arms and backs could hold, they were catastrophically unprepared for the 1,000 mile journey over mountain spines and through marshy jungles. Many died of exposure, dehydration, or disease. Some were caught by roving bands of Viet Minh and turned back or killed. Some were absorbed into villages along the way. A vanishing few made it to the safety of Saigon, where refugee camps had been established.

Word of the evacuation spread among the villages even before the Geneva conference established the 300-day grace period and a stampede began. A trickle of refugees became a torrent as Catholics descended on Haiphong by the thousands. All northern parish priests had tremendous influence, just like Father Thieu. They used their leverage to pry entire villages away from their generational homes for a life of blind uncertainty, and privation as a refugee. A volatile mixture of fear, hope, and religious obedience convinced these simple farmers to pull up roots that had grown deep and thick over centuries. Even the big city of Hanoi watched its population shrink alarmingly as bars, restaurants, and shops closed by the hundreds, leaving the conquering

Viet Minh to take possession of a capital that looked more like a ghost town.

The results of Catholic flight were devastating to the towns they left, but nothing compared to the tormenting hellscape experienced by the Haiphong refugees themselves. Thrown into a writhing pit of humanity with inadequate food, water, and shelter, and without cultural, legal, or religious moorings to anchor them, the camps descended into anarchy. Rape, theft, and murder joined hunger, thirst, and disease in the fetid squalor. The Four Horsemen of the Apocalypse had a trial run in Vietnam; bringing famine, war, pestilence, and death to the wretched people huddled along the muddy banks of the polluted Song Cam.

In Luong Dien, Father Thieu looked out a small window in the front of his church. A group of children were playing in the small plaza, chasing one another, squealing with joy. Thieu felt a crushing sense of shame. Soon he would uproot these children from their happy lives and give nothing in exchange but a promise he had no power to keep. He wondered how many would be happy in a year. He wondered how many would be alive.

The priest from Haiphong still had contacts who sent him news of the awful conditions in the refugee camps. With this invaluable information, Father Thieu was able to save his people from immediate misery, but he knew he could not wait forever. He would eventually have to tell them to leave. But when?

The bishop continued to send him letters throughout the summer, apprising him of conditions throughout the diocese, and the ongoing power struggle that had brought the world to their unassuming country. The entire situation was fluid and complex. The bishop wrote that the

Americans would soon be sending ships to assist the overtaxed French fleet. The logjam in Haiphong would be relieved. This was good news, but the clock was ticking. Father Thieu wondered how long he could stay in Luong Dien before the communists came to arrest him and persecute his flock. Leaving too early carried the risk that his people might die in the camps. Leaving too late risked the same at the hands of the Viet Minh. Death surrounded Father Thieu once again, just like 1945.

He began to drink *ruou cuoc lui* again.

In the spring of 1954, the newly married Dung and Dinh tried to adjust to married life. This was easy for Dinh. His life changed very little, except he now had a partner to share his bed. Dung was not so fortunate. Her world had been upended. The work was no more than she had been used to at home, but learning the unfamiliar rhythms and demands of her new family was taxing and frustrating. Sex was frightening and uncomfortable. She often felt like a piece of property, no more valued than a water buffalo. In quiet moments, Dung allowed herself the luxury of self-pity, recalling the night her parents told her they were giving her away. Their action, while traditional and somewhat necessary, took on the shape of betrayal in Dung's mind. She raged with anger at them one moment and longed to be back home with them the next. Dinh often caught her lost in thought and chastised her idleness.

"Dung, what are you doing?" he asked.

"Nothing, just mending some clothes."

"Well, keep your mind on your work," he said.

Dinh felt pressure to mold his new wife. He was mindful of the patriarchal society in which he lived. A man was expected to rule his wife so that she would bring honor to him. Though sometimes he felt sorry for her, and wanted to be more loving and patient with his sweet-natured bride, he obeyed the code of his people and took on the role of leader first, husband second.

Dung privately seethed under her new master, but complied without protest as a wife was expected to do. She, too, understood the rules of society and played her part. When she felt weary, she leaned on Paul's words to the Corinthians.

Love bears all things, believes all things,
hopes all things, endures all things.

She didn't believe things would ever get better. Indeed, "better" was such a foreign concept, it was not given time or oxygen to thrive and grow into a wish. Wishes were deluding and dangerous, like a drug. She had seen enough of life to disabuse herself of the possibility of happy endings for females. Hardship was a woman's true birthright, forbearance her greatest asset. Still, she never abandoned hope that the Lord saw her unhappiness and would someday deliver her. Until then, she would bear all things, endure all things.

One day, Dung overheard Dinh speaking with his father. Dinh was doing most of the talking, which was how their recent conversations usually went. Dinh got his news from Father Thieu, who had become a mentor and confidant to the ambitious young man. He was saying something about a battle between the French and the communists.

72

Usually, Dung kept busy with her work and didn't concern herself with politics, but she often overheard her husband's conversations which seemed to be taking on more intensity each week. She was aware that her country was at war and that the communists represented a grave threat to Christians like herself. From Dinh's urgent words, she surmised that the war must not be going well.

Dung did not question Dinh about the news. She kept quiet and minded her work. To allay her anxiety, she rubbed her rosary smooth and imagined herself a Corinthian, receiving Paul's letter.

A few days later, Dinh received the news of the fall of Dien Bien Phu. He was standing in Father Thieu's dusty office, watching his friend's hand shake as he brought a cigarette to his lips. The priest, usually brimming with self-possession and decisiveness, looked like a trapped animal—fearful and nervous.

"Dinh, I don't know what to do," the priest confided.

"What do you mean?" Dinh asked.

"The Viet Minh have won. They are in charge now. We have to leave."

"What?" Dinh whispered.

He remembered the promise he made to Dung on their wedding day. Now, the Viet Minh and Father Thieu would make a liar of him.

"We won't be able to stay. I already have been getting reports of Christians being attacked. It will only get worse now that the communists are in power."

"When?" Dinh asked, unable to speak more than a word.

His mind bogged down with incredulity. How could the mighty French, for decades the fearsome overlord, have been beaten by Ho Chi Minh's ragtag group of peasants?

"That's what I don't know. There are already thousands of people in Haiphong waiting for transport to Saigon. They are starving, and living like rats while they wait. I'm not sending my church into that."

Dinh finished the thought, "But if you wait too long, the communists might interfere with the evacuation."

"Exactly," said Father Thieu.

Once again, he was impressed with Dinh's quick mind. A long silence suffocated conversation as the two men pondered. Finally, Father Thieu spoke.

"We will wait. The monsoon is on its way which will slow the activities of the Viet Minh. They are unlikely to spend energy on a pogrom when they have to establish their government. We should have a few months."

"Shall we start warning people now?" Dinh asked.

"No, it's too dangerous. There may be communist sympathizers in Luong Dien who would get word back to the Viet Minh, not to mention the panic it would cause."

"Yes," Dinh agreed, "and it will give us time to grow and stockpile food for the trip."

Father Thieu was unsure about the necessity of stockpiling food. He envisioned a desperate flight rather than an orderly exodus. He did not correct his friend, thinking it best to keep everything as normal as possible until it was time to go.

"For now, don't tell anyone, not even your family. Our survival depends on our silence," Father Thieu said.

Dinh turned to leave. Father Thieu had one more thing to say.

"Dinh, when it happens, it will happen fast. You have to be ready to go at any moment. I don't know yet how I'm going to get word out to the whole parish, but when you get my instructions, you have to leave immediately."

Dinh nodded and left with a chill running the length of his spine. He exited the church feeling the weight of the secret he had been given and overwhelmed with the thought of their entire village vanishing. As he walked home, he made a list of the things he would try to take with him. It was a short list.

11

Seaman Jimmy Kimbrough was born in 1930 on a southern Appalachian plateau called Sycamore Mountain. The plateau was tucked into the corners where Alabama, Georgia, and Tennessee meet, its western bluff overlooking the wide Tennessee River below and its endless forests dotted with bright green patches of farmland. Sycamore Mountain was a hard place like Vietnam, settled by pugnacious Scots-Irish immigrants who spilled like molasses over the southern hills in the 19th century. These settlers were clannish, and violent by nature, rejected by the Scots, the Irish, and coastal Americans. They found their place in the hills and hollers of Appalachia, and withdrew to lives of drinking, fighting, timbering, and farming. On Sundays, they prayed to a stern Calvinist God before resuming war with their neighbors on Monday. Sycamore Mountain, isolated by steep sandstone cliffs, was an ideal place for this lifestyle. Outsiders were discouraged from moving to the area. African-Americans were threatened with death if they were found on the mountain after dark.

Jimmy Kimbrough was a product of this culture. He drank instinctively and heavily. His first drink was homemade moonshine at age ten. Drinking uncovered a nasty temperament. When drunk, Jimmy fought indiscriminately, with rage bordering on madness. At the age of 22, Jimmy got into a drunken argument with Bennie Cole in a roadside bar. The disagreement, over the bloodline of a local horse, turned violent and Jimmy killed Bennie. The next day, Bennie's father went to Jimmy's father and told him that if he ever saw Jimmy on Sycamore Mountain again, he would kill him.

When Jimmy returned home, bruised and hungover, his father was waiting beside the car.

"Boy, did you kill Bennie Cole?"

"Yes, Daddy."

In addition to being a brawling drunk and now a murderer, Jimmy was an unhesitating liar, but he knew better than to lie to his father. His father shared Jimmy's penchant for violence, having raised his son with the back—and the front—of his hand. His Dad was the only man of whom Jimmy was scared.

"You dumb son of a bitch. If you want to live, get in the house and pack a bag," his father said.

"Why?" Jimmy asked.

"Because his daddy is going to kill you if he ever sees you again."

Jimmy packed a suitcase and jumped in the car. His dad drove him off the mountain, past the sign with a warning message that read *"Nigger don't let the sun go down on your black ass on Sycamore Mountain,"* to a Navy recruiting station in nearby Chattanooga.

The new recruit was shipped to Great Lakes Training Station to learn how to be a sailor. His fighting ways, racism, and alcoholism went with him. Constantly in trouble, he was nearly thrown out, but Jimmy managed to scrape through basic training and was assigned to the *USS Montrose*, a transport ship based in San Diego that had seen action in World War II and The Korean War.

Seaman Kimbrough was a poor sailor— stupid, surly and insubordinate. His upbringing on Sycamore Mountain had instilled in him a reflexive antipathy toward authority, and an unconscious hatred of blacks. He was repulsed by the thought of sharing close quarters with African-Americans and planned to establish dominance immediately. When he arrived on the ship, he called out to Louis Washington, a hulking and popular African-American boatswain's mate from East St. Louis.

"Hey, boy, carry my duffel to my bunk," Jimmy said, smirking.

Louis didn't say a word, but removed his cap and walked meekly over to Jimmy and paused in front of Jimmy's bag. He then took one more step and punched Jimmy squarely in the chest, knocking him down.

"This ain't the south, motherfucker," Louis said, and walked away.

Jimmy lay sprawled on the floor and waited for the other white sailors to attack the black man. They didn't do anything other than point and laugh at Jimmy. He sputtered in outrage at what he considered a betrayal of his race, but he didn't dare fight the much bigger Louis Washington. He picked himself up, grabbed his duffel and slunk to his quarters. The humiliation burned inside him. He swore to himself that he would kill Louis Washington someday, but he had been emasculated, only capable of fantasizing about revenge, and too ashamed to admit to himself that he was scared of a black man. Jimmy avoided Louis and the other black sailors and fell in with a small group of like-minded men from Mississippi, Florida, and, oddly enough, Massachusetts. The blacks and even some of the whites on board mockingly called the group "The Klan." The Klan spent its free time huddled in sullen conversation, most of which was dedicated to bemoaning the state of the integrated Navy. They predicted a dire future for the country if full desegregation ever came to pass.

"We shoulda picked our own cotton," Klan members were fond of saying.

Operation Passage to Freedom employed the ships of Task Force 90, some 100 Navy vessels charged with moving hundreds of thousands of refugees from Haiphong to Saigon. It was a huge undertaking. The *Montrose* received orders to steam for Haiphong to join the task force.

Seaman Kimbrough had become a machinist mate aboard the *Montrose*. He and his shipmates had to make their vessel ready to receive thousands of refugees. Most of the sailors recognized the scale and goodness of the humanitarian mission, but not Jimmy. His disagreeable nature etched a permanent scowl on his face. In addition to his bilious expression, Jimmy gave voice to the acid in his heart. He turned out to be a well-rounded racist, hating not only blacks, but Jews, Indians, and women. His hatred of Asians was second only to his loathing of blacks, lumping Koreans, Chinese, Japanese, and Vietnamese under the catch-all term "Gook."

"Vern, why are we saving them goddamn Gooks, anyway?" Jimmy asked his friend.

"Hell, it ain't like the world don't have enough of them," Vern replied.

"I know," Jimmy drawled, "Did you know that these fuckers ain't even Buddhist or whatever, they're fuckin' Catholic. We ought to leave them where they are and let them kill each other. Less Gooks, less Catholics, and less communists, problem solved."

"Damn, Jimmy, you're brilliant," Vern said.

"Maybe I'll run for president someday," Jimmy snickered.

The machinists were tasked with building a toilet that could handle more than 1,000 refugees. One sailor came up with the idea to use 55-gallon drums. The machinists split three drums down the middle and welded them together to form a long trough. Planks were laid at intervals across the openings on which to stand or sit. A fire hose was attached to one end to spray the refuse to the open end where it fell off the ship's fantail and into the ocean.

When the *Montrose* docked at Haiphong, the sailors came on deck to see the sight. None were unaffected by what they saw. Many were overcome with emotion. A mass of humanity rippled as waves in a pond after a pebble has been dropped in it, radiating in every direction. Louis Washington shed a tear at the grandeur and pathos of the scene.

"Surely there ain't enough boats in the world for all these people," he whispered to himself.

Jimmy Kimbrough was impressed too, but wrestled his awe into revulsion at the sight.

"Jesus, look at this shit," he snarled.

The first load of refugees boarded the *Montrose* orderly and quietly. A few carried a sack of belongings thrown over their shoulders, but most were empty-handed. Many were shoeless. More than half wore the conical *non la* hat so common in the rice fields. Seaman Kimbrough and the members of The Klan mocked the Vietnamese as they walked up the gangplank. When he had his fill of ridicule, Jimmy extinguished his cigarette and headed to his bunk.

The *Montrose* set sail down the Cam River with its ragged passengers. As they entered the Gulf of Tonkin, a disturbance arose on the fantail. Vern ran to tell Jimmy what was happening. Jimmy was in his bunk, looking at a comic book.

"Jimmy, you ain't gonna believe what they are doing on deck," Vern said.

"What?" Jimmy asked.

"You gotta see this for yourself."

Jimmy and Vern arrived on the fantail. Half the crew had beaten them there. The sailors gathered to see what the refugees were doing with the homemade latrine the machinists had made. The Vietnamese had been given no instructions on the use of the latrine, so they began using it as a bath and laundry. Mothers gleefully used the clean running water to wash weeks of grime from their children. Clothes were doused and scrubbed.

The sailors laughed at the miscommunication. Jimmy sneered in contempt. The episode highlighted a problem that would repeat itself on every ship of Task Force 90. There was no reliable way for the Americans and Vietnamese to communicate. French was a language familiar to both, but the differences between the sailors' rusty high school French and the dialect of the Vietnamese French were too great to overcome.

In the end, Rome came to the rescue. Both the Navy chaplains and the Vietnamese priests spoke Latin in their Masses and used the dead language to bridge the communication gap. The Vietnamese priests threw back their heads in laughter when the chaplains informed them of the intended use of the trough. The priests passed the instruction along to the mothers, but it did not change behavior much. The ladies still washed their clothes and children in the upper end near the hose. The lower end was allowed to be used as a toilet.

Little by little, the challenges of transporting refugees were overcome. By the end of the operation, more than 300,000 souls would be relocated by the U.S. Navy. The Vietnamese even warmed to the sailors. In Haiphong, Viet Minh infiltrators had spread rumors about murderous sailors throwing passengers overboard. When they first arrived aboard, the refugees were highly suspicious of the Americans, but once they realized the rumors were baseless, they grew to adore the big men dressed in blue dungarees, chambray shirts, and little white caps the sailors called Dixie cups.

But trouble was nearby.

In Vietnam, trouble was always nearby.

12

A dull rain thudded against the soggy earth as night creeped in, pulling a black blanket over Vietnam. It was September and the monsoon seemed to be tiring of its rage. The earth turned to soup under months of precipitation. Mud was inescapable. The people of Luong Dien, exhausted from weeks of ceaseless toil in the rice paddies, slept like the dead in their huts as the rain's soothing rhythm beat against the rooftops.

A lone figure emerged from his residence and dissolved into the darkness. He was dressed in the traditional black attire of a farmer. A mud-stained *non la* sat atop his head. The blackness of the rain-soaked night absorbed the world into a formless void. Sky and earth were one in uroboric nothingness. There were no street lights or house lights to provide illumination. The farmer carried a small lantern to guide his steps along the road. Mud squished through his bare toes. He dared not wear the only shoes he owned for fear his identity might be questioned.

As Operation Passage to Freedom continued, the Viet Minh realized a large chunk of their population, and their power, was disappearing in the ships docked at Haiphong. Individual units began harassing refugees in an effort to discourage flight, but the people, mostly Catholic, kept leaving. By degrees, the communists stepped up their efforts to prevent people from fleeing. It began with whispered rumors and propaganda, then escalated into violence as soldiers forcefully prevented escape.

The man from Luong Dien used the darkness and rain as cover as he made his way toward Haiphong. He regretted the lantern which stood out like a searchlight against the black backdrop, but could not navigate without it. He hoped the rain would keep the soldiers inside for the night.

The journey from Luong Dien to Haiphong was 60 kilometers. The farmer estimated it would take at least 15 hours of constant walking to get there, assuming there was no delay or detour to evade roving patrols of Viet Minh. Traveling after dark was the best way to avoid soldiers, but the man knew he could not make the journey in one night. At some point daylight would catch him, and most likely the Viet Minh would as well. He prayed to Saint Christopher for safe passage.

Rivers were his greatest concern. A natural chokepoint, Viet Minh units often camped out at bridges to catch and turn back refugees. There were six rivers and innumerable canals on the route. The man figured he could wade across the canals, but the rivers were swollen from the monsoon—deep, swift, and full of dangerous tree trunks lurking below the muddy surface. Only a fool would attempt to swim across. As he walked, he practiced the lies he would tell the soldiers.

The farmer made it across the Song Tra Ly and the Song Diem Ho without seeing a soul. As he crossed the wide Song Hoa, the drab light of dawn fell lazily across the land. He extinguished his lamp and threw it in a ditch beside the road. He had packed two bananas and a small vase of *ruou cuoc lui* which he carried tied to a rope around his waist.

He ate one of the bananas and took a sip of wine to celebrate crossing half the rivers on his route without incident.

Daylight grew to its muted full strength, diffused by thick clouds which cast a depressing gray gloom over the earth. Thankfully, the rain persisted, which the man hoped would diminish the soldiers' enthusiasm for harassment. But this was Vietnam, where the people breathed rain like oxygen. He didn't count on luck seeing him through to Haiphong.

A sharp pain pierced the farmer's foot. He raised his foot and saw red mixed with the brown mud. He had stepped on a shard of pottery which left a gash.

"Holy Mother, deliver me," he whispered.

An injury could be disastrous. He leaned against a coconut tree and scraped the dirt from the oozing wound and poured *ruou cuoc lui* on it to cleanse and disinfect it. He grimaced when the alcohol hit open flesh and realized the cleaning would make little difference once he started walking again. He cursed his luck and weighed his options. There was only one. He had to keep walking. The searing pain forced a limp as he avoided putting the weight of his stride on the injured foot. His gait slowed. He had figured he could run away from the Viet Minh if all else failed; now he couldn't even do that. He wasn't a sitting duck, but a very slow-moving duck.

The Viet Minh caught him.

As the farmer was passing a house, a group of five young men, maybe teenagers, filed out of the hut and saw a stranger limping by.

"Hey, old man, where are you going?" the leader called.

Although the man was not yet forty 40 years old, his new limp made him look old. The young men were all carrying green bamboo staffs, heavy with water and rock hard. The farmer guessed their staffs served as weapons in lieu of guns.

"Little boys playing war," he thought.

The man stopped and looked at them. Though they bluffed courage, he could sense their weakness and embarrassment for accosting an elder.

"What business is that of yours?" he demanded.

He was used to wielding authority and instantly put the young men on the defensive.

"We have a mission to stop any refugees trying to escape," the leader stammered as his embarrassment grew.

"You're not going to Haiphong, are you?"

He seemed to shrivel with each word.

The man snorted, "Haiphong? I'm going to Ham Duong to get a buffalo. My regular animal died and I'm going there to rent one. I'm losing daylight making this trip, I have just cut my foot, and now you are delaying me even further. I'm not going to Haiphong, I'm trying to feed my family."

The boys shrunk before him. They looked at each other and bowed their heads in shame.

"We are sorry. Please forgive the delay. You said you cut your foot, can we give you a bandage?"

The farmer accepted the boys' magnanimous offer and wrapped his foot. He limped north. He had easily bullied the young men, but the episode frightened him. He had bluffed and they backed down. Had they been a bit surer of themselves, they might've cracked his skull with the bamboo poles.

The bandage helped tremendously, but his pace was still slowed by the injury. He crossed the Song Thai Binh without incident.

Two more rivers to go.

As the Red River approaches the sea, the land flattens. The main channel no longer has gravity to pull the river to its end, so the water backs up and fans out. Secondary channels form to carry excess water and a river delta is born. Distributaries stretch out like spider legs, dumping their alluvial treasure over a 2,700-mile triangle of land. The result is a watery web, a fantastically rich agricultural net which supports tens of millions of people.

Through this net of river and canal, farm and grove, the farmer made his way toward one of the largest delta rivers, the Song Van Uc. The man figured if he could cross it, his chances of making it to Haiphong would improve dramatically. He fingered the rosary hidden under his shirt and prayed for protection. Up ahead, the Song Van Uc loomed a half-mile wide, dark, and deceptively peaceful.

A small detachment of Viet Minh clustered at the southern end of the bridge spanning the Song Van Uc. The seven men were Viet Minh regulars, all having fought at Dien Bien Phu. They each had a Russian Kalashnikov rifle slung over a shoulder and took patriotic pride abusing refugees whom they considered French collaborators, traitors to the nationalist cause, and fanatical Christians.

The farmer saw them up ahead. He decided to use the buffalo line that had worked so well with the boys. That story combined with his natural authority and charisma might be enough to get him through the blockade. He strode up to the soldiers as confidently as he could.

"Let me pass, please," he said.

"Where are you going?" a soldier asked.

"Bac Sai Nghi," the farmer answered.

"What for?"

"Borrowing a buffalo from my cousin."

In one fluid motion, the soldier took the Kalashnikov from his shoulder, stepped over to the farmer and buried the butt of the rifle in the farmer's gut. The pain exploded through his body as he doubled over and fell face first into the muddy road. He gasped for breath. Finally, he rose to his knees, protecting himself with both arms folded across his midsection.

"You didn't come all the way from Thai Binh for a buffalo. Go back home Christian," the soldier said.

The farmer stammered, "What are you talking about?"

"Your accent gives you away, priest."

"Why do you call me priest?"

"I was raised in the church. You all speak with the same haughty, patronizing tone," the soldier said.

The man was outed. Too easily. He dropped the charade and made one last appeal to the highest authority.

"Don't you believe in God, son?"

"What has God done for us? Made us slaves to France! I believe in the one who has delivered us from French bondage, and his name is Ho Chi Minh."

The farmer's heart was broken.

"Oh, son, communism will be a much harsher master than you can imagine."

The soldier stiffened and looked like he might swing his rifle again.

"If you call me 'son' one more time, the next strike will be against your head. Now go home."

The soldier turned to his company and they all laughed.

The man sat down in the middle of the road; ashamed, beaten, and broken. He had been foolish to wait so long to make his escape. To make matters worse, he was responsible not only for himself, but for the evacuation of his village. He had failed them. Hot tears streaked his dirty cheeks.

He got up and shuffled aimlessly away from the river. His plan was dashed and he had no backup strategy. His failure had a crushing finality to it. He reached for the *ruou cuoc lui* but it was not hanging from the rope around his waist. He looked back toward the bridge and saw the vase lying in pieces in a puddle.

Smashed.

Just like his passage to freedom.

13

ather Thieu is gone," Dinh panted as he burst into his house.
He had walked to the church to pick up a piece of music. While
he was there, he stopped by the priest's office. The Father was
not there, nor was he in his residence. Dinh checked all the produce
markets frequented by Thieu. He was nowhere to be found. For a long
time, Dinh sat on the steps outside the church, waiting for his friend,
dreading his suspicions. While he waited, Dinh remembered something
odd he had seen in the priest's office on his last few visits. He returned
to the office to see if the strange items were still there. They were gone.
Electricity shot through Dinh's body. He sprinted home to tell his wife.

Dung was further from the priest's orbit and did not react to the
news with the same alarm. She could see her husband's panic and
attempted to reason with him.

"How do you know he's gone?" Dung asked. "Maybe he's visiting
someone in another village."

"No, he is a man of routine," Dinh said. "He never deviates from his
schedule. I'm sure he's gone."

"Perhaps someone was dying and he had to give last rites," she
offered.

Dinh lost patience with his wife's logical alternatives and employed
his trump card of evidence.

"Look," he said, "Father Thieu had some clothes hanging in his office lately. Regular clothes like a farmer would wear. He even had a *non la*. When have you ever seen him wearing anything but his cassock? I went to his office. The clothes were gone."

Dung listened and her husband's suspicions became clear. He must have worn the farmer's clothes as a disguise to fool the Viet Minh. She was convinced.

"But why?" she asked, "Do you think he has abandoned us?"

Dinh hated the question. He thought so highly of the priest, but the possibility that Thieu had forsaken them had to be considered. He hadn't said anything to Dinh before vanishing, which planted doubt about his motive.

"I hope not," he said.

"What do we do now?" Dung asked.

While Dinh had been consumed with the reasons behind the disappearance, he hadn't considered the ramifications for his family and friends. Dung was practical. She had a way of cutting through the theoretical to get to the issue at hand. Dinh admired his wife's ability to avoid emotional hijack.

"I don't know," he said.

To Dung, this was a stunning admission. Her husband had been decisive to the point of being obnoxious, always so sure of himself. His doubt was both frightening and endearing. Dung felt both pity and loyalty. It was the first time she had a positive thought about Dinh in the nine months they had been married.

The situation was indeed troubling. Bands of Viet Minh now paraded openly in the streets of Luong Dien. They were callow bucks mostly showing off, but their hubris intimidated all the townspeople except Father Thieu. He was the people's champion, unafraid to confront the boys and send them scattering with heads hung low. Now he was gone. His flock was all alone.

Father Thieu was in shock. He sat on the side of the road and processed his anguish and physical pain. He had not been a victim of violence since his youth, and marveled at its power. One rifle butt to the belly was all it took to shatter weeks of preparation, and worse still, his pride. For an hour he sat motionless as the pain pulsed in waves. The soldiers on the bridge noticed he had stopped walking. They calculated he would be no more trouble, but kept a casual watch on him in case he needed a reminder.

The priest was loathe to leave the bridge and head back to Luong Dien. To go south was to surrender. North, across the bridge, was his salvation and that of his people. As he sat, the sharp pain in his gut turned to a manageable ache, and as his pain subsided, and so did his despair. He began to formulate alternatives, even considering the suicidal act of swimming the Song Van Uc.

As the priest was lost in thought, a large group of people, maybe 20 or more, walked past him toward the bridge. He wanted to warn them, to exercise his God-given authority and stop them from the disaster which awaited them on the bridge. He did not. The physical attack had demolished his confidence, his legitimacy. He was embarrassed to call himself a priest. The old sin, pride, had crept back into his life and deluded him about the strength of his influence. Unquestioned among the hundreds of people in his parish, his stature

95

became nothing in the face of raw physical power. He decided he was a coward, the biggest fool in all of Vietnam. He stayed silent as the group walked by.

"Hey, you," a voice whispered from the stand of mangroves behind the priest.

Father Thieu turned around and saw a figure hiding among the trees.

"If you want to get to Haiphong, come with me."

"What do you mean?" Thieu asked.

The voice became impatient.

"Do you see that group headed for the bridge? The soldiers will be distracted with them for about two minutes. If you want to escape, quit asking questions and come now."

The priest slipped into the woods and followed the stranger. The two made their way to the river. Concealed from the soldiers' position, a sampan was tied to a tree.

"Get in," the man ordered.

Thieu got in. The boatman untied the rope quickly and pushed off.

"Where are we going?" Thieu asked.

"Sao Do, but first we have to get out of here. If the soldiers see us, they might start shooting. They really didn't like you. Are you a priest or something?"

"Yes," Thieu answered.

The admission tasted like bile in his mouth. He imagined the boatman's contempt for his weakness.

"That figures. They don't like priests. The Viet Minh consider them French puppets."

The man stopped talking as they drifted downstream toward the bridge. As the sampan drifted silently under the bridge, a commotion could be heard above. Shouts and screams erupted overhead as the refugees began fighting with the Viet Minh. The awful sounds of conflict echoed against the underside of the bridge, then all was quiet. As the sampan emerged from under the bridge, the men heard a different sound.

Music.

At first the sound was as soft as a breeze, but got louder as more voices joined the singing. Father Thieu craned his neck to see what was happening. The people on the bridge had joined hands and locked arms. They were singing!

He leadeth me, He leadeth me
By His own hand, He leadeth me
His faithful follower I would be
For by His hand he leadeth me

The soldiers had been beating them ferociously with their rifles, sparking panic that almost scattered the group. But then it happened. Without command or coordination, the group joined arms and stared down the soldiers. The Viet Minh were confused by the simple power of unity, transfixed by the spontaneous, almost supernatural way they organized, as if God had whispered instructions in the ears of each one. And then they began singing. And walking. Individuality disappeared. Fear dissolved like fragrance on the wind, replaced by iron courage that could not be penetrated even by the threat of death. The group became a machine, a holy tank which plowed through the Viet Minh with faith and song. As one, they moved across the bridge, leaving the perplexed soldiers to wonder what just happened.

And when my task on earth is done
When by thy grace the victory's won
E'en death's cold wave I will not flee
Since God through Jordan leadeth me

The words swelled in Father Thieu's heart and flooded his eyes. He watched the spectacle—the *miracle*—with open-mouthed wonder and elation he didn't expect to experience until he stood in front of the Lord on Judgement Day. The group sang all the way across the river, then released their grip on each other and kept walking as if nothing happened. The priest crossed himself and began whispering the Lord's Prayer.

"Our Father, who art in….."

"Hey you!" shouted a voice on the bridge.

The sound cracked the air like a rifle shot and broke the sacred spell cast by the singing tank. Father Thieu looked to the sound and saw the soldiers on the bridge staring at him.

"Time to go," the boatman said calmly.

He reached across the priest and instantly cranked the motor, sending the sampan skidding down the river.

The two men remained quiet for a long time. Father Thieu was exhausted physically and emotionally. He sat catatonic on the bench as the boatman expertly steered his vessel along tributaries and canals that crisscrossed the land. Soft rain pattered hypnotically, breaking the surface of the river into a million tiny waves. Finally he spoke.

"I saw God on the bridge."

"What?" the boatman replied, not sure what the priest meant.

"I saw a breath…a disturbance in the air above the people. Like waves of heat rising from the road on a hot day. It was God, protecting his people just as he did when Moses parted the Red Sea."

"Hmm," said the boatman, not sure how to respond.

"Didn't you see it?"

"No," said the boatman, "I guess the Christian God is only visible to those who believe in him."

"You're not Catholic?" Father Thieu asked.

"No, I'm Buddhist."

"Why are you helping me?"

The boatman took a deep breath and exhaled heavily.

"I was having a bad day. Fish weren't biting. Motor was giving me trouble. I was worried the Viet Minh might take my boat. They have been confiscating boats because fishermen have been helping the Christians cross rivers. In short, I had fallen into self-pity, bitterness, and attachment to the world, and began to suffer from my anxieties. I decided to meditate for a while in the grove of trees beside the bridge. Before you walked up to the soldiers, I had been practicing the metta and karuna."

Father Thieu interrupted him, "I'm sorry, I am not familiar with those terms."

"Metta is a feeling of compassion toward all beings. By practicing metta, the Buddhist overcomes anger, ill will, and hatred. Karuna is metta in practice, an active form of sympathy that is willing to bear the pain of others. When I saw the soldier attack you, I was moved to extend karuna and share your burden."

"That took courage," Father Thieu said. "Thank you."

"Courage is the highest form of Buddhism," the boatman said, "It is a willingness to let go of the ultimate attachment—life itself—for a friend.

"Greater love hath no man than he who is willing to lay down his life for his friends," Father Thieu muttered.

"What did you say?" the boatman asked.

"John 15:13. It is a verse in our Bible. It sounds a lot like what you just said."

"Maybe our religions are more alike than people think," the boatman offered with a smile.

Father Thieu smiled back.

The boatman deposited the priest on the far side of the Song Lach Tray, the last of his journey's six rivers. The outskirts of Haiphong were visible from the river bank.

"Be careful," the boatman warned, "Viet Minh own the city outside the refugee camps. You will have to weave your way through town to avoid them. Good luck."

"And to you as well," Father Thieu said. "Thank you."

He disappeared into the trees.

Like a cat, the priest padded silently through the streets, ducking into alleys when patrols came stomping noisily along the street. The soldiers were lazy in the city, more interested in bars and prostitutes than catching Christians. By the hundreds, lone refugees like Father Thieu slipped through their fingers like grains of sand.

But the ease of movement for a single person highlighted a problem. There was no way the entire population of Luong Dien could get through to the embarkation center. They would have to find another way to get the people on one of the ships. As he passed through the gates of the refugee center, the priest convinced himself that an answer would be found by going forward, but he doubted the sincerity of his rationalizations.

He was processed quickly, and sent to the ship which would take him to Saigon. Guilt overcame him as he realized his heart had lied to him about his intentions. He boarded alone, ashamed that he had turned a blind eye to the weakness that drove him to flee.

A smirking seaman named Jimmy Kimbrough stood on the railing above the gangplank, watching the dirty, shoeless, wreck of a man entering the ship. He sniffed in contempt and took a long draw on his cigarette.

14

The *Montrose* bounced along the South China Sea. The dying monsoon thrashed out the last of its seasonal strength, bending rain sideways across the open decks of the ship.

Below, Father Thieu and 1,000 other Vietnamese regretted their decision to flee with each bout of nausea. The disorienting pitch and roll of the ship soured every stomach, filling the bunking areas with the rotten stench of vomit. The anxiety of relocating, which had set up residence in every heart, was replaced by the immediacy of wrenching physical misery that lasted for three days.

When the priest wasn't lying on his mat or throwing up in a bucket, he made conversation with the ship's chaplain, a squat sailor from New Jersey with a jolly expression etched into the folds of his lumpy face. His name was Father Perrone. The two men spoke in halting Latin. On the third day, Father Thieu asked Perrone if he could give confession. The American removed his eyeglasses, which were too small for his face, and nodded in kindly assent.

"Forgive me Father, for I have sinned," Thieu began.

Father Perrone watched as the penitent struggled under the weight of his guilt.

"I have abandoned my people," he continued.

Thieu paused to let the full weight of the truth sink in. His eyes filled with tears. He then told Father Perrone of his journey to Haiphong.

"I convinced myself that I was scouting an escape route for them, but I was really running away."

He broke down and started to sob. Father Perrone grasped his shoulder in sympathy.

"We all fall short in our efforts, Father," Perrone said. "Pride and fear seek to separate us from the love of God, but the Lord understands our weakness, and extends His grace to us eternally. Succumbing to sin is the easy path that we all walk sometimes. He recognizes this. That's why He gives us unlimited chances to repent and atone. We find favor in His sight anytime we choose to pursue the difficult thing…the right thing."

Father Thieu strained to open his heart to the words of reconciliation and hope. Father Perrone continued.

"Are you prepared to do your penance to God and your people, Father Thieu? If so, I will tell you how to make this right."

Perrone spelled out his plan and Father Thieu flinched in dread. Father Perrone ignored Thieu's body language and concluded his advice with a deadline.

"We will arrive in Saigon in about an hour. There will be a two-hour debarkation window, after that we will sail back to Haiphong. I wish you peace in your decision."

When the *Montrose* steamed out of the Mekong River three hours later to return to Haiphong, it had one extra passenger. This passenger chose to go back north to do the right thing.

It would be a difficult thing.

Christians of North Vietnam began to curse themselves and despair. They wanted to escape the strengthening reign of the communists, but by October 1954 they had waited too long. Their first choice had been to go directly to Haiphong where the ships of Task Force 90 were waiting, but this option was squeezed off as the Viet Minh steadily closed their grip around the port city. Panicked, the refugees started racing in all directions; west into the mountains and across the border into Laos, south to reach the safety of the 17th parallel, and east to the edge of the Gulf of Tonkin to flag down passing boats.

Most were caught and forced back home. Some tried again and again to escape. Others gave up and decided to take their chances under communism. Chaos and fear reverberated through the population. Those who remembered the famine of 1945 said it felt the same way, as if the devil himself had set up shop in their beleaguered country.

In Luong Dien, fear paralyzed the residents. They had put their faith in Father Thieu and he had vanished. They did not know how to proceed without their leader. As the village learned that the priest was gone, the Viet Minh youth found out, too, and filled the power vacuum left by Thieu's disappearance. Their harassment and bullying increased. Violence escalated as the child soldiers beat anyone who challenged them. Like a silent boa constrictor, the insidious presence had slithered in and wrapped itself around the village.

Dinh Doan watched helplessly as the events unfolded. He nervously smoked cheap Haiphong cigarettes one after another to allay his tension. Dinh thought about trying to organize his neighborhood into an escape party, but he did not know where to go. The news that Haiphong was largely controlled by the Viet Minh had filtered through the region. Dinh confided in Dung that he thought they missed their chance.

"I was wrong to put my faith in Thieu. We waited too long and now we're trapped," Dinh said.

"What will we do?" Dung asked.

"I don't know," Dinh answered.

His wife, never an initiator of physical affection, walked over and wrapped him in a fearful hug. He hesitated, then put his hands on her shoulders.

In the evening of the eighth day after the disappearance of the priest, Dinh lay in his bed next to his sleeping wife. Evening rain tapped intermittently outside. Dinh fell into a fitful sleep. In the hazy dimension between consciousness and sleep, reality is corrupted by untethered, mischievous subconscious. Absurdity is validated by dream action, which is simultaneously independent and under the control of the dreamer. As Dinh entered the somnolent murkiness, he heard his name called outside.

"Dinh!"

As he took his place on the spongy stage of dreamworld, he became an actor in his own play. The spirit of the monsoon had called to him. The spirit wanted Dinh to come outside and let his body be dissolved by the rain. Dinh would join a puddle, then a trickle, then a stream, then a river. He would be carried to the sea to feed the monsoon.

Dinh argued with the spirit. He couldn't go, he pleaded. He was now married and had to provide for his wife.

"Dinh!" the spirit called again forcefully.

"I can't go with you, I have to fight the Viet Minh somehow," Dinh said.

"Dinh!"

Dinh thought the spirit was rude to keep calling his name while they were having a conversation. It happened again, and he was jolted back to consciousness.

"Dinh, come out!" the voice said.

Dinh sprung from his bed to see who would come calling so late.

Dripping wet, wearing black farmer's clothes, Father Thieu stood before him. Still groggy, Dinh stared at him blankly.

"Where have you been?" he asked.

"I'll tell you later. Right now, we don't have much time. We have to go," the priest said.

Thieu gave Dinh a few instructions and disappeared into the blackness. Dinh stood in his doorway for a moment, wondering if this was part of the dream.

"What's going on?" said a voice behind him.

It was Dung.

"Why did you jump out of bed?"

Dinh looked at her and realized he wasn't dreaming.

"That was Father Thieu. He said we have to go."

"What?" she asked, "Where has he been?"

"I don't know."

"When do we have to leave?"

"Now."

Within minutes, Luong Dien was a beehive of silent activity. Neighbors were awakened and given instructions to go to the church. In less than an hour, the church was full of nervous Christians anxiously whispering to one another. They had been instructed to leave everything behind except a blanket.

Finally, Father Thieu burst into the sanctuary and closed the doors. A few people had lit candles to light the room. He told them to extinguish them for fear the Viet Minh might discover them. They sat in the dark and listened to the priest tell them the only life they had ever known was about to end. Gasps and quiet sobs softly pierced the blackness. He then told them what they were about to do. Objections filled the air.

"I can't swim."

"What if we get caught?"

"Who will take care of my buffalo?"

Thieu brushed aside their fears.

"We have no choice. We cannot make it to Haiphong, and we cannot wait any longer. God is not here anymore. We have to go where He waits for us."

And so they did. Everything was left behind. All the possessions that grounded them to life and to the only place they had called home for generations would be abandoned without a moment to reminisce. Animals, clothing, cooking pots, ancestral altars, furniture, pictures, and the houses that held them would become artifacts of a ghost town, a hundred tiny museums without any visitors. As instructed, the only thing each person brought along was a blanket. Father Thieu told them they would need that once they got on the giant ship called "Muen-tross."

Father Thieu thought smaller groups would stand a better chance of eluding Viet Minh patrols, so he sent his flock to the sea in waves of 20. Dinh led the first wave. His group was made up of his family, Dung's family, and a few neighbors. Dung's friend Mai, now betrothed to Dinh's groomsman Tuan, was in their group. Dung and Mai held hands as they walked in the dark. Each carried a blanket in the other hand.

The groups were instructed to walk along the road. If they saw a patrol, they were to duck behind houses, hide behind groves of trees, or swim across canals. Under no circumstances were they to confront the Viet Minh. Dinh sent two of his cousins ahead to act as scouts. Shortly after dawn, his scouts came running back to him.

"There's a patrol up ahead," one of the cousins reported.

"How many?" Dinh asked.

"About five or six. We saw them at the next junction. One of them has a rifle."

Dinh had seen a rifle only once in his life. The name alone made him tense. He gathered his group together.

"We will cut across the fields here. The road will curve back into our path after the junction. Everyone must stay silent, no matter what," Dinh instructed.

"There is a canal out there," Tuan offered.

"Then we will cross it," Dinh said.

The walk quickly became a slow muddy slog. The farmers were used to working in the paddies, but moving at a farming pace was much easier than crossing them at speed. Frustration seeped into the group. Blankets were dropped in the mud. The people kept churning; Dinh at the front, Tuan in the back.

The canal was swollen from the monsoon. The group stopped at the edge and looked at Dinh. He studied the water for a moment and lowered himself silently into it. It was cold. He turned and saw the hesitant faces of his group. He motioned sharply for them to get in and they did. Children swam across with ease and emerged on the opposite side shivering. The water came up to the necks of the shorter women.

One by one, Dinh's group crawled out of the canal. Everyone's blankets became waterlogged and heavy, so they were left in the canal or on the bank. The one possession they were to carry to the south was abandoned within the first hours. If they made it to the south, they would do so owning nothing but the clothes they wore.

The road was regained without incident, but the cold canal and the fatigue from crossing muddy fields drained the group's energy. Some of the older people had to be assisted, younger children had to be carried. Progress was excruciatingly slow. Dinh furrowed his brow with anxiety, knowing the youthful vigor of the Viet Minh could pounce upon them at any moment.

Through divine intervention, or its close cousin dumb luck, Dinh's group made it without further sightings of the Viet Minh. The wet refugees huddled on the beach and shivered while they waited for other groups to arrive. A pernicious mist hung in the air, drawing heat from their bodies. Sand burrowed like an opportunistic parasite under their clothes. In the distance, the sea boiled with malicious whitecaps. A few hours prior, everyone had been sleeping peacefully in a warm bed. The realization that they had traded the possibility of communist oppression for the reality of immediate misery sank in as body heat drained out.

Either from shame of their naiveté or fatigue of hypothermia, the people said nothing. Father Thieu's words, "God is not here anymore," intended to be a call to action, were transformed into a sentence to Hell. They sat on the beach and shivered without protest, consumed with despair and regret. One by one, following groups of refugees arrived at the beach in the same condition; wet, cold, and wondering why they agreed to flee. Some spoke of their adventure of eluding the Viet Minh patrols, most just joined the huddled mass and bore their suffering in silence.

Father Thieu and his group were the last to arrive. Dinh noticed that the people were moving much faster than previous waves that had staggered to the beach. At first, Dinh attributed this to the hypnotic influence Thieu had over his parishioners, but Dinh soon saw the reason for the group's rapid pace.

The Viet Minh were coming.

15

The South China Sea quieted to a whisper as the last of Luong Dien's refugees arrived on the beach. It was as if the sea anticipated a fight was about to break out and didn't want to distract the combatants. Thieu's terror-stricken group arrived with six Viet Minh soldiers right behind, mocking and whooping.

"Where are you going?"

"This is not the way to Haiphong, traitors!"

"Your God is not going to save you!"

With the addition of Thieu's group, the number of refugees on the beach numbered around 400. At the sound of conflict, adrenalin surged through the hypothermic Christians who stood up and forgot their misery.

With a booming voice that belied his small stature, Father Thieu shouted, "Go to the sandbar!"

All heads turned to watch him sprint past the group toward the water.

Vietnam's Moses was urging his flock to cross the Red Sea, only there wasn't salvation at the other end, just an undulating black grave that stretched to the horizon. As Moses had pursued foes, Father Thieu had to contend with his own brand of Egyptians. The six Viet Minh soldiers ran after the priest to block the exit to the sandbar.

Over the dunes came another, larger company of soldiers. Yet another was spotted hustling up the beach from the south. Still another came from the north. The refugees were soon surrounded by more than 50 soldiers, most bearing poles or sugarcane sticks. A few had rifles. The Catholics froze in fear.

The Viet Minh took up positions near the water's edge to prevent passage to the sandbar. Panic ignited and spread through the people, and they stampeded like spooked cattle toward the soldiers. The armed soldiers began swinging their sticks indiscriminately, hitting men and women, old and young alike.

A brawl broke out. The men shouted as they fought. Women and children screamed and cried. Kicked sand filled the air like confetti. The unarmed men of Luong Dien outnumbered the soldiers but were no match for the young men with weapons. Father Thieu was once again punched in the gut as he had been on the journey to Haiphong. His people lay bleeding and concussed. Everyone was covered in a layer of wet sand. After a few minutes, all the people, including the Viet Minh, became exhausted and stopped fighting. Gasping for air, Father Thieu gathered his congregation away from the water's edge. The Viet Minh regrouped between them and the sandbar.

"Go home, Christians," shouted a Viet Minh leader, "you're not leaving."

"We have the right to pass to the south. Your own leader, Ho Chi Minh, signed the agreement," said Father Thieu.

"Show me Ho Chi Minh's signature and I'll let you pass."

The soldiers laughed.

"Why do you care if we go?" Thieu asked.

"Go? Go where? Are you going to swim to Saigon?"

They laughed again.

"That is our concern. If we die on the sandbar, why do you care?"

The soldier thought a moment and then came up with a terrifying answer.

"Because we will need your sons to help us conquer the south."

The Viet Minh surveyed the groaning Catholics splayed on the sand. If they had been wise, they would've pressed their attack and scattered the refugees. They could have isolated them in small groups and sent them running back home. The people were already exhausted from the skirmish and the wet march to the beach. They had no fight left in them. One more push would have broken them.

Instead, the soldiers looked out over their victory in satisfaction. Or pity. Or a mixture of the two. Whatever they were feeling, it froze them in place for several crucial minutes. One by one, the refugees staggered to their feet. Color returned to the sandy faces. The look of the people puzzled the Viet Minh. It wasn't rage or resignation. It was something else. They looked beatific. Serene. Without command, they closed ranks and formed a phalanx. Father Thieu spoke again.

"We are going to the sandbar now."

"Are you going to walk through us?" the Viet Minh officer asked.

Father Thieu didn't respond. He turned to Dinh.

"Dinh, give us a song."

Dinh started singing instantly as if the song had been planted in his mind for the occasion. Dinh sang the first line solo.

Salve Regina mater misericordiae

Vita, dulcedo, et spes nostra, salve

The choir members joined next, adding luxurious harmonies.

Ad te clamamus, exsules, filii Hevae
Ad te suspiramus, gementes et flentes
In hac lacrimarum valle

The plaintive notes of *Salve Regina* lilted across the beach with the lightness of a butterfly and smoothed the water. The people formerly of Luong Dien reached out to grasp the hand nearest them and pulled in close. The townspeople didn't understand the language, but they knew the words to the beloved hymn. They joined the choir and sang unconsciously.

Eia ergo, Advocata nostra,
Illos tuos misericordes oculos
ad nos converte.
Et Jesum, benedictum fructum ventris tui
noblis, post hoc exsilium ostende.
O Clemens: O pia: O dulcis
Virgo Maria

The mysterious words took the shape of a spell, as if speaking the language of God himself. The song resonated outward, as if propelled by the breath of angels, into a force majeure far beyond mere decibels, sailing high into heaven and back with frightening power. Father Thieu had learned the lesson of the miracle he witnessed on the Song Van Uc Bridge. Now he was going to receive his own miracle.

The Viet Minh were reduced by the spectacle. Blasted by sonic waves and an unseen preeminence, the soldiers wilted into impotence. The people began to walk toward the soldiers without aggression, repeating the final verse over and over.

O Clemens: O Pia: O dulcis
Virgo Maria

The company of soldiers parted. There was no violence, no spoken threat. As if by magnetic repulsion they simply moved out of the way. They moved and watched impassively as the Catholics walked into the narrow trough that separated the beach from the sandbar. The water was not deep. The refugees sloshed through it quietly, the only sound the swooshing of water around their legs, and the murmuring surf. The Viet Minh looked on as they climbed the sandbar, perplexed by the faith that possessed and propelled these Christians.

A sandbar is the product of ceaseless violence. Water and wind thrash the earth, grinding and pounding rock into fine grain. Currents rip and slash at the coast, pushing sand to and fro in fits of rage. Sometimes the sand is mounded into a shifting island. Impermanence is its essence, a beach with no foundation. A sandbar owes its existence to the temperamental sea and takes its own enigmatic character from its maker.

Onto this turbulent swath of semi-solid ground, the refugees from Luong Dien staked their lives. The sandbar was big, 50 meters wide and nearly a kilometer long. It plunged like a sword into the South China Sea. The far end was a foreboding place, stretching precariously above the abyss. Four hundred souls made their way to the end. There they would receive deliverance or destruction.

Father Thieu said a prayer and then explained what would happen next.

"I was brought here by the great American ship called the *Muentross*," he said. "The sailors instructed me to be here at midday today. They will stop and pick us up. Have faith, God will deliver us."

Dung wasn't so optimistic. The fear that had kept her off the sandbar as a child returned to torment her. It was only because she felt God Himself on the beach that she found the courage to come this far. The supernatural peace and power she felt on the beach vanished. She was scared again.

"What will we do if the ship doesn't come?" she whispered to Dinh.

"Shhh," he responded. "The Americans will save us."

Dung did not probe further and kept an anxious eye on the swirling water.

Overhead, the agnostic sky promised neither deliverance nor doom. It hung like a pale canvas stretched across the earth, unblemished by smudges of benign blue or angry black that might portend an outcome. The tenuous land under their feet pledged nothing either. It might support them. It might crumble beneath them and toss them into the sea. Neither heaven nor earth contained hope or hopelessness. The people of the sandbar, moments ago cradled in the hands of the Creator of Heaven and Earth, were now in their own little purgatory. They waited for judgment which would be upon them within the next few hours. Whether or not the *"Muen-tross"* showed up remained to be seen. One thing, however, was certain to return.

The tide.

Since the day the earth acquired water, the tide has functioned on a non-negotiable schedule. At its height, water would flood the sandbar, covering it by two meters. The only thing the people could do was pray the Americans would get to them first.

They waited and prayed the creator of the tide would delay it.

The sea began to rise.

16

Some of the Viet Minh soldiers grew bored with the refugees cornered on the sandbar. They left the beach to pursue refugees who were actually fleeing. Fleeing refugees were much more interesting than stationary ones. Some of the soldiers stayed to gawk at the tragedy about to unfold on the sandbar. Two of the men who remained on the beach watched in fascination as the people walked to the far end of the sandbar. They looked at each other with arched eyebrows, the unspoken signal humans use when in the presence of insanity. The Christians, they surmised, were surely a cult and were about to commit mass suicide.

"The tide will be in soon," one said.

He lived a kilometer from the beach and was familiar with its movement.

"Why would they do this?" the other asked

"I think they are trying to flag down a passing ship. Many bodies have washed up here in the last few weeks, probably trying the same thing."

"What will they do when the tide rises?" the other asked.

"Unless their god has a very big boat nearby, they are going to drown."

On the sandbar, which now looked like an island, Father Thieu led his flock in prayer and urged them to sit down and save strength. To take their minds off the tide, he told the story of his return from Saigon.

"The walk to Haiphong was long and hard. I walked through the night to elude patrols, but I got stopped twice by soldiers and beaten up once. A kind Buddhist saved me and took me to the city on his sampan. I had to sneak through the streets of town to avoid the Viet Minh. It would've been too long and dangerous for all of us to make the journey. I decided to board the "*Muen-tross*" to see if The Lord might deliver an answer there. I sailed to Saigon. On the ship I met a priest who told me they had rescued refugees straight from the beaches."

The telling was difficult for Thieu. He remembered the whole adventure in granular detail, but the emotion that kept bubbling to the surface was the shame he felt when, in his heart, he abandoned his people. He suppressed the feeling and continued.

"The captain remembered this sandbar and offered to drop me off so I could bring you here. I was put in one of their landing boats with a jittery, fearful sailor named *Kim Broh*. His name was stenciled on his shirt. All the sailors wear the same style of shirt with their own name written on theirs. We sailed toward the beach but stopped 100 meters short and he ordered me to swim. I got in the water and he turned the boat to go back. Over the past eight days, I have been scared for my life, beaten, exhausted, and so seasick I thought I would die, but none of those was as terrifying as swimming in the black ocean with nothing but the sound of the surf to guide me. I was so alone."

The people listened in astonishment. Some took courage from their leader. A few were struck by the recklessness of it all. None of them said anything. Thieu concluded his story with a promise.

"God brought me through all this for a reason. He will not abandon us in our hour of need."

The water continued to rise.

Tides are inextricably bound to the story of humanity. Long ago, the moon was ripped from the womb of nascent Earth and tethered in the sky. Distance produced a contentious interdependence. A tug-of-war ensued as Earth and moon pushed and pulled at one another. Like a child of divorce, the Earth's seas became the victim of quarrelsome celestial spheres. As the moon traced its bitter path across the face of the earth, the petulant satellite sloshed ocean water in daily fits of gravitational pique.

The waters were condemned to restless existence. Back and forth they moved, beckoned by lonely moon, held by jealous earth. But in that sleepless ocean, a secret seed soon bloomed. The mixing, churning, breaking currents revealed the blueprint for life, which sprang forth from tidal pools and covered the earth. Our own biology traces our tidal legacy. Our veins still run with saltwater. Estrus mimics the moon's cycle. To return to the ocean is to feel the faint memory of returning home. We are children of the tide.

The tide was the beginning of life, but for the 400 refugees from Luong Dien, the rising water looked more like the end of it.

Dung looked across the horizon. She absentmindedly lifted a clump of wet sand and ground it between her fingers. She looked at her talkative friend Mai who was more fearless than she. Mai's face was devoid of the optimistic buoyancy that marked her carefree style of living. She looked miserable and scared, too. She did not speak.

The water had spilled over the edge of the bar and was now creeping toward the outside of the group. Those on the edges closest to the water stood up instinctively. Soon everyone was standing. Within minutes, all 400 were standing in water. Muffled sobs broke the eerie silence. All eyes strained to the north, willing the *Montrose* to appear on the horizon.

It did not come.

It should've been here by now, Father Thieu thought.

The tide continued its inexorable rise. Dinh tried to lead the people in song, but the growing panic crowded out the enthusiasm which had been so powerful just an hour earlier. After only a few bars, the song sank into quiet depths. The water reached Dung's knees and she felt hope draining from her soul. She held onto Dinh. Quiet sobs around her became piercing wails.

From the time the refugees arrived on the beach, the sea had been calm. Wind and waves had become silent as the drama unfolded. In the midst of all the other life-threatening events, it was one difficulty Father Thieu was thankful they had not faced. But then it came. A soft breeze caressed the faces of the people. Initially, it felt like a refreshing relief from the close humidity within the huddled group, but in reality, it was a harbinger of death coming up from the south.

The sea had risen chest high when the waves began their grim harvest. The first person to be taken was the frail widow Hoa. She was small and weak. A wave knocked her over and swept her off the sandbar. Shrieks of horror ricocheted through the women. Her body would be discovered several days later when it washed up on the beach. Then another wave came and took the old man who lived three doors from the Doan house. His name was Minh and he always had a mischievous twinkle in his eye and a piece of sugarcane for neighborhood children. His head could be seen bobbing for a few seconds as he was carried away. It soon disappeared.

Five more were swept away by swirling black currents. In surging panic, the people had stopped watching for the ship and fixated on the menacing waves. They missed the sight of a boat crossing the horizon and heading straight for them. By the time someone looked up and shouted, "Ship!" the vessel was only a few miles from their position.

It was the *U.S.S. Montrose.*

There was no rejoicing on the sandbar. Only wide-eyed terror.

On the bridge of the ship, a lookout named Adamson was wielding a pair of binoculars, scanning the beaches. He called to Captain Trent.

"Captain, refugees ahead."

"How many, Adamson?"

Adamson looked twice and whistled in awe.

"Hundreds, sir. Maybe two or three hundred, and sir…"

"Yes, Adamson?"

"They are standing in the middle of the ocean."

17

Helmsman, bring us to the windward side of those people, distance, 200 yards!" Captain Trent barked. "We don't want to get hung up on that sandbar."

"Captain, shall we deploy the Papas?" a junior officer asked.

Papas were better known as Higgins Boats, the famous flat-bottomed amphibious assault transports used in World War II battles such as Normandy and Iwo Jima. The wooden craft had a ramp on the front which dropped onto the beach to quickly discharge soldiers. *Montrose* had used her Higgins Boats to send troops into battle on Okinawa in WWII and Inchon during the Korean War.

"No," the captain said, "tide's too high on that sandbar to drop the ramps on the Papas and I don't want those people trying to climb over the sides. Send out the life rafts."

Adamson spoke up again.

"Sir, there are about ten soldiers on the beach."

"Thank you, Adamson," said the captain, "We'll fix that."

The ship's loudspeakers crackled with a call to action.

"Now hear this, man all life raft stations. Rescue teams report to your stations. Man the forward deck gun."

The sailors came pouring out of rooms, donning their Mae West life vests. Gunners swiveled the big 40 millimeter cannon—the one that

127

shot down two kamikazes in World War II—toward the beach. The sight sent the remaining Viet Minh onlookers scattering over the dunes. Both Louis Washington and Jimmy Kimbrough were on a rescue team. They scrambled to their station. The deck officer came in and briefed the mission.

"Alright, we have counted 416 people in the water. They are standing on a long sandbar that is submerged in four to five feet of water. Two-foot waves are rolling in, so do the math. Some are swimming and getting exhausted. Two Papas will tow life rafts to the sandbar. Each raft will have a crew of two. Get those people in the rafts as quickly as possible. We are almost at high tide so we can expect some nasty currents to start developing, so stay out of the water. Under no circumstances should you get in the water. Got it? Alright, let's get those boats moving."

The sharp sound of forced air whooshed throughout the ship as rafts were inflated. As fate would have it, Jimmy Kimbrough and Louis Washington were the last sailors to board a raft. Jimmy saw Louis in the raft and halted for a moment.

"Aw, shit," Jimmy muttered.

"Do you have a problem, sailor?"

It was the deck officer.

"Naw sir, I just don't like working with niggers."

The officer roared, "Get in that fucking boat!"

Jimmy hopped in like a scolded dog and the two shoved off.

"Hey Washington, you ready to go Gook fishing?" Jimmy said with a nervous laugh.

Louis looked at him with disgust and said, "Shut up, you idiot."

The sandbar was mostly a memory now; a murky, transient connection to solid earth. The tallest refugees were able to maintain contact with the sandbar but shorter men and most women had to bounce off the bottom and tread water for a few seconds before bouncing again. Children had to be held above the waves. They were passed around to save their mothers from exhaustion. Everyone had to hop up with each cresting wave.

The people fell into an existence somewhere between life and death. They did not speak or look at each other. The cold water and exhaustion had shut down brain function to bare minimum. There was no hope, no fear, only silent resignation. They mechanically bounced up and down and passed the children around. It seemed like a dream when the rafts started coming toward them.

The rafts continued to float toward the silent people. It wasn't until the first raft reached the edge of the group that life returned to their eyes. Within seconds, hope returned, followed by hot panic. Like a school of fish moving as a single organism, the people began to beat the water in a desperate attempt to swim to the rafts.

Screams of rage and anguish filled the air as the people fought their way to safety. They climbed over one another, punched, and pushed their way past their neighbors. The rafts were soon surrounded by fighting Vietnamese. Some chose to bypass the rafts and swim straight for the *Montrose*. Sailors on the deck threw lifebuoys at them. The current culled several and folded them into the deep forever.

Sailors on the rafts pulled people in as quickly as they could, shouting in English to keep calm. The refugees didn't understand the language, not that it would have mattered. Panic has a language of its own. It screams urgency and survival. It drowns other forms of communication in a neurochemical flood. Even Father Thieu, who had led his people with uncommon courage, abandoned his faith to fear as he fought his way into a raft.

Dung was pulled from the sea and thrown into the bottom of the raft by the strong arms of Louis Washington. Dinh still had enough power to pull himself in and he flopped down beside his wife. When her strength returned, Dung stood up to find her parents and brothers. She saw them in another raft and began to bawl in relief. Dinh's family made it into a raft as well.

It took Dung a few minutes to compose herself. She then scanned the rafts for Mai. She could not see her in any of them. Dung looked at the struggling people still in the water and did not see her face. She then saw a black head floating atop the swells. The head rotated. It was Mai, eyes wide and mouth open in a frantic attempt to gulp oxygen to feed her failing muscles. A wave rose up and hit Mai in the face, forcing water into her lungs. She coughed and went under.

Jimmy Kimbrough saw too, and with an instinct that belied the hate in his heart, jumped in the water and swam towards Mai's bobbing head. Jimmy was light and wiry. He skimmed across the water, burning vital energy in a sprint to get to Mai. He reached her, grabbed her limp body and pulled the string to inflate his life vest.

Nothing happened.

The Mae West was equipped with a canister of compressed carbon dioxide which forced air into the vest. Some of the sailors foolishly removed their canisters to carbonate drinks. Seaman Kimbrough was one of those sailors. He thought he would never need to use his vest in an emergency. When he realized his error, it was too late.

"Aw, shit," he drawled.

Jimmy turned to swim back to the raft with Mai in tow. To his horror, the raft was now twice the distance he swam to get Mai. A current was pulling them out to sea. Jimmy fought the current as long as he could, but his strength faded fast. His head, and Mai's, slipped below the surface for the last time, never to be seen again.

Louis had been frantically pulling refugees from the water and didn't see Jimmy leave the raft. When there were no more people to pull in, he turned to find Jimmy missing. One refugee was wailing, pointing at the open water, and speaking rapid Vietnamese that Louis could not understand. He looked to the area where she was pointing and saw nothing but waves. In the chaos, no one but that single refugee saw what had happened to Mai and Jimmy.

The rafts were towed back to the *Montrose* and began to transfer the refugees. Those who had strength climbed up the cargo net that had been thrown over the side. The young, weak, and elderly were transferred with a winch and basket.

Four hundred and sixteen people walked onto the sandbar. Four hundred and two made it onto the decks of the *U.S.S. Montrose.*

Dung Vu and Dinh Doan and every member of their families survived to begin life anew in the new nation of South Vietnam.

Father Thieu, the battered, broken, exhausted leader of the escapees lived to make his second voyage to Saigon.

Dung's lifelong friend, Mai, made her new home in the mansion of her new husband, Thuy Tinh, mythological Lord of the Waters, maker of monsoon and tides.

Jimmy Kimbrough, murderer of Sycamore Mountain and the most despised crew member on the *Montrose*, died a hero. The crew shook their heads at the irony, wondering how the captain could stand to suspend the truth long enough to write a lying letter to Jimmy's parents praising his many great qualities and esteem amongst the crew.

"Wouldn't that be funny if he got the Navy Cross?" one said, alluding to the Navy's highest award.

They all laughed bitterly. Even the other members of the Klan mocked
Jimmy's mortal heroics.

After the life rafts were stowed, Louis Washington found a quiet room and closed the door. He wept, his great back heaving with sobs of grief. He didn't understand why. He had no love for the despicable Jimmy. He didn't know any of the 14 souls who perished in the tide. But he felt loss. In some inaccessible corner of his soul, he believed life, in all its ugliness and brutality, was sacred and he mourned its end.

Louis cried himself out and exited the room. He emerged onto an open deck just in time to catch a brilliant sunset. Streaks of slanted light tore holes through the clouds, throwing bright shafts onto the sea ahead. New tears came to Louis' eyes. Tears wrung from his soul by the sight of sublime beauty, tears only the hopeful cry. Louis was a hopeful man. He lingered at the railing and watched the sun gather enough strength to spread a rainbow over the water.

The monsoon was over.

Part 2

Thanh An, Can Tho, South Vietnam

18

I came into the world at a dangerous time, in a dangerous place. I was born on January 9, 1965, right at the beginning of the American War, or as the Americans called it, the Vietnam War. The war nearly killed me more than once. It deflected and defined my life's trajectory. It was a wellspring of horror and hope, death and rebirth.

My mother said I was the most difficult of the eight babies she delivered, not that giving birth in a poor Vietnamese village would have ever been considered easy. There were no epidurals to be administered or doctors to inject them. A close friend or relative served as obstetrician. A bamboo stick to bite was the only pain relief available. Despite the difficulty, I arrived healthy and Mom survived to have four more children.

My name is Doan Minh Chuong and my parents were Dinh and Dung Doan, formerly of the village of Luong Dien in North Vietnam.

Ten years before my birth, they made a daring escape from Ho Chi Minh's northern communists. Mom and Dad arrived in Saigon after three days traveling on an American Navy ship called the *U.S.S. Montrose*. They spent a year in a dirty refugee camp along with thousands who were also waiting to be relocated. Nearly one million northerners had migrated south before the border was sealed. The southern government disastrously underestimated the number of migrants and struggled to relocate the new arrivals.

Mom and Dad finally got an opportunity to settle in a new community in the Mekong River Delta. The government drained a swamp near the river called Song Hau, crisscrossed the land with a grid of canals and sent refugees there to farm it. The entire village of Luong Dien was assigned to this new village called Thanh An in an area called Kinh Rivera. *Kinh* is the Vietnamese word for canal, and *Rivera* is a colloquialism of the French word for river. As the redundant name suggests, our lives were defined by the water which braided the land.

Smaller canals branched at right angles every kilometer or so from the big feeder canal called Kinh Cai San. Each smaller *kinh* had a designating letter. My parents settled on a five-acre farm on Kinh B, three kilometers from Thanh An. They built a shack and began producing rice and children.

In the north, Ho Chi Minh's victory over the French turned into disappointment. He vanquished the colonial occupiers only to see his country split in two. Worse still, an even stronger presence replaced the French in a long line of foreign occupiers.

Americans.

The great country—big, rich, and powerful—was the champion of western civilization, the bulwark against the alarming spread of communism in the world. The Americans originally signaled support for the liberation of Vietnam in the 1940s, but when it became obvious that communism would be included in the bargain, the United States balked and threw its support first to their French ally, and later to the newly formed government of South Vietnam. They poured money and advisors into the new country to stabilize and legitimize the government.

Ho was undeterred by the giant standing in his way. The goal of a unified, liberated Vietnam still eluded him, yet his patience never wavered. North Vietnam embarked on a mission to weaken the southern government and help collapse it from within. The key was to do so without provoking the Americans into direct conflict, at least until the North was ready.

To this aim, a trail was built through the jungle which secretly funneled fighters and supplies from north to south. It was called the Ho Chi Minh Trail. Tens of thousands of northern soldiers infiltrated the south and began guerilla operations designed to apply relentless pressure on the southern government. The concerned Americans watched events unfold, but insisted South Vietnam had to put down the insurgency themselves. Meanwhile, the growing communist militia embedded in the south organized themselves into the National Front for the Liberation of the South, better known as the Viet Cong.

Despite the warning signs, Vietnam remained a backburner issue throughout the Eisenhower administration of the late 1950s, but with the arrival of a new decade and a new American president, things would soon change. Vietnam would move to the forefront of the consciousness of the new administration as well as the entire nation.

John F. Kennedy was a young man when elected president in 1960. He was also the nation's first Catholic leader. His short term was dominated by crisis management and responding to communist ambitions throughout the world. The Berlin Wall was built. The Bay of Pigs invasion became a national embarrassment. The Cuban Missile Crisis tested the young leader's nerves. Laos was on the brink of succumbing to Marxism.

Kennedy's reputation, and that of the nation, was in jeopardy. Determined to draw a line in the sand, he said, "Now we have a problem making our power credible and Vietnam looks like the place [to show it]." With those words, the two countries were bound together in a terrible destiny which would destroy countless lives and scar a generation.

The world continued to unravel. Kennedy was assassinated in 1963. His successor, the bellicose Lyndon Johnson fully supported the conventional wisdom called domino theory, which predicted the fall of all neighboring countries if just one adopted communism. Johnson inherited this position from his predecessors Kennedy, Eisenhower, and Truman, albeit without their circumspection. If allowed to turn communist, South Vietnam might be the domino that would knock over Laos, Cambodia, and the rest of Southeast Asia.

That was good enough for the pugnacious Johnson, the Texan with a Texas-sized chip on his shoulder. He did not possess the prudence of his presidential forebears, but in fairness, he was put in a bind by the actions of the increasingly violent Viet Cong. Ho Chi Minh had his chess pieces in place. He was finally ready to confront the U.S. He made a statement ominously similar to one he made to the French decades earlier.

"If the Americans want to make war for twenty years, we shall make war for twenty years. If they want to make peace, we shall make peace and invite them to tea afterwards."

Johnson chose war. In a sharp departure from previous policy which limited direct military action, American troops were sent to Vietnam by the tens of thousands. At the end of 1964, there were just over 20 thousand American soldiers in South Vietnam. By the end of the following year, there would be a quarter million. At the war's peak, US armed forces would number more than half a million. North Vietnam and South Vietnam would each field more than a million men, while the Viet Cong guerillas moved another 100 thousand in and out of the shadows.

Young Vietnamese men who might otherwise have been building paddy dikes and listening to the monsoon were asked to die for politics that had nothing to do with growing rice. Young American men who might have been building cars and listening to rock-and-roll were asked to die in a place they couldn't even find on a map.

Me? I was just trying to survive my childhood. In Vietnam in the 60s and 70s, that would prove to be no easy task.

19

Life on Kinh B was blissfully removed from rising political tensions in the late 50s and early 60s. The growing communist threat that seemed to be materializing out of thin air all over the south did not make it to Kinh Rivera. This gave my parents time to establish a new life. Mom and Dad worked harder than ever to build rice fields and a house from the ground up. The work was constant and backbreaking—farming all day, constructing a house at night. Somehow, they found time and energy to make babies.

My brother Doat, born in 1956, was the first to survive. Mom had her first child in 1955, but the boy died of fever within days of being born and had not been baptized or named. Older sister Thi Tuyen came after Doat in 1961. Then, in 1965, it was my turn.

Within two months of my birth, American Marines landed at Da Nang. The city in the central part of the country was home to a vital airport. The Marines' mission was to protect the airport, relieving the South Vietnamese Army to go fight the Viet Cong. Their arrival marked the first U.S. ground force in the country and the beginning of a long, sad period for both countries. It also coincided with some military-related news much closer to home. On a clear March day, Dad came rushing into the house holding a letter.

"What's wrong?" Mom asked.

"I've been drafted," Dad said.

"What does that mean?" she asked.

"I'm being forced into service in the army."

"You're going to war? I don't understand. Who is forcing you?"

"The government," Dad said.

"They can do that?"

"Yes."

"Where do you have to go?" she asked.

"Thu Duc. It is near Saigon."

Dad did not tell her Thu Duc was the site of infantry school, where he would presumably learn how to be a frontline soldier. He saw no need to worry her prematurely.

"When do you leave?" Mom asked.

"*We* leave tomorrow," he said.

Mom was stunned, but didn't respond.

We? She thought. A husband's word was law in a Vietnamese household. There would be no discussion. She didn't protest though the thought of dragging two young children and an infant to war twisted her stomach in knots.

"You will stay with your parents in Tan Phu until I can find housing. It doesn't make sense for you to stay here. You can't manage the farm and the children by yourself. Your parents can help and you will be closer to me."

Mom dipped her head in a bow of obedience and started packing, burying her anxiety in action.

Saigon, she thought.

The year in the refugee camp had been a degrading experience. Living in dehumanizing density, the camp had been a tortuous combination of noise, stench, and sickness. Mom had preserved her sanity by praying the rosary and recalling her uncomplicated days with Phu, the water buffalo. She would sometimes close her eyes and dip her shoulders from side to side, imagining she was riding him to the beach, recreating his unhurried stride.

She shook her head in disbelief. When she left Saigon ten years earlier, she had hoped never to see it again.

The next day, our little family was heading for the city on a bus carrying all our possessions, which consisted of two cooking pots and a few clothes. Nine-year-old Doat thought it a grand adventure. It was the first vehicle he had ridden that wasn't a water buffalo. His sharp eyes took in the passing scenery. Mom spent her time wrangling me and four-year-old Thi Tuyen. Dad smoked one cigarette after another and did not pay any attention to us.

The 200-kilometer journey lasted ten hours. The route took us across the breadth of the Mekong delta and its many brown arms. Two of the rivers had to be crossed by ferry, each one requiring a long wait to board. Over the course of the day-long trip, the rusted bus was stopped more often than not. Chickens in bamboo cages clucked in soft disapproval at the delays. The pigs on board gave no protest, but they did emit a disagreeable odor.

The utter flatness of the land offered no change of perspective. All the earth was extravagantly clothed in layers of monochromatic foliage. Only the gray road below and a sliver of blue above broke the monotonous green walls. Verdant folds which enveloped us pulsed with heat and humidity. The bus, crammed with sweating passengers, became a sauna. Animal smells magnified in the heat until the inside of the bus could've been mistaken for a barn. I was a slippery, hot, little pig in my mother's arms. She had no choice but to hold me and suffer my body heat. Thi Tuyen got cranky. Even Doat the enthusiastic traveler became disenchanted with the journey and begged to return home.

Eventually, banana and bamboo groves and rice paddies gave way to clusters of houses, shops, and churches. The scattered settlements grew more connected as we rode. A strange smell wafted into the open windows. It was a malodorous mixture of exhaust, food, trash, vegetation, and human waste. Smoke from thousands of cooking fires and poorly maintained vehicles hung thick and ugly in the air. An unfamiliar sensation began to vibrate the bus. At first it was a distant rumble, like thunder from a far-off storm. As we got closer, the ominous sound grew until it became a crashing cacophony of machine and man, stabbing at our peaceful country souls with invisible knives made of noise.

We had reached Saigon at last.

The city's 1.7 million inhabitants crawled over it like fleas on a dog's back. In the country, poverty can be disguised as simple living. There, a measure of dignity is still possible, but in the city, poverty is dirty, repulsive, and pathetic. Simplicity is transformed into want. Decency spirals into debasement. Mom clutched her rosary as dread welled inside her. Dad smoked another cigarette.

Saigon's Tan Phu district had been the site of refugee camps at the end of the French War. After the camps were deactivated, some of the refugees stayed. My maternal grandparents were two such people. The life-threatening exodus from North Vietnam had been traumatic for them and they swore to never move again. Despite the city lifestyle which was unnatural to them, they remained true to their word. When most of the villagers of Luong Dien moved to Kinh Rivera to start over, they stayed behind and built a house in Tan Phu. We moved in with Ong and Ba (grandma and grandpa) while Dad figured out how to find something more permanent.

Draftee Dinh Doan reported to Thu Duc, on the other side of the winding Song Sai Gon. When he came home two weeks later, he was Private Dinh Doan. He was wearing a plain green uniform with an audacious red ascot billowing out of his shirt like a sail. Trouser legs disappeared into black boots which rose above his ankles. Mom smiled with pride despite her misgivings about the whole situation.

Dad brought home good news from his training. While at Thu Duc, he passed a test which gave him the equivalent of a high school diploma. With his newly achieved academic status, he would not be assigned to an infantry company. Instead, he was sent to the supply corps. They needed men who could follow written instructions and work independently. In addition to farming, housebuilding, directing the choir at church, and fathering children, Dad had found the time to teach himself to read, write, and do basic arithmetic. His ambition probably saved him an early death in battle.

"You look very handsome," Mom said with a bow and a grin.

"Thank you, I have more good news," Dad said.

"Oh?"

"Because of my job, I will be able to come home each evening. We can start building our own house."

"But where will we build it?" Mom asked.

"I spoke to your father. He wants us to build here, next door to them."

Mom smiled bigger than ever.

20

Mom's happiness did not last long in Tan Phu. The war was in full swing and Saigon was center stage. Being the capital of South Vietnam, it was the prize the North coveted most. The slippery Viet Cong easily infiltrated the city to commit acts of terrorism—setting off bombs, engaging in skirmishes, assassinations, and creating mayhem throughout the city. Once their mission was complete, they dissolved into the fabric of the city like black-clad phantoms.

Tan Phu had no strategic or political value and was not a target, but war is an indiscriminate, messy thing and we were casualties nonetheless. Our wounds were psychological and emotional, invisible yet as traumatic as any physical wound. Anxiety flooded our bloodstreams with muscle-tensing adrenalin. Fatiguing vigilance added a physical cost to our mental strain. My family was constantly reminded of the danger and death which stalked nearby. The night sky flashed with beautiful, deadly light; soundwaves from distant explosions drummed the walls of our house, and closer blasts vibrated the ground and disturbed the dust overhead, sending it showering down upon us. We existed in a state of unrelenting stress.

The non-stop battering even affected my unusually stoic father. Dad decided Tan Phu was too dangerous, so he moved us to another Saigon district, Chi Hoa. We stayed with relatives for a few days but war found us there, too. We moved again to a refugee camp inside a school. After a few weeks of living in the cramped conditions with three small children, my parents realized there wasn't an ideal place for a family anywhere in Saigon. They resigned themselves to living with the war the way one coexists with a noisy, inconsiderate roommate, so we moved back to Tan Phu. There they began building a house.

Dad worked all day for the army, delivering supplies and mail. He rode with his friend Khan Tran in the big American truck called a *Deuce-and-a-half*. Khan drove while Dad handled directions and the manifest. The two made a good team. Khan was stocky, jovial, and earthy. He possessed an innate grasp of real things like driving and repairing the truck. He threw the gears of the big rig with authority and panache as he bounced happily in the driver's seat.

Dad was his opposite. Stiff, cerebral, and responsible, my father excelled in the conceptual world of music and numbers. He was highly organized and driven, perfectly suited to manage cargo with precision and seriousness.

"Hey, Dinh, why don't we stop and have a few beers on the way back to base?" Khan would repetitively ask, seldom eliciting more than a tired grin from his partner.

He thought his friend too uptight, and persisted in his efforts to keep Dad from collapsing under the weight of his own gravitas. Dad's personality didn't speak the language of mirth. His DNA only carried strands of sobriety. He secretly lamented the deficiency as he watched Khan's effortless ability to connect with others. He had to be satisfied with the vicarious humor of those around him. He was glad to have Khan to supply sustaining levity while he worried about the job at hand.

"Hey Dinh, that prostitute we just passed was winking at you. You want me to drop you off and pick you up later?"

Dad rolled his eyes in annoyance as he studied the figures on his clipboard, but secretly he enjoyed Khan's easy banter. It helped take his mind off the dangerous job they were doing.

After a long day in the service of the republic, Dad came home to more work. The house had to be built and there was no one to do it for him. Luckily, bureaucracy had not made it very far into the lives of average Vietnamese citizens. There were no building codes, which meant anyone could throw up four walls and a roof and have a dwelling. Using our grandparents' side wall as one of our own gave Mom and Dad a jump on the process. Each night for several weeks, the three-person construction crew labored at the walls. Doat held a lantern while Mom mixed cement and Dad laid bricks. A few studs and sheets of corrugated tin were obtained for a roof and we had a home.

Shortly after our house was finished, another home was built using our side wall for support. And so it went until nearly the whole street was a solid wall of homes. The dwellings were small. Ours was three meters wide and fifteen meters long. Rooms were partitioned by curtains. Outside walls were limewashed and some were painted pastel greens and blues.

Once the house was complete, Mom and Doat went to work on a bunker. They filled rice bags with sand and stacked them. Three walls were erected and topped with a piece of plywood. More bags were piled on top and we had a bomb shelter. The space inside was tiny, a dark crack big enough for three children. An adult could also wedge herself in if she turned sideways. Sometimes Mom would join us, but she was usually out of the house selling vegetables at the market. This left poor Doat, not yet eleven years old, responsible for the survival of himself and two younger siblings.

We used the shelter often. The air raid siren regularly shattered the peace with its urgent scream. Every time he heard the apocalyptic howl Doat was jolted into immediate panic. Until I was old enough to run on my own, I was grabbed by the nearest person and carried like a sack of rice to the shelter. Mortar and artillery shells rained with frustrating frequency. Even when all was quiet, simmering anxiety kept everyone on edge, waiting for the next round of falling bombs and that god-awful wail of the siren.

I guess we were lucky. Some houses in our neighborhood took direct hits, killing everyone inside. Depending on the size of the shell, many houses could be destroyed or damaged with a single blast. In Tan Phu it didn't take much. Everyone built their houses with the same flimsy materials and methods my parents used. Dwellings were constructed to withstand the monsoon and nothing else. One day, our luck almost ran out.

The familiar sound of the siren still startled us. Doat picked me up and yelled at Thi Tuyen to hurry. We crouched in the bunker and waited for the familiar thump of distant explosions. The sound we heard wasn't a thump. It was something far worse.

A blast from an explosive device delivers layers of destruction. The first and most dangerous layer is the blast wave. Energy released during a detonation compresses air particles and shoves them outward at supersonic speed. These invisible particles slam into anything in their path with astonishing force. If they collide with a human being, the

150

damage can be severe to deadly. The body was not designed to handle such a blow. Eardrums split, limbs are severed, organs rupture. Traumatic brain injury can cause lasting, sometimes permanent, damage.

Then, there are the other effects of an explosion. Shockwaves, shrapnel, and extreme heat from a blast can wound or kill with merciless redundancy. It is a weapon of indiscriminate brutality, killing soldier or civilian without prejudice.

The shell landed in the street in front of our house. The blast wave shook the ground so violently it pulled the earth from under our feet and threw us to the ground. Oxygen was pulled from our lungs. The sound was too big for our ears. We 'heard' it through our whole bodies which seemed to be ripping apart cell by cell. By the time we reflexively cupped our hands over our ears, the blast wave was long gone. When the air returned to our lungs, we lay on the floor crying, incapacitated for several minutes.

The shelter did its job. Aside from being badly shaken, we emerged intact. As we made our way toward the front of the house, Mom was screaming as she ran down the street. She had been at the market and was not home when the shell dropped. I can only imagine the horror she must have felt as she ran home, petrified that she might find three dead children.

When she saw us, she wailed in overpowering relief. She covered us in kisses and tears. She praised Doat for his quick action. She was so happy she didn't see what the bomb had done, but soon her awareness expanded to see the terrible destruction wrought by the explosion.

The front wall of our house, and the house of Ong and Ba, had been demolished. Houses across the street did not fare so well. Three of them were piles of rubble. An eerie silence descended on the scene as emerging neighbors realized that death had paid our neighborhood a call. Anguished cries here and there broke the trance and men sprang into action searching the debris for survivors.

Seven neighbors lost their lives that day. By the time Dad got home, cleanup was well underway. He looked at his missing wall and turned to Mom. She quietly told him the names of our neighbors who were now dead. He dropped his head for a moment in a gesture that looked like prayer. After a few seconds, he lifted it to address Mom.

"Start mixing cement," he said.

21

I n the Year of the Monkey, 1968, the war was not going well for either side. The Americans brought their war machine to Vietnam expecting a quick victory. Like the Chinese, Mongols, and French before them, they seriously underestimated the Vietnamese will to fight. Ignoring hundreds of years of history, President Johnson doubled down on his bad bet, sending more and more troops to die in the rice paddies and jungles. Approval for the war among American citizens steadily declined.

Things weren't any better in Hanoi. The communist capital had been badly mauled by the American bombing campaign called *Operation Rolling Thunder.* Northern leaders were gravely concerned that if the bombs continued to fall, their ability to support the southern military effort would be ground to dust. They needed to break the looming stalemate which would only benefit the continuation of the two-state status quo. An audacious plan was developed over years to launch attacks at multiple locations throughout the south. The purpose of the offensive would be to ignite a civilian uprising in the south that would overthrow the already teetering South Vietnam government and force the Americans to the bargaining table. An agreement was reached by the generals to proceed with the operation, dubbed the *General Offensive and Uprising.*

Ho Chi Minh was briefed on the plan and gave it his blessing. The old revolutionary was in his late 70s and his heart was beginning to falter. He wouldn't live to see the end of the decade or the cause to which he dedicated his life. He had relinquished power in 1965 but still held the title of president and continued to contribute to the vision that had driven him for nearly 60 years. His influence, though waning, still resonated through the Vietnamese Politburo. He retained one skill set that was unmatched by any of his successors. In his long career, Ho had seen more of the world than anyone in Vietnam and had a pragmatic perspective which reflected his travels.

As a young man he spent time in the United States and immersed himself in its unique culture. Ho had an innate grasp of the intricacies of American politics and their heavy reliance on popular opinion. In the years leading up to the approval of the *General Offensive,* he had repeatedly insisted that the attack be launched in the year of an American presidential election. He wanted the attack to push growing American dissatisfaction into the limelight surrounding the election. Ho understood the way to beat the superpower was not through direct confrontation of its overwhelming military, but by turning the American public against the war.

Ho got his wish. The offensive was scheduled for 1968. President Lyndon Johnson, the man most responsible for the war, would be up for re-election. With luck, a successful operation could turn the election into a referendum on the war.

The Politburo wanted to maximize their chances against the superior firepower of the Americans, so they pulled a few tricks. First, they decided to begin the attacks on the first day of Tet, the biggest holiday in Vietnam. Then, they announced to the South Vietnam government they would observe a seven-day truce to observe Tet.

The South Vietnamese Army took the bait and allowed nearly half its soldiers to take leave for the holiday. The American commanders were more circumspect. Their intelligence officers noticed a sharp increase in traffic along the Ho Chi Minh Trail near the end of 1967. Also, battles erupted along the Cambodian border as northern forces sought to draw the southern and U.S. armies away from the coastal cities. The Americans knew something big was coming, but they couldn't quite put their finger on it. Their biggest failure was a lack of imagination. They couldn't imagine the scale of what was about to happen.

Still, U.S. chief General Westmoreland acted prudently and ordered 15 battalions to be moved from the Cambodian border to protect Saigon. He also suggested the Vietnamese cancel leave for their soldiers. The southern generals declined, citing concerns of morale and an unwillingness to give the communists a propaganda victory.

My father was one of the soldiers released for Tet leave. So was his friend Khan. Khan drove Dad to within a few blocks of our house.

"Khan, let me out here, I need to go to this market."

"Sure thing Boss."

Khan pulled up beside the store and watched Dad climb down to the street. Khan grew serious for a moment and fixed my father's eyes.

"Hey Dinh, if anything happens, we have a big underground bunker with plenty of room for you and your family."

"Thank you, friend, but I'm sure we'll be fine. What kind of Vietnamese would attack on Tet?"

Dad made his purchase in the market and happily walked home to begin preparing for the holiday celebration.

Meanwhile, the Viet Cong loaded their guns and waited.

22

D ad's home!"

Doat and Thi Tuyen squealed and jumped up and down as Dad came into the house early in the day. I jumped, too, in imitation of my siblings.

"Dad, why are you here?" Doat asked as he eyed the *mai vang* branch Dad was holding.

"The army is giving me some time off for Tet," Dad said.

"Tet, Tet, Tet!" Thi Tuyen screamed.

Even though she was only six, she fully grasped the material aspects of the holiday. Tet meant new clothes, delicious food, family, and money for herself, Doat, and me.

"Dad," Doat interjected, steering the conversation away from Thi Tuyen's starry-eyed fantasizing about the bounty of Tet, "is the war over?"

"No," Dad said," the North has declared a ceasefire in observance of Tet."

"Cease...fire?" said Doat, bewildered by the term.

"The North's army is going to stop fighting for seven days, so our army is, too. Since nobody will be fighting, my commander gave me a few days off."

STRANGERS ON THE WATER

Doat and Thi Tuyen danced in circles, overcome with delirious joy. Dad fashioned a stand from two stray pieces of bamboo and inserted the *mai vang* branch. He moved a homemade table to the center of the small room and placed the branch on it. The blooms of the *mai vang* flower, known scientifically as *Ochna integerrima,* consisted of five spade-shaped yellow petals and a cluster of red stamen in the middle. The colorful display instantly brightened the dull room. The three of us stood transfixed by the sublime sight, as if a piece of heaven had materialized in our house.

"Tomorrow morning there will be some red envelopes hanging on the branches," Dad said, "Do you know what will be in them?"

"Money!" Thi Tuyen screamed.

Dad laughed at her enthusiasm.

Mom walked in the house and removed her *non la*. She had been selling her vegetables all day throughout the district. She sat down heavily and dropped her baskets beside her. She was tired but her face showed a look of satisfaction. Currency was a fluid concept in her business. Sometimes she received cash, sometimes she bartered for other food. Most days it didn't matter what she received since all the money went toward food anyway. On this day, however, she was on a mission to acquire all the supplies needed for Tet, including new clothes for her children, money for the red *li xi* envelopes, and food for the Tet feast. Her baskets were loaded with pork, rice, beans, and banana leaves, clothes, and money.

"Looks like you had a good day," Dad said, admiring the overflowing baskets.

"Thank you," she said, "I want to start the New Year with as much good luck as we can get."

Mom placed a tattered faith in the Lord's promise to provide, but she also hedged her bets, accepting good fortune from any source if it helped her feed her hungry, growing children. She struggled against her swelling belly to get up from the chair. In a few short weeks she would have another mouth to feed. Dad's army salary amounted to little more than cigarette money for himself, so the success or starvation of her family would be on her already overworked shoulders. Feeding a family in peacetime was hard enough, the food shortages inherent in war made her precarious supply chain even more tenuous.

But that was a worry for another day. She had done well this day. She stood up, took a long breath, and launched herself into preparations for the next day's celebrations.

Tet Nguyen Dan means "the feast of the first morning of the first day." It is known simply as Tet, and is the biggest holiday of the year in Vietnam. Based on the lunar calendar, it is both the first day of the year and the first day of spring, usually occurring at the end of January or early February. It is the official birthday of every Vietnamese citizen.

The legends that animate the celebrations have developed over millennia. There is not one supporting myth, but many. Stories of gods and kings, flowers and animals, love and war have all been woven into the Tet canon, giving it complex, chaotic layers of meaning. The overarching theme, though, is renewal. Tet gives us a clean slate; a chance to begin again and live a better life.

The luck that Mom counted on played a big part in the rituals of Tet. The preferred observance of the New Year contained specific directions for securing coveted good fortune. The house had to be cleaned top to bottom. Broken items were repaired or replaced. Debts were to be paid and old quarrels settled. Three days' worth of food had to be prepared ahead of time because it was bad luck to cook during Tet.

While Dad finished repairs, Mom began cooking *banh chung,* the traditional food of Tet. Dad finished mending a chair and called me, Doat, and Thi Tuyen to listen as he told the story of the invention of *banh chung.*

"Many hundreds of years ago, there was a prince named Lang Lieu. The prince was the 18th son of King Hung Vuong VI. His mother was estranged from the king and did not receive an income, so his family was poor. While he was still a boy, his mother died, and because the king disliked her so much, he did not bring Lang Lieu into his home."

"Did he have to live outside all the time?" Thi Tuyen asked.

"Shh," Doat said, "let him finish."

"Years passed and the king felt old age creeping into his bones. He decided it was time to find the heir to the throne, so he gathered all his sons together, even the neglected, orphaned Lang Lieu. The king told them of his plan to pass his kingdom to the one who could present him with the most delicious food. The king really loved his food.

The rich sons of the king rode to distant lands to find the most exotic ingredients and the greatest chefs, but Lang Lieu was too poor to travel and buy expensive food, so he stayed home and despaired of winning the contest. Then, in a dream, a fairy whispered in his ear. The next morning, he gathered some items from local farmers and did just what the dream fairy told him. He combined sticky rice, pork, and mung bean paste into a square cake, wrapped it in banana leaves, and baked it. He then made a round cake with the leftover sticky rice.

"One time, Mama let me help her make *banh chung*, I helped her wrap the banana leaves..." Thi Tuyen interrupted.

"Shhh," Doat scolded again.

"The recipe was delicious, so he decided to present it to his father as his contest entry. When the big day arrived, all his brothers returned with their extravagant dishes. They laughed at Lang Lieu's simple, unadorned creation, but the king liked its rich flavor and texture. He asked Lang Lieu about the shapes. His son told him that the round cake represented the sky that all live under and the square was the earth that contained all the things that sustain life.

The king was impressed. He asked Lang Lieu where he obtained the ingredients for such a delicacy. When Lang Lieu told him he had bought them from farmers in nearby villages, the king was overcome. Not only was this son's dish the best tasting, but he had honored his father's kingdom by using its own products. Lang Lieu was crowned king and became the founder of a dynasty which lasted for hundreds of years, and we get to eat the creation that made him king."

At the end of the story, Dad sent us to bed with a promise that he would wake us at midnight to bring in the New Year. We were especially excited about the fireworks, which were exploded to scare off any evil spirits which might bring bad luck. I fell asleep quickly, dreaming of streaks and bursts of color burning transient holes in the black sky.

I was awakened by Thi Tuyen and Doat standing over me.

"Get up, Chuong, Tet is almost here!"

I sprang out of bed and Thi Tuyen unfolded my new clothes. As she dressed me, Doat instructed me on the correct Tet greeting to say to my parents.

"You say *'Security, good health, and prosperity',*" Doat said, "And then you get a *li xi* envelope."

"And money!" Thi Tuyen happily interjected.

We made our way to the front of the house. Dad had set up some chairs for us to sit on while we watched the fireworks. We sat fidgeting in our chairs in anticipation. When the clock struck midnight, we heard the first boom. It was here. Tet had arrived.

My father sat upright at the sound of the explosion. When he heard the second, he stood up.

"What's wrong?" Mom asked.

"Those are not fireworks," he said as the color drained from his face.

23

An khang thinh vuong. Security, good health, and prosperity.

Nothing is so antithetical to security, good health, and prosperity as war. War is an affront to the happy nature of Tet. Where Tet motivates a slate-cleaning renewal of spirit, war doesn't clean the slate or even leave the slate dirty. It breaks the slate into a hundred pieces and scatters them among smashed blocks, splintered beams, and shattered glass shards. War doesn't refresh life, it maims and extinguishes life with slashing shrapnel and flesh-piercing bullets. Red is the lucky color of Tet. It represents the sun's life-giving warmth. Red is also the color of war; the color of cold, sticky blood splattered on walls and pooled beneath the bodies of its victims.

The Viet Cong swarmed through Saigon, but not like an army that storms into town from some distant land. They were already there. They had been there for months, tucked away in safehouses throughout the city. They had walked into the city unmolested while the American forces were responding to the diversionary attacks on the border. The Viet Cong soldiers were indistinguishable from other citizens as they poured into the city by ones and twos. They talked like us. They dressed like us. They didn't even carry weapons. Those were smuggled into town in trucks carrying flowers, fruit, and rice.

They *were* us, Vietnamese to the core, but with one difference. When the clock struck midnight on January 31, 1968, we celebrated life. The communists destroyed it. Even the name of the holiday became perverted by the North's betrayal of our shared principles. *Tet Nguyen Dan* became known to the rest of the world as *The Tet Offensive*.

"Get in the bunker!" Dad shouted above the encroaching booms and the rising staccato of small arms fire.

Mom picked me up and screamed as a deafening blast fell close. Doat and Thi Tuyen ran into the house to get to the bunker in the backyard. Mom was right behind them with me in her arms. We stumbled through the narrow rooms as falling cups, bowls, and pots clattered on the floor after a blast wave hit the house. The *mai vang* branch Dad bought a few hours earlier had been knocked off the table and was trampled underfoot. The cash-stuffed red *li xi* envelopes which had mesmerized Thi Tuyen were still attached to the branch. The four of us emerged from the dark house and squeezed into the shelter.

"Where's Dad?" Doat shouted.

He was not with us. A minute later, he emerged from the house and entered the shelter. He worried that the Viet Cong might know his identity and address, so he had taken time to shut the steel scissor gate that served as our front door, hands shaking as he secured the door with a heavy chain and padlock.

The five of us wedged into the tiny bunker as hell rained from the night sky. Rockets exploded in every direction. The rockets, 122mm Soviet-built Grads, were simple, cheap, and could punch a hole in the earth six meters wide and two meters deep. Each blast was lethal up to 163 square meters. It usually carried a payload of scored steel which fragmented into nearly 4,000 pieces of deadly shrapnel. Its biggest flaw was control. It was unguided, so once it was fired only God knew where it would land. This feature made it more of an instrument of general terror than a precision weapon with which to kill enemy soldiers. Anyone caught in the blast radius would be ripped to shreds by jagged flying steel and likely bleed to death from their wounds. It was the devil's own sword—indiscriminate and cruel.

Each blast destabilized our shelter of stacked sandbags. The tiny space got smaller as the bags shifted toward the open center.

"Dad, the bags are going to fall on us!" Doat screamed.

"We'll be all right, the shelling will stop soon," Dad replied.

Mom wailed with each explosion. I screamed in uncomprehending terror. Thi Tuyen whimpered softly, while Doat fretfully scanned the sandbags for a breach.

Dad was mistaken in his estimate. He had guessed the attack was just one of the garden variety actions the Viet Cong launched regularly. He didn't know that we were in the middle of the largest offensive of the war. He didn't know that more than 80,000 northern troops had been unleashed on more than 100 cities and towns throughout the country. He didn't know that this was Ho Chi Minh's make-or-break gamble to buckle the South's will to fight.

But none of that mattered. As the rockets continued to fall through the night, Dad became increasingly worried if our luck against the 122s would hold. We didn't rest. The shelling was near constant. The air in the close space was spoiled by our exhalations and body heat.

Creeping claustrophobia became nearly intolerable yet we dared not venture outside.

Finally, as the day broke into an overcast pall, Dad made a dangerous decision. He knew we couldn't chance much time outside the relative safety of a shelter, but our little rathole was rapidly becoming unbearable. He also held no delusions about the integrity of our bunker in the event of a direct hit, knowing we would all be killed instantly if it happened.

"Stay here, I'll be back to get you," Dad said as he vanished into the house.

Between booms, we could hear him removing the chain on the front door. Mom, on the verge of nervous breakdown, did her best to recite the rosary. Doat and Thi Tuyen looked in open-mouthed horror at the door through which Dad disappeared, sure he would be blown to pieces. I screamed at the sound of each explosion.

Within minutes that seemed like hours, Dad returned.

"Come quickly," he said.

Everyone obeyed without hesitation and walked into the house.

"Dung, put all the food in a sack. Children, take the *li xi* envelopes off the branch and put them in your pockets. We may need the money to buy food."

While I clung to Mom's leg, she started gathering the *banh chung* and dried fruit dish called *mat* we were supposed to eat for the Tet feast. Doat and Thi Tuyen scalped the *mai vang* of its envelopes. Meanwhile, Dad went to the backyard well to fill the bucket. As he neared the well, he could hear a voice rising up from the deep hole, crying for help. Dad peered over the edge of the well and could see a face staring up at him. It was his brother-in-law, Xe.

"Xe, what are you doing?" Dad asked

"I came to get in your shelter, but when I saw you only halfway inside, I knew there was no room. An explosion happened while I was thinking about where I could go. I panicked, so I went to the safest place I could see," Xe said.

Dad threw a rope in and pulled Xe out and instructed him to bring up a bucket of water. Dad went back inside to find jars to fill with the water. When all the supplies were rounded up, we went out front. Fires raged in the houses of some of our neighbors. A few dead bodies slumped against walls or splayed grotesquely in the street. Ugly smoke hung ominously over the scene.

It was quiet. Relatively. We could still hear the distant rat-a-tat of Russian-made AK rifles and the anguished cries of the injured, but the pulverizing loudness of the 122s, the sound which battered our brains and constricted our lungs, had stopped for a moment. As if we suddenly remembered the necessity of breathing, we reflexively inhaled a deep lungful of noxious air and coughed out the dirty fumes. We were joined in the street by Mom's parents, Ong and Ba.

"Come on," Dad said, as he picked me up.

Mom was carrying the food, Xe had the water, and Doat held Thi Tuyen's hand. We trotted as fast as we could toward Khan's house, climbing over rubble and gawking at the dead. When we reached Khan's house, we went straight in without knocking or waiting to be invited inside, which in normal times would've been an embarrassing breach of Tet etiquette. We scurried through his disheveled rooms to

167

his backyard. There, lying flat on the ground, was a set of heavy steel doors. The doors looked like they had once been standing but had since fallen over. Dad went to the doors and stomped one of the doors three times with his heel.

"Who is it?" came a muffled voice from below.

"It's Dinh," Dad said.

The doors were unlatched from below and opened. Khan stepped out with an American revolver in his hand. Dad looked at it and raised his eyebrows at his friend. Khan ignored the gesture.

"Come in," Khan said. "Watch the steps, they're steep. Here, give me the baby."

Dad waited until Khan stuffed the gun in the back of his pants and handed me over. Khan carried me into the bunker. Mom struggled against the unbalanced weight in her belly to descend. When we were all inside, Khan went back up and closed the doors. One small lantern sat in the middle of the room and fought vainly against the darkness, casting haunting flickers upon everything it could reach. Everyone sat on the dirt floor with backs against the cold block wall.

"Where did you get that gun?" Dad asked.

"Oh, Boss, you know me, always talking to people, always making friends. Americans, you may not know, are generous people."

"A soldier just gave you his pistol?" Dad asked incredulously.

"No, he didn't give it to me. He helped me…acquire it," Khan said with a grin.

"I don't want to know," Dad said as he looked toward the ceiling, pretending to avert his eyes from the petty crime that surely played a part in Khan's possession of the revolver.

Khan ignored Dad's eye roll and addressed the occupants of the shelter, now numbering fourteen.

"There is nothing to worry about. We are safe here. We have food and water and the protection of this bunker. Nothing will get to us here."

Dad wasn't convinced by Khan's assurances. He had seen craters made by the 122s and was certain that a direct hit would annihilate us all. He kept his concerns to himself.

Khan turned to Mom and noticed her vacant stare. He tried to engage her with his constantly buoyant manner.

"Dung, I hope you brought some of your famous *banh chung*!"

Mom didn't react. She handed Khan the bag and wrapped her arms around me. Booms from renewed rocket attacks vibrated through the bunker doors. I cried in the dark. Mom cried too.

24

The Tet Offensive was ambitious. The Viet Cong and North Vietnamese Army regulars struck Saigon with 35 battalions. They had six targets throughout the city marked for takeover, including Tan Son Nhat Airport. Our district, Tan Phu, was immediately west of the airport, so we were in the direct path of the advance. Three battalions rolled over us from the west and two came from the south. While the communists didn't target civilians, neither did they go out of their way to spare us. We were the expendable masses.

Rocket fire continued throughout the day, shaking the bunker and sending me into crying fits with each blast. Everyone was exhausted from fear. No one spoke. No one prayed. Even Mom, the dedicated Catholic, was too shell shocked to recite the rosary. The sad flickers from the lamp added to the feeling of hopelessness. The light of life itself seemed to be growing dimmer with each blast.

None of the bunker inhabitants had a watch. Time degenerated into day or night, marked only by light seeping through small cracks at the edge of the doors. Dad kept a bored eye on the crack and when the light seemed to fade, he suggested that Khan accompany him outside to check on things. As the two men stood up, the rest of the group stirred from their stupor.

"Dad, I need to use the toilet," said Doat.

The words worked like a spell on the others who suddenly remembered their own full bladders. As Dad considered the wisdom of allowing people to take turns going to the outhouse in Khan's yard, a nearby blast knocked the two men into each other.

"We will bring a bucket for you to go in," Dad said as he and Khan climbed the wooden stairs and opened the doors.

A rush of burnt air replaced the stale, heavy air we had been breathing for hours. While they were outside, the two men spoke openly of the fear they kept secret from their families.

"Dinh, what's going on?" Khan asked.

"Something big," Dad said. "Ho Chi Minh must have known that half the army is on leave."

"But it has been going on for hours. How could they launch an attack this large on such short notice?" Khan asked.

"You're right. There is no way they could've smuggled this much firepower into the city over the course of a few days. They have been planning this for months," Dad said.

Khan shook his head.

"And they did it on Tet. Shameful."

"Yeah," Dad agreed, "let's get our stuff and head back in, I don't want our families to worry."

The two walked through the house to collect their items. They peeked out the front door and saw a squad of Viet Cong, distinguishable from the North Vietnam regular soldiers by their civilian clothing, running down the smoke-filled street carrying two rockets and a launching tube. Dad and Khan retreated back through the house. A few seconds later they were in the shelter carrying a bucket of water, an empty bucket that would be the makeshift toilet, and a small bottle of oil for the lamp.

The doors were latched and the bucket was passed around. When everyone had relieved themselves, Khan carried the bucket out to dump it in the outhouse. He returned and the doors were fastened again, sealing in the gloom that hung alongside the bad air in the bunker.

We stayed there through the night and into the next day. There was nothing else to do, so we ate all of the *banh chung*; chewing without tasting, swallowing without savoring. The explosions waxed and waned but never completely stopped. The sharp crack of AK rifles filled the space between booms. In the afternoon of the second day, the oil for the lamp ran out and we were immersed in darkness. The light seeping around the door edges formed a hazy rectangle above us, the only reference point in an otherwise infinite void. It seemed to withdraw from us until it became an inaccessible portal so far away it might as well have been the moon.

The rectangular light faded and so did hope. It had been a beacon, a promise, a star by which we could navigate back into the world of the living, and now it was abandoning us too. The light grew dim until it disappeared. We sat in total darkness.

The bunker that gave us the best chance of survival was now a tomb. We were buried alive in a grave we had walked into gratefully. The percussive thump of the 122s continued through the night, momentarily rippling the surface of preternatural stillness, then disappearing into the consuming blackness that absorbed everything, even our thoughts. The screams that had clawed their way out of my lungs after each explosion lay silent. Each explosion had been a knife thrust through my ears into my brain, setting off a cascade of anxiety that pooled in my throat and then rushed out like a crashing wave. But without light, sound had no reference point, no foundation. Without shadow, how do we know there's anything to create a shadow? It was no longer frightening. The dead aren't scared anymore.

The war had finally killed me—not physically, but emotionally. I stopped crying. What is the use of crying when you no longer exist?

Outside our lightless hole in the ground, the North's great gamble was losing steam. The communists' massive assault was audacious but had a fatal flaw. Instead of concentrating their forces on just a few targets, they had spread them over 100 cities and towns throughout the country. The thin assault was quickly subdued by the superior firepower of the Americans and the unexpected ferocity of the previously disrespected Southern troops. Also, the fabled uprising that would overthrow the despised southern puppet government didn't materialize. The North had taken it as an article of faith that the people of South Vietnam were just waiting for the right moment to join the revolution. They weren't. They were too busy hiding from the fury and chaos of the haphazard offensive.

Saigon, the biggest prize of the Tet Offensive, slipped away as well. The Viet Cong attacked their six targets throughout the city and were beaten back from each one. One of the main objectives, Radio Saigon, was temporarily captured by a squad of Viet Cong carrying a recording of Ho Chi Minh. On the tape, "Uncle Ho" urged the citizens to awaken and overthrow the colonial usurpers. The soldiers loaded the tape for playback and began the broadcast they hoped would ignite the peoples' righteous clamor for socialism.

Nothing happened. The mission, while bold and creative, was not thoroughly planned. They went to great lengths to occupy the radio station, but they did not protect the transmission lines leading to the broadcast tower. When the studio was overrun, quick-thinking station workers simply cut the lines and prevented the message from being heard.

The North was beaten. In every facet of the offensive, the communists suffered staggering losses. Somewhere between 35,000 and 40,000 northern soldiers were killed, as opposed to fewer than 5,000 South Vietnamese and American deaths. The people did not rise up and take over the government. On the contrary, they were incensed that the communists had launched an attack on Tet. The Viet Cong ceased to exist as a cohesive fighting force and would spend the rest of the war in small-scale rural action.

Northern leaders were despondent over their Tet failure. Their miscalculation had cost them dearly. They were on the verge of annihilation and had nothing to show for it.

Except one thing.

One miniscule thing that would change the outcome of the entire war.

25

Scientist Ed Lorenz famously asked, "Does the flap of a butterfly's wings in Brazil set off a tornado in Texas?" It was the beginning of a theory widely known as the butterfly effect, an illustration of the idea that small variances in the conditions of complex systems can have profound effects on the systems' outcomes. Lorenz's idea became the basis of chaos theory.

On February 1, 1968, as my family was hiding in Khan's bomb shelter, the butterfly's wings were flapping on a nearby Saigon street. It was a small drama, insignificant in the outcome of the Tet Offensive, but one which would change everything in Vietnam including the trajectory of my own life. Nguyen Van Lem, a Viet Cong guerilla, was arrested for the murder of a South Vietnamese officer, Lt. Col. Tuan, and seven members of his family. He was captured and brought before the chief of the national police, General Nguyen Ngoc Loan.

Loan did not hesitate. He calmly walked over and told the arresting soldiers to back away. He produced his pistol and shot the handcuffed Lem on the street at the exact moment American journalist Eddie Adams captured the execution in a haunting, perfectly-timed photograph. In the photo, Loan had his back to the camera. His outstretched arm held a pistol which was pointed at Lem's head. Lem was dressed in a rumpled plaid shirt. As the bullet entered his skull, shock waves spread across his face and tossed his thick black hair.

The butterfly in Saigon set off a tornado in the United States. The picture captured the savagery of war like none before it, shocking in its immediacy and brutality. Americans were outraged. Support for the war collapsed despite the overwhelming Tet victory. After the battle had been won, General Westmoreland sensed North Vietnam's army was at its breaking point. He requested 200,000 more troops to crush the communists and end the war.

The American public would have none of it. Adams' picture created a firestorm of opposition and Westmoreland was denied his troop surge. On the cusp of victory, America began its long and costly withdrawal. The Tet Offensive had been a tactical disaster for the North. They did not achieve a single objective and lost tens of thousands of men. And yet, a single photograph with less physical power than a butterfly's wingbeat gave North Vietnam a stunning strategic victory. Within three weeks, Lyndon Johnson announced he would not seek reelection.

The picture went on to be called "the photo that lost the war."

About the time the light left the eyes of Nguyen Van Lem, it returned to ours. It was the morning of the third day. The rectangle of light returned. Pathetic as it was, it was something tangible, a lifeline in the boundless abyss. Daylight seeped into our tomb, entered our eyes and stimulated our brains. If light still lived, maybe we could live again too.

The rockets had stopped falling sometime during the wee hours. In our delirium and exhaustion, we didn't notice it, but Dad did. When the absence of explosions persisted for a few hours, Dad broke the silence. He spoke in a voice as clear as mountain water and it startled everyone.

"Khan, I think it's over. Let's go check it out."

"Dad, I want to go, too," said Doat.

"No, son," Dad said, "if it's over, everyone can come out in just a few minutes."

The two climbed the stairs and opened the doors as Doat sulked. The light flooded the bunker and overwhelmed our eyes. We shielded them from the burning brightness. The men closed the door and we were plunged back into darkness. When they returned, the doors were flung open. Khan and my father stood above the opening.

"You can come out now, it's over."

Doat ran up the steps. Thi Tuyen assisted me while the adults below helped my very pregnant mother. We emerged from the bunker blinking in the full intensity of daylight. It wasn't a bright day. It was the kind of overcast one would usually call gloomy, but we didn't care. It was light and it was precious. I ran around Khan's backyard releasing three days of pent-up energy. The act was strictly a biological impulse. There was no joy in my robotic motions. Thi Tuyen and Doat tried to play with me, but they, too, were exhausted and didn't last long. Our new Tet clothes were streaked with dirt and wrinkled from living in them for three days. Mom watched us with unfocused, uncomprehending eyes as Dad and Khan whispered to each other.

"Come on, we have to go home," Dad announced.

We maneuvered our way over and around the debris in Khan's home to the front door. The front wall of his house had been knocked backwards by a blast and leaned precariously over us as we exited onto a street transformed into an ineffable hellscape. Homes were blasted into piles of blocks. Walls which were still standing were either charred with soot or pockmarked by shrapnel. The air was heavy with smoke. Fragments of shrapnel lay scattered like confetti in the streets along with bullet casings and possessions blown out of houses after direct hits. Tan Phu was in ruins.

And the bodies. When we made our way to Khan's bunker on the first morning, there were a few corpses here and there. Two days later, the scene was breathtaking. Soldiers lay stiff in the streets with blood-stained clothes marking the places they were shot. Assorted weapons—AK-47s, pistols, rockets, and launchers—were close to the bodies, some still clenched by dead hands.

The civilian casualties were more gruesome. Direct hits from 122s blew people to pieces. Arms and legs protruded from rubble. Those not killed by a blast were shredded by shrapnel and left to bleed out in agony. Still others met their end from bullets, collapsing houses, or fires.

As we walked toward our house, the shrieking began as survivors discovered dead family members. The sound grew in volume and desperation as more people exited their damaged or demolished homes. A crescendo of grief enveloped the neighborhood. It sounded like the tortured screams of hell itself.

I held onto Mom's pant leg and looked up at her for guidance. Her face was like stone, looking ahead, staring past the grisly scene. When we reached our street and she could see our own neighbors wailing, she could no longer hold her composure. She went to them, embraced each one and cried with them. Then she and Dad helped their friends dig through the rubble for survivors.

There weren't any. The combination of blast wave, shrapnel, and falling walls proved grimly efficient at ending life. Heads were cracked and pressed into unnatural shapes. The long black hair of some of the women shrouded their faces, stuck in place with dried blood. Limbs were broken, pulled out of socket, or separated from bodies. Mouths were contorted in frozen agony.

As I stared at a decapitated corpse in morbid fascination, an imperceptible toll mounted silently inside me. Under normal conditions, the brain receives stimuli through our five senses, processes them, and responds. The stimulus/response cycle is the common denominator of all living things, the thing that separates us from the inanimate earth on which we live.

But the human brain is not so simple. A slipshod construct of complexity and contradiction, ours is the Rube Goldberg machine of evolution. It is three brains in one—the lizard brain, the mammal brain, and the human brain—layered one on top of the next as our ancestors continued to survive, adapt, and evolve. Each section controls a part of the whole, and all three struggle to direct behavior. Writer Arthur Koestler famously said it is the only example of evolution providing a species with an organ which it does not know how to use.

The stimuli of the Tet Offensive were multifaceted and overwhelming. All my senses were activated, flooding my young brain with too much information—all of it bad. Whether it was the sound of exploding rockets slamming like sledgehammers against my ears, vibrations that buzzed through my skin telling me danger was too close, the acrid smell and taste of burnt gunpowder, or the sight of death and destruction in all directions, every piece of information was sending an urgent message…

RUN.

I didn't run although my lizard brain was screaming at me to do so. My mammal brain said to stay with Mom because, for mammals, Mom means safety. My poor human brain, undeveloped and confused, didn't know what to do, so it shut down.

For five years.

26

I t was a bitter victory. The South had won the battle, but at a terrible price, most of which had been paid by the civilian population. More than 14,000 civilians perished in the attacks, including many of my parents' friends. Some 630,000 South Vietnamese became refugees, including us. Our house was one of 70,000 made unlivable by the battle. Unlike the first time our house had been crumbled by a rocket blast, my parents did not begin to rebuild right away. The destruction was too widespread to bounce back quickly. Also, because our home was strategically located near the airport, Dad had been convinced to find shelter out of the way in case the North came again, so he and Mom packed a few kitchen items and clothes, and we walked through the ruined city to Chi Hoa, five kilometers east on the outskirts of Tan Phu.

The trip produced our family's first war casualty. Unexploded rockets stuck out of the ground and protruded from walls like barbs. We had no option but to take our chances and move fast. Uncle Xe walked ahead of the group to act as a scout. Dad kept an eye on him and steered us away from harm anytime Xe stopped and pointed.

An explosion ripped the air and Xe fell.

"Stay here!" Dad shouted at us as he sprinted to his brother.

Xe was wide eyed and breathing heavy.

"My back! My back! It hurts! Dinh, help me!" Xe panted.

He howled in pain as Dad rolled him over. The back of Xe's pants were red with blood, but Dad could see no other wounds.

"Xe, I have to remove your pants to see where you are hurt. O.K.?"

Xe grimaced and agreed. Dad pulled his pants down and saw two bright red wounds on Xe's buttocks. A piece of shrapnel cut cleanly across his backside, giving him symmetrical wounds on both cheeks, as if someone had removed a slice from two round hams.

Dad laughed without thinking and immediately felt ashamed. Xe stopped grunting long enough to take offense at Dad's callousness.

"Why are you laughing? It's not funny!"

"I'm sorry, Xe. It's not funny. The good news is that your wounds are not serious."

"Well, what's funny about getting shot in the back?" Xe demanded.

"It's not your back. It's your…um…ass."

"What? I got shot in the ass?"

"Not *in* the ass," Dad explained, "More like across it. Here, let's get the bleeding stopped. You will be sore for a few days, but you will be fine."

We traveled to Chi Hoa without further incident and stayed as refugees at a school for a few weeks. When Dad felt it was safe enough, we returned to Tan Phu and my parents rebuilt the house. The baby that Mom carried through the horrific attack arrived right on time, healthy and strong as a water buffalo. My parents named her Kim Tuyen, not to be confused with my older sister, Thi Tuyen.

Five years passed without depositing normal childhood memories. The Tet Offensive left a lifetime of psychic scars, but remained an open wound for the length of our stay in Saigon. I like to think that my brain was healing itself of the trauma of Tet and couldn't spare the energy necessary for memory curation. Only a few, broken, hazy fragments are scattered here and there. Most were negative events etched with strong emotion.

I remember yelling at my cousin Linh to get out of the apple tree which grew in front of our house.

I remember Mom sending me to get eggs at the chicken house down the street. The building was long and contained hundreds of clucking hens. The offensive stench of ammonia wafted far from the source. The sound and smell of the chickens frightened me.

I remember seeing an orange sky on nights when the North attacked some place in the city.

I remember running to the shelter. Over and over and over. It is a scene that has replayed in my head like a skipping record.

Despite the blank pages in my memory, my older siblings have assured me that I grew up normally. I started school. I played in the street. I had friends. I smiled and laughed just like any kid, but none of those things registered. Instead of a living scrapbook filled with moving pictures, sounds, and smells of childhood, all I have is a musty attic, crisscrossed with cobwebs, splotched by scenes of discomfort and the terror of Tet.

There is one exception to the barren, ugly landscape of my early memories. Mom was always seeking ways to provide for the family. The vegetable trade just didn't produce enough income, so being an enterprising businesswoman, she diversified and began weaving sedge mats to sell in the market.

Sedge grass has been used by humans for eons. Archaeologists have found evidence of its use in bedding 70,000 years ago. Weaving is also ancient, dating back some 12,000 years, making it one of the oldest human crafts. Sedge mats had become synonymous with Vietnamese culture, a ubiquitous household item. They were used as mattresses, seating, and floor coverings. Making a mat was painstaking work requiring physical stamina and mental concentration. Within the last couple of centuries, machines have largely taken the place of hand weaving, but in 1968, poor Vietnamese still used a manual loom.

The weaving process was fairly simple. Strings were attached to one end of the frame of the loom and stretched across to the other side. This was called the warp. Long shafts of sedge grass, called weft, were then threaded under and over the warp strings, creating the weave pattern. A heavy wooden bar, called a beater, pushed the weft grass into place. These steps were repeated hundreds of times to create a mat.

It was tedious work but possessed of simple beauty. When my parents worked the loom together, the process became rhythmic. They labored without speaking, yet communicated profound truths that bypassed the crude, sloppy mechanism of sound sliding across an auditory nerve into a bumbling consciousness which is so often inaccurate at translating words into meaning. Their effortless teamwork at the loom penetrated far deeper, planting seeds of virtue directly into my subconscious. I even got a glimpse of love among the threads of warp and weft.

The easy harmony of my parents' graceful motions seemed like a dance. I must have watched for hours. Absorbing. Remembering.

When Dad was around, he and Mom could make a mat in a day. Most days he was working with the army, so Mom had to find another partner. The person she usually pressed into service was less experienced and far less enthusiastic.

In the aftermath of Tet, schools were closed for the remainder of the term. As a result, Doat found himself involuntarily employed. On the days that Mom sold her vegetables in town, he was put in charge of his three younger siblings, even baby Kim Tuyen. Thi Tuyen and I were easy to manage, but Doat struggled to care for Kim Tuyen. He didn't know what to do when she cried, so he cried along with her. If he thought she was hungry, he carried her down the street to a lactating aunt. It was a measure of our poverty that a young boy would be trusted to manage an infant, but Doat faithfully cared for his sister and Kim Tuyen survived.

Doat also had to assist Mom with weaving. Suffice it to say he did not share my appreciation of weaving's balletic qualities. In fact, he hated it. Each morning before she left on her sales rounds, Mom woke Doat to weave for a while. He made no protest. Backtalk to one's parents didn't exist in Vietnam, but Doat found a passive-aggressive way to vent his displeasure. Whenever he was bored or tired and wanted a break, he pushed the sedge too hard through the loom, causing the long blade of grass to split. Work was stopped while Mom patiently repaired the weft.

She never scolded him or lost her composure. She was too kind. As the years have passed, I have become awed by this virtue she possessed in such abundance. Hers was a life defined by hardship, yet neither famine, war, nor inescapable poverty blemished her spirit. She persisted in a way only the faithful can persist.

Her trials were far from over in 1968. Her persistence had many tests yet to endure.

27

C huong, where are you?" called my friends Khanh, Lap, and Thang as they stood on the dock looking for me.

I broke the river's surface slowly to avoid any telltale splashing. Peeking over the gunwale, I could see them though they couldn't see me. . I slapped the water to get their attention.

"I win!" I laughed.

"Come on, Chuong," Lap said. "Let's play again."

I slipped my head under the brown water, letting my fingertips slide along the smooth underside of the sampan to guide me to the other side of the boat. I climbed out of the water and punched Khanh on the arm.

"You're the seeker this time," Khanh said.

My three friends disappeared into the water and I counted to ten. I was about to jump when Mom came around a corner and called to me.

"Chuong, I need your help."

"Okay, Mom, I'm coming."

Our game of water hide-and-seek would have to be postponed. Though I could not see my friends hiding amongst the clot of tied boats, I called out to them.

"Hey guys, I have to go. See you later."

I ran across the unpaved main street of Thanh An and ducked under the board that served as a counter for Mom's vegetable business. Dripping wet, I began serving customers, haggling over the price of water spinach called *rau muong* and jute vegetables called *rau day.*

The year was 1973, the Year of the Buffalo. Dad was still employed with the army of South Vietnam, also called the ARVN. He had served faithfully and efficiently and was rewarded with a promotion and transfer to the base at Long Xuyen. The base was about 35 kilometers from our old home in the area called Kinh Rivera, so Dad moved the family back to Thanh An, the sleepy little town at the mouth of Kinh D, just a few kilometers from our old rice farm.

Moving out of Saigon was therapeutic for me. Attacks on the city did not end with the Tet Offensive of 1968. War was a constant companion there, a loud and destructive presence that kept everyone on edge. When we traded the harrowing, reoccurring tragedy in Saigon for the bucolic quiescence of river life, I healed. I never heard another bomb explode. I never saw another mother cry in anguish as she held her dead child. My brain began to process life without the extra weight of fear. I began making memories.

Thanh An was a trading village on the banks of Kinh Cai San, one of thousands of canals dug in grid-like regularity throughout the Mekong Delta. The canal system and attached farming land had been constructed for the hundreds of thousands of refugees who fled the north at the end of the French War in 1954. My parents, along with most of the neighbors from their village in North Vietnam, had settled along these canals surrounding Thanh An and started life over.

Dad sold our original farm when he was drafted into the army in 1965. When we returned to Kinh Rivera in 1973, he bought a place in town so Mom could continue her business. Our house looked much like the one in Saigon— a narrow, two-story building made of limewashed block. The house was one of several which bordered a small open space which served as the main marketplace for Thanh An. A corrugated tin roof attached to the front of our house created a covered porch from which Mom conducted her trade.

Mom appreciated doing business from a stationary location. Her days as a *ganh hang rong* (street vendor) in Saigon were brutal on her small frame. Carrying a bamboo pole with two balanced baskets of merchandise on each end would be exhausting in perfect conditions, but in the oppressive heat and humidity of Vietnam, it was punishing. Fruits spoiled quickly in direct sunlight, and she struggled to sell waterlogged produce during the monsoon.

The market stall in front of our house was perfect. Mom could sell her fruits, vegetables, and sedge mats while keeping an eye on her expanding brood. In 1971, while we were still in Saigon, Mom gave birth to brother Tien. My older sister Thi Tuyen was nearly a teenager and had strong maternal instincts, which was also immensely helpful to Mom. Thi Tuyen cooked, cleaned, and helped care for Tien, freeing Mom to run the business.

Shortly after the business was up and running in Thanh An, Mom discovered I had a knack for selling. I had an innate grasp of the give-and-take of negotiation and she put me to work whenever things got busy. On the day she called me from my game of water hide-and-seek, I rested my wet arms on the counter, narrowed my eyes, and engaged in battle with crusty old Mrs. Hong, a notorious and aggressive local cheapskate. She was sweaty and fleshy and had beady little eyes that disappeared behind her fat cheeks as her contempt rose.

"How much for this jute mallow?" she demanded.

"One-hundred dong," I coolly replied.

"That's outrageous!"

"It has been selling fast today at this price," I said.

"Not to me," she said.

I slowly ratcheted up the pressure.

"Suit yourself, but if you change your mind later, it might not be here."

She sensed that her bullying strategy was not working, so she changed course, probing to find my weak point. The sweat poured across her face and her beady eyes glinted in the sunlight.

"Listen, Chuong, I don't have 100 dong. You know my husband has been ill and hasn't been able to work. I'll give you 40."

She shoved a wad of bills at me as if her offer sealed the deal.

"Forty? Mrs. Hong, I can't sell this at 40. We have a large family and my father is away at the war."

She fumed at having the pity tables turned on her. As she regrouped, I looked in her basket at the other items she purchased from other vendors.

"I'll tell you what. I will sell you this mallow for 40 dong if you give me three eggs," I offered.

She was almost apoplectic.

"Three eggs!" she nearly shouted. "I paid 25 dong apiece for these eggs. Are you trying to rob me?"

"Not at all. But if it will help us come to an agreement, I will do it for two eggs."

She fumed with indignance as she slammed the money on the counter and gently laid two eggs on top of the bills.

Mom witnessed the exchange and gave me a proud smile. She was finishing her own transaction but did not receive any money for the water spinach she gave the customer. I noticed and asked her as she made an entry in a small notebook. The pages of the notebook were curled and dirty.

"Mom, why didn't they pay?"

She sighed.

"Sometimes people don't have money with them, so I let them take items on credit. They promise to pay me back soon."

"Have any of them paid you back?" I asked.

"Not yet, but they will. Jesus taught that we must love our neighbor as ourselves. We just have to be patient."

She smiled serenely, but behind her smile I saw doubt. I glanced at her book. It had a lot of entries.

28

D ad's home!"

I was sitting in the house when I heard the familiar sputtering engine pull up in front of the house. Dad had kept his Honda XL250 from our days in Saigon. He had brought it with him when we moved to Thanh An and now used it to travel to and from the base in Long Xuyen. He didn't make the 35 kilometer journey every day. He spent most of the week on base and came home for the weekends. It was a treat when he came home. Doat and Thi Tuyen were teenagers, surly and hard to impress, but Kim Tuyen and I were overjoyed when Dad came home. He brought us each a piece of candy. Even the teenagers smiled at that.

Mom appeared in the room and smiled at Dad but did not embrace him.

"Welcome home, husband. You are just in time for supper," she said. "Children, please make a place for us to eat."

Kim Tuyen and I raced to arrange sedge mats in a circle and we all sat. Mom and Thi Tuyen brought out two big bowls, one with rice and the other with water spinach and caramelized fish. Mom also had a small pot of soup called *pho* and the traditional condiment called *nuoc cham*, a dipping sauce made from anchovy fish sauce, garlic, sugar, and lemons. It was very salty and tart. She placed the entrée in the middle of the circle where we could all reach with our chopsticks. As custom dictated, Mom kept the rice and soup pots near her so that she or Thi Tuyen could refill bowls as requested.

Suppertime was an inviolable tradition in our house. Dad insisted that each of us had to be home so we could eat as a family. Conversation was forbidden during mealtime. Mom was exempted from this mandate so that she could correct Kim Tuyen and me when our manners slipped. Still, she barely spoke above a whisper and never made eye contact.

"Chuong, don't eat your soup like you are trying to drain a lake."

"Kim Tuyen, chew with your mouth closed, please."

After our silent supper was finished, Dad spoke to me.

"Chuong, you will become an altar boy," he said.

"Yes, Father, but I don't know how to be an altar boy," I replied.

"After Mass tomorrow, you will stay behind and let Father Tao teach you."

Mass in rural Vietnam was held each morning at four a.m. so farmers could get a jump on their tasks in the coolest part of the day. The Catholic Church, *Nha Tho Thanh An,* was the biggest building in town, a cruciform structure made of simple blocks. The church was regularly painted white, but the relentless rain and humidity of the Mekong Delta stained it a splotchy beige. It had a wraparound covered porch which stretched from transept to transept. The columns of the porch and roof fascia were painted flamingo pink. The tall gable featured a large cross at its apex which was outlined with pink neon lights. The cross stood high above the trees and buildings of town and was visible everywhere and at all times. It had a subtle yet authoritative effect. It beckoned parishioners to come worship and also judged us like a glowing eye in the sky.

Unlike the heavily ornamented churches of old Europe, the inside of the church was spare. Stained glass windows were plain aquamarine, narrow, and regularly spaced. A few pieces of traditional statuary dotted the sanctuary—The Blessed Mother, St. Joseph, and the Via Crucis in relief on the walls.

After Mass, Father Tao walked me and my friend Khanh through our duties and then took us to the choir room. He handed each of us a cassock and surplice and gave us strict instructions to wash it the night before we were scheduled to serve. Father Tao was a serious man, grim and joyless. He never smiled or displayed any warmth of spirit. He warned us he would tolerate no monkey business, which was a shame because I specialized in monkey business. I didn't hear anything else he said as I was thinking about monkeys dressed as altar boys, swinging on jungle ropes across the sanctuary. As the priest wrapped up his warnings, I made it my young life's goal to engage in as many shenanigans as I could get away with.

Being the second son in a highly patriarchal society meant the pressure to carry the family honor was not on my shoulders. That was Doat's burden. I was free to pursue my Tom Sawyer lifestyle, which I did with gusto. Thanh An was to me what St. Petersburg was to Tom, a source of limitless adventure to a small boy with imagination and opportunities. My short career as an altar boy promised another avenue of mischief.

When Khanh and I were released from Father Tao's morose grip, we ran out the front doors. Painted over the doors was *Matthew 11:29.*

Take my yoke upon you and learn from me,
for I am gentle and humble in heart.

We raced into the palm lined courtyard. Lap and Thang were waiting on us.

"Let's go swimming," Lap said.

"Yeah, there's a barge coming. Chuong, you can swim out to it," Thang added.

I declined.

"Sorry, guys, Mom said I have to help her in the market."

With a promise to find them as soon as I could, I walked home. When I rounded the corner, Mom was finishing up a sale by making another mark in her notebook. There were no other customers around, so she went into the house. I stopped for a few seconds and thought about going to the canal, but conscience overcame me and I went in the house to check in with her. I found her on her knees in the kitchen, digging at the dirt floor with an old spoon.

"Mom, what are you doing?"

I startled her and she grabbed her chest.

"Chuong, you scared me! I need to buy some fruit when the Pineapple Ladies come to town tomorrow."

She kept digging until a small jar was unearthed. She opened the jar and let me look inside. The jar was about half filled with gold and silver coins. Mom explained to me that our paper currency, the *dong*, was unreliable in its value and often worthless. Whenever exchange rates were favorable, she traded *dong* notes for coins.

198

Mom dug out a few coins and returned the jar to its hole. She scraped dirt over the jar and put a heavy pot on top. She whispered a plea that I would not reveal the buried vault to anyone and suggested I go play, probably hoping I would soon forget her secret. I was more than happy to take her offer, but I didn't forget. I charged out of the house toward the dock. As I ran, I remembered the words over the church doors, *for I am gentle and humble in heart.* It occurred to me Jesus must have been a lot like my mother.

When I reached the canal, my friends were standing on the dock where the ferry crossed over to Kinh D. They were dripping wet.

"Why are you up here?" I asked.

Thang pointed north. A long barge of rice was lumbering to the port at Rach Gia. It occupied over half the width of the canal.

"Go Chuong, you can do it," they said.

I had developed a reputation as the daredevil of the group. Being the smallest, I operated from a position of assumed inferiority. To compensate, I became highly competitive and took stupid risks like climbing onto a moving boat.

I jumped in and swam to the barge. It sat low from the weight of its cargo. A thick dockline hung off the side. I grabbed hold and hauled myself on deck. My friends cheered as I raised my arms in triumph. The commotion was enough to get the attention of people waiting on the ferry. They began pointing and laughing. With an appreciative audience, I did a little dance. This was enough to rouse the boat's captain, who followed the pointing fingers and saw a wet, skinny stowaway dancing on his vessel. He came charging out from the wheelhouse to evict me. I began running toward him to build drama, planning to dive off the boat just before he caught me. It would be the grand finale of the impromptu performance.

It would have been great. My status as the bravest kid in Thanh An would have been assured. But the deck was wet and slippery. I lost my footing and careened toward the captain. At the last moment I tumbled off the boat into the water.

I didn't come up.

29

A sucking current pulled me under the barge, tumbling and disorienting me. I didn't know which way was up, so I reached around frantically until I found the smooth hull above. I searched in blind rage for the edge, but it did not present itself. My lungs throbbed as they filled with noxious carbon dioxide. Muscles accustomed to limitless oxygen screamed in petulant protest. A mutiny formed, body against brain. Dumb muscles didn't know they were submerged, they only felt the ache of urgent need. I wrestled against water and against my own body to maintain control of the unraveling situation.

Life is usually measured in years or decades. We throw away minutes, hours, even days, because we operate under the illusion of abundant time. When the sun is high and the rice stalks grow thick and yellow, we luxuriate in confidence that time is on our side. Even when want strikes, the reserves of fat and water that have evolved over eons of survived famines and droughts promise days and weeks to seek replenishment. We hang on even in the direst situations, willing to endure prolonged agony in exchange for a promise—vouchsafed by generations who survived and passed on their genes—that time brings relief. Tenacity is a form of faith, a belief in a benevolent future that lasts as long as reserves hold out.

But there is no bank of oxygen within us. It is the most abundant yet transient of resources. We gulp in great lungs full of air every few seconds and save none of it. Our greedy tissues light fire to every molecule of oxygen to stay warm, stay alive. If we are plunged into an alien environment without immediate access to life's gas—outer space or under water, perhaps—our blithe confidence turns to howling panic within seconds. If not rectified, lifespan is reduced to mere seconds.

On the dock, the previously appreciative crowd gasped in horror. They strained to see a black head pop out of the muddy water. Nothing appeared and they leaned in, growing more alarmed with each passing second. Khanh, Lap, and Thang began to whine mournfully, unable to move, unable to turn away from the place where their friend was about to die.

My strength was depleted and my will was overcome. I could not hold back the riotous demands coming from every part of my body. Water—the first womb, the giver of life—was about to become a murderer. In one final stroke of rebellion, my diaphragm seized, forcing me to inhale. The brown water was cold and heavy in my lungs. I coughed it out and drew another liquid breath as my head broke the surface.

"There he is!" my friends shouted. They jumped in and swam out to me. They dragged my limp body onto the dock and screamed for me to wake up. Chaos swarmed inside me as organized energy, tenacious but fragile, dissipated. Without oxygen to fuel the fires of being, my cells immediately began the pitiful work of dissolution. I was dead.

I don't know what happened next. Maybe my friends shook me. Maybe my dimly functioning brain sent one last message down deteriorating neurons to the diaphragm, telling it to spasm one more time. Maybe God touched my abdomen and pressed the water from my lungs.

Whatever it was, I coughed. Water seeped from the corner of my mouth. I coughed again and more water came up. The great fire was lit again. I rolled over and heaved, emptying my lungs and stomach. My friends laughed, cried, and patted me in relief. When my strength returned, I walked home and stayed there the rest of the day. I didn't say much, I just had an inexplicable urge to be near my family. In the afternoon as the sun was melting over the edge of the rice paddies, the regenerative power of forgetting was already working in me. A boy in another part of the world might have developed a lifelong fear of water, but in the Mekong Delta there was no escape from its ubiquity. To be hydrophobic in Thanh An would have been to shun life itself. Still, a lesson was learned. I never climbed onto another barge again.

A near death experience might change some people, make them better behaved, softer in word and deed. As far as I could tell, my brush with the hereafter didn't do much to alter my personality. But I had to be careful. Dad was the choir director. It would not do for such a prominent person in the village to have such a reckless reprobate for a child. Everyone knew him, and by extension, everyone knew me. It was a stifling state of affairs for an artist in mischief. Every town has its busybodies—the incorrigible gossips who live to cluck their disapproval of the moral degradation running rampant in every town on earth, in every age since Adam and Eve were evicted from the garden. Our gossips made short work of juicy news. On lazy days in the market, I could track the speed of news as the sellers whispered across stalls.

God's own supernatural eyes may have penetrated deeper into the soul, but the surface perception of the gossips carried a more immediate and certain threat. Accordingly, I kept my devilment as stealthy as possible.

It wasn't that my hijinks were premeditated acts of basic evil. They were simply random opportunities for a laugh that presented themselves to a boy with too much energy, like the time I taught myself how to use Dad's bicycle. Bikes weren't children's toys or recreational devices in those days, but a serious mode of transportation. Dad used it extensively for errands around town, but left it at home while he was stationed in Long Xuyen. I fancied the bike, the pleasing aesthetic of triangles and circles, the marvelous simplicity of its action, and the everyday accessibility of one of the world's greatest inventions, so I took it upon myself to learn how to ride it. But the bike was far too tall for me to ride traditionally. If I sat on the saddle, I could not reach the pedals. I had to develop another strategy.

First, I tried the "skateboard method." I stood on one pedal with one foot while pushing with the other. This worked fairly well, but something was unsatisfying about it, as if I dishonored the spirit of the bicycle's inventor by riding his contraption so incompletely.

I figured out that I could put both feet on the pedals by stepping through the triangle and stretching out and up to grasp the handlebars. It was an ungainly pose. I twisted like a snake around the frame of the machine to get both feet on the pedals and both hands on the bar. The bulk of my scrawny mass was too far forward and off to one side, giving a center of gravity that made the bike unstable and hard to control.

As they say, necessity is the mother of invention. While necessity had no part in this enterprise, desire made a good substitute. The feeling of gliding on wheels was intoxicating for a boy who had only ridden in any kind of vehicle twice in his life. Soon I was wheeling my way precariously through town, parting clusters of townspeople who hurled curses in my wake. The old timers laughed at my circus act from the relative safety of the road margins, but within days the novelty faded and I melted into the ordinary comings and goings that constituted traffic in Thanh An. In the chaotic milieu of motorcycles, bicycles, pedestrians, buffalo-driven carts, and the odd automobile here and there, a boy wrangling an oversized bike receded into near invisibility.

Good thing, too. I developed an affection for riding that bordered on addiction. In every spare moment, I swooped around the square and up and down the main street. Mom decided to put my new hobby to good use. She sent me running errands up and down Kinh Cai San. Once I was sent on a pre-dawn run to Kinh B to pick up some fried tofu. Just down the street from our house, another seller, Mrs. Thu, was setting up her melons on the roadside for the day's trade. It would prove an unfortunate place to display her wares.

Though my unorthodox riding style was unbalanced, I had developed enough confidence to go with speed, which unsurprisingly did not improve the stability of the business. As I headed out, I bounced up and down on the bike, my skinny legs pounding the pedals, fleshy pistons beating out an accelerating rhythm. Just as I reached maximum velocity, I careened off the roadway and sliced through about six of Mrs. Thu's melons.

I was mortified. I braced myself for the onslaught sure to envelop me when Mrs. Thu saw what I had done. I imagined that she would come at me, slapping and cursing, and then she would tell my parents. Then I would be in real trouble.

Nothing happened. She had vanished inside a house for a moment and did not hear the sickening sound of melons being punctured. I had an instant. The instant contained a decision. I should have stayed put and taken my punishment. I should have offered to reimburse her for the damaged merchandise. I should have done the right thing, after all, I was an altar boy. What good is an impious altar boy?

Truth was, I didn't reflect much on my status within the church hierarchy or the disrepute my order would suffer from debasement within its ranks. I thought about the punishment that would descend upon me when my father found out. I jerked the bike out of the slushy mess and ran away.

Somehow, I got away with it. Darkness, the sinner's best friend, covered my getaway. An hour later, I would have been identified by the omnipresent eyes of the village. I didn't waste time mounting the bike, but pushed it down the street, my sandals beating out a rapid flip-flapping tempo on the dusty road. I hid behind the corner of a nearby house. When Mrs. Thu discovered the damage, she wailed in outrage. Spittle flew from her mouth as she pledged violence if she ever found the vile culprit. After a tirade that lasted several minutes, she began cutting the melons. She would have to sell them in pieces at a discount.

I spent most of the day a nervous fugitive. I figured the best way to avoid being named a suspect was to remain out of sight. I hid behind Mom's selling counter and watched Mrs. Thu selling her melon slices.

I expected her wrath to remain unsated until her criminal was apprehended and brought to justice. To my surprise, she didn't remain angry all day. I even saw her laughing with her customers a few times. This puzzled me. The margin between enough and want was slim in our village. In my undeveloped and inexperienced mind, I imagined my thoughtlessness had created a great disaster for Mrs. Thu. Yet there she was, going about her business as if nothing was out of the ordinary. I didn't yet understand the resilience of the Vietnamese poor, but in the annals of setbacks weathered by our battered people, the loss of a few melons hardly registered.

Such perspective is not innate. It is not passed down like instinct grooved into the folds of DNA. It is only developed through the hard business of living. I would have to put in many more years before such recondite knowledge would become accessible. For the time being, I trafficked in the rough emotions of the neophyte—fear, mostly.

Hours passed. Fear was slowly crowded out by expanding guilt. Fear ignites hot and burns out fast, but guilt burns long and constant, like a lump of coal, scorching the excuse-maker with penetrating moral clarity. I decided I must go to confession.

On the day of confession, I went to Father Tao and bared my ugly, stained soul. I was sure he would prescribe a full accounting of my deeds to Mrs. Thu and my parents, whereby my self-loathing would be made external and transformed into other forms of psychic and physical punishment. It was slowly becoming apparent that suffering in one form or another was an inextricable part of life.

Father Tao surprised me. Instead of sentencing me to public penance, he told me to recite the Hail Mary five times and go and sin no more.

That's all? I thought.

Here I was, prepared to go to the gallows of parental punishment, and the judge—God's own judge—let me off with less than a slap on the wrist.

Five Hail Marys? What a bargain!

I had beaten the system! I raced through the words and bolted out the door, free to continue on my wayward path with a clear conscience.

30

Regardless of country or culture, there is a certain barbarity to childhood. Children organize themselves by the law of the jungle, forming pecking orders reminiscent of lower mammalian cousins. It is a world often fraught with intimidation and brute force, but it welds steel into the personality. Such metallurgy was fortifying my younger sister, Kim Tuyen as she made her way through the jungle.

Kim Tuyen was three years younger than me, but nearly as tall. Where I was bony and sinewy, she was muscled and compact. She possessed a cat's graceful motion, power and potential wound into her frame like a spring. God chose to infuse her with a healthy dose of confidence to match her physical strength, imprinting her with natural authority and influence.

We became a team. With her bulldog athleticism and my underdog tenacity, we took on all comers in street soccer. I was quiet and calculating. Kim Tuyen was brash and uncompromising. The world's game in Thanh An looked much as it did in any third world town in South America or Africa— contested on dirt roads full of rocks and obstacles, devoid of the manicured green fields of Europe and the U.S. Skinned knees and bloody feet were bright red badges of honor. Quarrels broke out over fouls. Bodies were shoved and slammed in retaliation. Kim Tuyen didn't shy from any of it. She was the consummate tomboy.

"Chuong, pass the ball!" she would shout.

If I failed to comply, or worse, turned the ball over to the other team, incriminations rained on me. Still, we worked well together and won more than we lost.

Kim Tuyen was tough as nails, but she was not immune to the cruelty of the village mean girls. Every town has these female wolf packs which assert and maintain dominance through a dark talent for psychological warfare. Thanh An was no different. We had our share of slandering bullies and one day two of them bared their fangs to my sister.

I was searching for Kim Tuyen. Lap and Thang had challenged us to a game. Kim Tuyen was not often found inside, but I could not find her in her usual haunts, so I went inside the house on the unlikely chance that she was there. I found Mom, digging in the floor of the main bedroom.

"Mom, what are you doing?"

She jerked upright and gasped.

"Chuong, you scared me! You are quiet as a mouse. I was just getting out some coins to pay the Pineapple Ladies."

"What happened to your jar in the kitchen?" I asked.

Her stricken face flashed a quick panic at the realization I had remembered catching her in the act of digging up money once before.

"Oh, I like to keep my money spread out in case someone finds one of my hiding places. It's important you don't tell anyone about this. We will need this money someday."

"O.K., Mom."

I was more interested in finding Kim Tuyen than contemplating the reason for Mom's nervous behavior. I walked toward the back of the house, mussing four-year-old brother Tien's hair as I passed him.

I found Kim Tuyen hiding in a crevice between two walls. She was folded into a tiny ball, her arms wrapped around her legs and her head buried between her knees.

"Tuyen, what's wrong?"

She raised her head and sniffled. Her eyes swelled with tears.

"Hong and Thuy were mean to me."

"What did they do?" I asked.

"They laughed at me for playing with boys. They said I wasn't a real girl. Then they started shoving me and calling me a boy until I ran away."

I wedged myself in the crevice beside her and sat there until she cried herself out. As she sniffed and sobbed, anger welled inside me. And then thoughts of revenge. And then a plan.

"I will get those two tomorrow," I said. "Do you want to go play?"

She did. We found Lap and Thang. Kim Tuyen tore through them with fury.

The next morning at Mass, Father Tao made a surprise appearance in the dressing room to have a meeting with us altar boys. He led us in the vesting prayer as we donned the cassock and surplice.

"O Lord, the portion of my inheritance and my Chalice, You are He who will restore my inheritance. Invest me, O Lord, as a new man, who was created by God in justice and the holiness of truth. Amen."

Then he dove into the purpose of his presence.

"Boys, in the last few months, someone has decided to become a prankster. The candles don't light when they are supposed to, someone put grass in the thurible which smoked and stunk up the service, and yesterday, someone unscrewed the clapper on the bell so it would fly off when rung. Mass is not playtime. It is holy. You are in the presence of God and you will worship Him with reverence. You can be sure that He sees everything you do here even if I don't, and although He may choose not to punish you for your sin, I most certainly will if I catch you. Do you two understand?"

We nodded meekly. When Father Tao left, Khanh turned on me.

"I told you not to do those things. Now we're in trouble," he said.

"Relax," I said. "There are twenty other altar boys. He doesn't know who did it, he's just trying to save himself the trouble of an investigation."

"Well, are you going to knock it off?" Khanh asked.

"Yes, Father Tao scares me a little bit, but he would tell my dad and that scares me a lot. I just have one more crime to commit and then I'm done."

"Oh, boy," Khanh fretted. "What are you going to do now?"

"Not much, just a little payback."

Khanh rolled his eyes.

"Just don't get caught, please."

One of my jobs during Mass was to help Father serve Holy Communion. I was in charge of the paten—a small, brass plate with a long handle attached. It looked like a fancy gold frying pan with no sides. I held the paten under the chin of every supplicant to prevent crumbs of the consecrated host from falling to the floor. When it was their turn, Hong and Thuy kneeled at the altar rail.

Khanh was on Father's left, I was on his right. As he paused in front of each person to share the body of Christ, Father Tao made a quarter turn away from me to retrieve a wafer from Khanh's plate. There was a rhythm to his movements I could measure and anticipate, but risk was high. The timing had to be perfect to escape Father's detection. To assault someone while they were taking communion surely would be the gravest sin, and more immediately, get me dismissed and probably beaten at least twice—once from Father Tao and once from Dad.

Father Tao stopped in front of Hong and spoke the solemn words, "The body of Christ broken for you," and handed her a wafer. The three of us shifted one person to the left and I placed the paten under Hong's chin. Father turned away from me to pick up a wafer for Thuy.

WHAM!

I lifted the plate with as much force as I could muster over the short distance and struck the jawbone of the ass. Hong looked at me with perplexed, silent fury and stuck the wafer in her mouth. I glared at her with narrow eyes as she chewed. Thuy witnessed the attack and awaited her fate in wide-eyed dread. We shifted to the left. Father turned.

WHAM!

The sound made as brass found bone was negligible. Father Tao never knew two of his parishioners were attacked by an altar boy during the most holy moment of Mass. I got away with it, but it was a foolish, reckless act. In retrospect, I could've avenged Kim Tuyen anytime, but I like to think I understood the power associated with the place, the moment, and my position. There I was, a representative of the church, smiting sinners like an avenging angel dressed in white. The girls had to look up at me and the cross that hung above the altar behind me. Our respective positions gave my illicit actions authority, both physical and supernatural. Plus, it was audacious as hell and extremely satisfying.

My plan worked. The girls never bothered Kim Tuyen again.

31

The war seemed so far away. We never saw a soldier (other than Dad) or any other sign of the desperate struggle consuming our country. Saigon was less than 200 kilometers from our quiet green corner of Vietnam, but it might as well have been on another continent. I spent my time in Thanh An in contented ignorance.

The war, however, was coming for us.

After the Tet Offensive in 1968 changed public perception, the United States began a long and costly withdrawal from the war. By early 1973, all American combat forces were removed from Vietnam. The ARVN was left to defend the country by itself, a job for which it was neither equipped nor motivated to do. The North's army along with the Viet Cong guerillas ratcheted closer and closer to the capital. In the spring of 1975, resistance collapsed and the cities of Hue and Da Nang were overrun. The North's forces quickly marched south and encircled Saigon with 100,000 men.

Sometime in early April, Dad showed up at home in the middle of the week. This was odd. We usually only saw him on the weekends.

"Hi Dad!" I shouted when I saw him.

I was at that impressionable age when a boy still worships his father as an infallible demigod.

"Hello, Chuong," he said flatly and disappeared inside the house.

I never expected or received much attention from my father, it was not the way of our culture for fathers to be affectionate to their children. Still, in my two second assessment, I could tell something was wrong. There was some minute physical nuance that gave my subconscious a sense of foreboding; perhaps it was a slight inflection of his voice, a tiny slump of his shoulders, or a creased facial muscle. Whatever was eating at Dad became an undefined heaviness within me. I followed him to the door of the house but did not enter. I knew he wouldn't tell me directly why he was home. I hoped to get the information through eavesdropping.

I heard mumbling voices inside the house, but couldn't make sense of the few words that came through clearly. Dad was doing most of the talking, as usual, with brief, solicitous offerings from Mom.

"Chuong, come play with me."

It was Kim Tuyen.

"Shhh, I'm trying to listen to Mom and Dad," I said.

"Dad's home!" she exclaimed and pushed past me into the house to greet him.

My attempt at surreptitious listening ruined, I followed her in the house. He gave a sad smile to Kim Tuyen as she rushed to embrace him.

"Dad, why are you home?" I asked.

My attempt to play it cool was overcome by not only my enthusiastic sister, but my own impatient curiosity.

"I'm not in the army anymore," he said.

He didn't say anything else, though more—much more—practically radiated from his pores. I was too frightened to ask additional questions. Frightened of Dad, naturally, but also frightened of the terrible thing that weighed so heavy on him; frightened of knowledge I might regret possessing. I decided that ignorance was the safest, most comforting course of action, so I took Kim Tuyen outside to play marbles in the dirt.

When Dad said he wasn't in the army anymore, he omitted the fact there was no army. The South had been beaten. Except for the few battalions making a last stand to defend Saigon, the army had disintegrated. Soldiers at Long Xuyen Base burned their papers and uniforms and dissolved back into the rice farms from whence they came, hoping against hope that the communists would lose their appetite for reprisals once there were no enemies left to fight. But communists are naturally fearful. Their ability to govern relies on coercion rather than consent, suspicion rather than trust. Control of the populace must be guarded with utmost vigilance and preserved with unflinching brutality.

During the Tet Offensive in 1968, the Viet Cong occupied Hue for many weeks. When the ARVN regained control, they found mass graves. During the short occupation, the communists had executed anyone suspected of counterrevolutionary activities. Evidence of such activities had been scant or even non-existent. But no matter, to the communist, even the tiniest seed of liberty was a weed—an existential, fast-growing threat. Due process was a luxury they could not afford, so they had preemptively killed by the dozen. Victims included ARVN officers and Roman Catholics. Word of these atrocities had filtered through the ranks of the army. This was on Dad's mind as he destroyed the records he had kept so diligently for years.

The end came on April 30, 1975, the Year of the Cat. General Duong Van Minh, newly installed as president because the previous two presidents had resigned a few days earlier, made a radio broadcast announcing the surrender of the army and dissolution of the southern government. Six years after his death, and some 60 years after he began his quest, Ho Chi Minh's dream of a liberated, united Vietnam came to pass.

Word spread quickly through the countryside. Without radio or television, news of our surrender was carried remarkably fast on foot and by boat. In markets and house-to-house, urgent words were shared. The people of Thanh An, mostly Catholic, emptied their homes and shops and gathered in small clusters on the streets. Anxieties were explored in hushed tones as if the communists had already installed listening devices in town. I expected PAVN tanks to come rolling through the streets at any moment.

Tanks never came to town. After a brief spasm of rumor and dire speculation, life returned to normal. The farmers went back to farming. Markets teemed with pineapples, fish, water spinach, mangoes, and sedge mats just as before. Rice and cargo continued their chaotic dance up and down the canal.

His decade as a soldier complete, Dad returned to farming. With a loan from his parents, he bought a two-hectare plot on Kinh D, the tributary canal which branched off Kinh Cai San on the opposite bank from town. He took Doat and Thi Tuyen with him to build a house, while

Kim Tuyen, Tien, and I stayed in Thanh An to help Mom with her business.

Shortly after the communists ascended, the monsoon also swelled with power, streaking the sky and filling the earth. The paddies of our new farm lay fallow beneath the water, resting and recharging for the next season. The rains retreated in November and water that had flooded the fields receded. By Christmas, brown earth was once again visible. On Christmas day of 1975, my youngest sibling—a brother named Tam—was born.

The day after Christmas, communism finally made it to Thanh An. Two PAVN soldiers stood at our door, a red star on their hats ominously announcing their allegiance, Kalashnikov rifles slung over their shoulders.

"Are you Doan Van Dinh?" one of the soldiers asked in a thick northern accent.

"I am," Dad answered.

"You supported the army of the traitors with your service, is this correct?"

"I served in the Army of the Republic of Vietnam," he answered.

The soldier sneered in contempt.

"You will report to reeducation training in Long Xuyen two weeks from today. Here are your orders."

The soldier shoved a letter at Dad and the two turned and walked away.

32

The North celebrated their victory by renaming Saigon after their beloved former leader. Communication between the outside world and the newly christened Ho Chi Minh City was stopped so the communists could begin molding their new comrades without the sanctioning eyes of the western powers upon them.

Repression is a dirty business, and cruelty is its indispensable currency. Taking a light hand to vanquished foes may foster a spark of loyalty for the new regime, but it may also provide oxygen to the smoldering orange coals of resentment that could flame into rebellion. Totalitarian governments do not take this chance. Their power rests on the twin pillars of fear and force—fear of the latent force of people and the use of force to make the people fear the government—rather than on ethics, rule of law, and trust between governor and governed.

With this cynical understanding of history and bleak interpretation of humanity, the new rulers from Hanoi rounded up between 200,000 and 300,000 men—Catholics, soldiers, businessmen, teachers, postal clerks, etc.—and detained them in re-education camps. The word 're-education' sounds benign enough, like something one has to do after failing high school algebra. Even the Vietnamese name *hoc tap cai tao* advertised a place of transformation and re-creation with an opportunity to remake oneself into a better, more complete member of the new society.

The reality of the camps made a mockery of the salubrious title. They were in fact a bitter reminder that man is a fallen creature, all too eager to give expression to the darkness that resides in his heart, all too willing to use any scrap of power against his neighbor. Revenge, not reconciliation, was the primary expression of the power wielded by camp authorities.

The government announced the program as a gentle correction for the wayward Southerners and a means to assimilate them back into polite society, but Hanoi either lacked the resources to manage the camps humanely or lied about their intentions. The happy talk of benign reconciliation devolved into ugly reality as the camps were left to make their own rules. Each camp was run according to the dictatorial whims of its warden. Unsurprisingly, the worst side of human nature festered and grew in these men like a malignancy.

The government quietly classified offenders as war criminals under international statutes, which allowed them wide latitude in the detention and treatment of the prisoners. No one was ever charged with a crime. No trials were held. No sentences were passed. When the program was announced in 1975, officials laid out a 10 day "course of study" for low-ranking soldiers and a one month course for high-ranking officers. Dad received a letter instructing him to bring enough paper, pens, clothes, mosquito nets, food, and money for 10 days, which sounded like a caring reminder letter parents might get before sending their child to summer camp. When Dad headed off to his camp in January of 1976, we said goodbye with our wishes that his 10 days would pass quickly.

A month later, he was still not home.

Dad had entered a realm of discarded decency. Any hopes he may have harbored regarding the beneficence of the new masters was shattered as he watched the gates closing behind him. A foul-smelling guard had walked up to him and punched him in the gut.

"Over there, you stupid farmer," the guard growled while pointing to a group of men lined up nearby.

Dad straightened up and staggered to the group. They began shuffling away as he struggled to join them.

The men were led to a grove of trees and ordered to cut them down. Furthermore, they were pitted against another company of inmates in the task. The group which felled the most trees would be given commendations in their records. The losers would have to complete 'compensation work' on the next rest day.

And so it went. The men were put to work building barracks, digging wells, cutting forests, planting crops, and most dangerous of all, clearing minefields. In the evenings, the men were forced to attend indoctrination sessions. Topics were the usual communist tropes on the glory of labor, the evils of capitalism, and the crimes of the recently defeated puppet state in Saigon. Prisoners were forced to write confessions over and over for their actions in the war.

They were worked to exhaustion, physically and emotionally, and given starvation rations. Underfed, dehydrated, and mentally drained, the men became ill from diseases like dysentery, malaria, and tuberculosis. Treatment for sickness and injury was nearly nonexistent and many prisoners died. Bodies of the dead were thrown into mass graves dug by the inmates. The smell of rotting human flesh, an odor

Dad had not experienced since the famine of 1945, released horrifying memories he thought were safely locked behind the door of forgetfulness.

Dark tentacles of cruelty wrapped every moment and probed every crevice of the prisoners' minds. There was nothing to do but obey, yet obedience didn't provide shelter from assault. Innocuous facial expressions could result in a savage beating if a guard perceived it to betray the slightest irreverence. Schoolchildren were brought on field trips to the camps and urged to curse, spit, and stomp the bare feet of prisoners as they marched to and from work.

Dad lost 20 pounds in the first month. Skin began to sag from his bones and his eyes sunk into his head. Weakness hung like lead weights in his muscles. Without padding fat and water in his cells, sharp edges of bone pushed against the dry bag of skin, sending pain radiating through every corner of his body, denying him sleep and the release contained in each night's little death.

One day about a month after he arrived, my father received a visit from two angels. He was sitting on a bench outside his barracks, too tired to contemplate the rapidly approaching date when death would make its final claim on his life, but feebly wishing it would come soon. A guard approached him and ordered him to stand.

"You have visitors in the main office," the guard said and then turned to go back from where he came.

Dad shuffled across a dusty field to the whitewashed block office and waited for permission to come inside. He was led to a small conference room where his wife and his mother were waiting. When they saw him, both women gasped in horror and ran to hug him gently.

They brought him food and placed it before him. Tears streamed down Mom's cheeks as she watched his frail hands shake with the effort of bringing food to his mouth.

The guards put a quick end to the visit, bursting in the room after 20 minutes, ordering Dad back to his barracks. The guard then turned to the women and said the warden would like a word with them. They were ushered into his office and stood before him as he wrote on a paper, pretending not to notice them. Finally, he raised his head and condescendingly surveyed them.

"The war criminal Doan Van Dinh is your family member, correct?"

"Yes," they replied.

The man tapped a file sitting in front of him with a nervous finger.

"According to his record and his confession, he will have to be here for a few more months."

"Months?" Grandmother asked incredulously. "He was supposed to be here for 10 days. It has been over a month."

The man shrugged his shoulders.

"How many months?"

"That depends on his progress," said the warden. "He has a strong spirit and he's a natural leader. We have to be sure he is fully committed to the people's government. We have to be sure he will not become a counter-revolutionary once he returns home."

"He will be faithful, I promise," said Mom, her eyes brimming with tears.

"We will be the judge of that," the warden said.

The two women hung their heads and turned to leave. The warden cleared his throat and spoke softly.

"There is the possibility that a prisoner's term can be shortened by payment of a fine."

Mom looked up and began to speak, but Grandmother touched her arm lightly to stop her.

"I assume the fine should be brought directly to you, sir?" Grandmother said.

The man smiled with his crooked, dirty teeth.

"Yes," he hissed.

On the bus ride back to Thanh An, Mom remained silent as she processed everything she had just witnessed. Finally, she spoke.

"Why did you stop me from asking how much the fine would cost?"

"Because it's not a fine," Grandmother said. "It's a bribe."

It took several weeks of selling land and water buffaloes, but Grandmother accumulated a pouchful of gold coins. She went back to the camp and stood in front of the warden.

"I am here to pay the fine for Doan Van Dinh," she said, "I would like to take him home today."

The warden snorted, "Today? Impossible."

Grandma placed the bag of coins on his desk. The warden opened the bag and gleaming gold filled his eyes. He stood up and placed the bag in his pocket.

"A very generous gift, but I'm afraid his processing will take a few days," he said.

Grandmother patted her pocket to make coins inside jingle.

"Today, if you please," she said.

"Let me see them," the warden demanded. Grandmother pulled a bag from her pocket which was equal to the first. She opened it for his inspection but did not hand it over. She was playing a dangerous game. The difference in power between the two was absolute. If he wanted, the warden could have taken her money and thrown her in prison. Her impudence was nothing but a brazen bluff.

The warden eyed her for several seconds. He was a wicked man who didn't hesitate to use barbarity against his inmates. Nor would he feel an attack of conscience for the breaking of an insolent old woman. But he was more animated by venality and laziness than cruelty. He weighed his options. He could keep this reckless woman, her son, and her money, or he could take the money and have two fewer hassles to deal with.

He smiled with his rotten teeth and called for a guard to fetch her son. When the guard brought him into the office, the warden walked over and whispered in his ear.

"You are on probation. We will be watching you, so if you make one misstep, I will bring you back and all your mama's money won't get you out."

"How long is my probation?" Dad asked feebly.

The warden laughed, "As long as you live in this country."

We marveled at the withered man who entered our house. The joy we anticipated turned to shock as we surveyed the bag of bones before us. His head was the only thing that didn't shrink. It was too big for his emaciated body and looked as if its weight might snap his tiny neck. I was afraid the lightest touch or even a heavy breath might crack a brittle bone, so I kept my distance from him.

Not only had his physical strength melted away, but the spirit that filled him with confidence and dignity was shattered as well. He sat in the house and stared vacantly at an empty wall and the happy reunion became a silent vigil.

33

I n time, Dad's physical strength returned. His spirit, unnourished by the food that restored his body, remained dimmed by storm clouds that hung over his soul. His eyes were vacant portals to a black abyss where he resided—broken, scattered, and lost. I watched him surreptitiously at dinner time as he picked absently at his food, eating without purpose or interest, staring at nothing with unregistering blankness. I wondered where he was when he retreated into the caverns of memory and fantasy. Was he fighting the guards? Was he running from them? Was he reliving the beatings or the torture of bottomless hunger? I longed to reach out to him, but the dictates of our culture prohibited such sentimental familiarity with one's father. So, I watched and worried.

I went about the business of going to school and helping Mom, and tried to get used to the uneasy presence. We lived with a ghost who barely spoke. Sensing an opportunity one day, I asked him if I could quit school as some of my friends were doing. The question touched a deep place that roused him from his stupor. It made him straighten up momentarily and deliver a clear and resonating, "No." After his resounding denial, he slumped his shoulders and retreated to his inner cave.

When he regained enough strength to return to the farm on Kinh D, I was relieved. We loved our father, but his presence had become draining, like an inadvertent vampire sucking energy from those around him. I thought Mom would be happiest of all, what with her reduced caretaking duties, but she did not seem to be buoyed by the lightened mood in the house that his return to the fields created. She had her own mysterious heaviness which robbed her attention. As the monsoon of 1976 wrung impossible amounts of rain from the clouds which banged angrily against our tin roof, Mom increasingly spent her spare minutes poring over the receivables in her notebook. The worn record looked like some time-beaten ancient manuscript. Humidity kissed and curled the ragged pages. One day she handed me the book and asked me to look over the names associated with the debts. The number of entries had grown exponentially since I first noticed it.

"Chuong, if you see any of these people, let me know or tell them I need to talk to them," she instructed. "They all owe me money."

I began to see a side of her I didn't know existed. I had considered her to be utterly submissive, but in desperation she found her backbone. She grew more insistent with the debtors who came to her stall. Very few paid their balance. Most said they didn't have money to pay her back. Some promised to come back the next day and pay, but none did. Some who balked at repayment were even brazen enough to ask for more credit.

Mom's aggressive collection efforts didn't have the desired effect of balancing her books, but they drove away the freeloaders. When credit flowed freely, they were the nicest customers we had, overflowing with friendliness and gratitude. But when there was no more credit to be had, the moochers' effusive charm dried into indignant avoidance. We could see them visiting other vendors but they ducked their eyes and quickened their pace as they walked by us.

There comes a time in a child's life when he begins to see his parents in the harsh light of reality, a final umbilical severing that emancipates us from the childish belief in parental omnipotence, an awakening to the disappointing fact that parents are stalked by weakness, haunted by mistakes, and made vulnerable by life's unceasing difficulty. I saw it in Dad's empty eyes when he returned from prison, and now I watched as my mother was broken. She was not weak. She had survived the vicissitudes of a hard life, from the macabre scenes of famine, to the displacement of her home, to the shrieking terror of war. Through it all she had retained her dignity and her faith. Indeed, she seemed to draw strength from her Jobian trials.

Her ability to withstand previous suffering was due in no small part to the impersonal nature of events. A faceless malefactor like the French, or the Japanese, or the Viet Minh, or Ho Chi Minh, or the Viet Cong was always behind the grief that enveloped every decade of her life and gave her some measure of separation from it. War was indiscriminate. It affected everyone and made commiseration possible.

But this wound was exquisitely personal. She had been betrayed by friends. She had been deceived and robbed by those who touched her hand in gratitude, smiled and laughed with her, wished her well, and complimented her babies. Each lie, each theft—numbering in the hundreds according to the notebook—was a knife's plunge in her flesh. She agonized over being duped by so many. The memories of those lies replayed over and over until they metastasized from her brain and burrowed deep in her heart where they oozed black tar and tried to grow roots. I watched Mom fighting the cancerous bitterness each time she clutched her rosary like it was a piece of driftwood in a drowning sea.

The spiraling losses mounted and one day her options ran out. I was returning home from school and found her on the floor, crying. Beside her lay a collection of small containers which had been excavated from holes she dug throughout the house. Her hands were dirty from the effort.

"Mom, what's wrong?"

"I don't have any money and the Pineapple Ladies are coming tomorrow."

"Nobody paid today?" I asked.

She shook her head.

"What are we going to do?"

"I don't know," she said. "Go get your father."

In a driving rain, I boarded the rickety ferry that crossed Kinh Cai San. More than once, I had seen this overloaded boat capsized in the canal and heard the shouts of rescuers. Every time it happened, at least one life was lost. I shuddered as more and more people crammed themselves into every inch of the craft.

Safely across and off the ferry, I climbed the bank and drove my bare feet into the warm mud of the path that ran alongside the canal. Crossing the canal between the town and the farms was like going back in time. Thanh An would never be mistaken for a modern city, but it had streets, block buildings, shops, and even an occasional car passing through.

Kinh D was medieval in comparison. There were no roads or electricity. Houses were mud huts. Huge water buffalo grazed in the small spaces between houses and the path. In my urban life, I never developed an easy familiarity with the ubiquitous farm beast and was terrified by their size and horns. My mother's sweet stories about the love she felt for a buffalo she had cared for in her youth did nothing to ease the distrust I felt for the giants. I suspiciously eyed each buffalo I passed and prepared to jump in the canal should one of them charge. None of them ever gave me so much as a glance.

As I walked, three ghostly figures appeared in the distance, partially concealed in the mist. The smallest of the three men was wearing a *non la.* The other two leaned in, pointing fingers at him and gesturing aggressively. I slowed my pace so I wouldn't run into the trouble. When the two men finished, they turned and walked my way. I picked up my pace so I wouldn't arouse suspicion of spying. As they passed, I lowered my head in respect and got a glimpse of pistols strapped around their waists. They were soldiers. The man in the *non la* saw me and began walking toward me with a familiar gait. It was my dad. He looked careworn, but his face brightened slightly when he saw me.

"Dad, what were those soldiers doing out here?"

He shrugged, "Oh, they were just checking on me to see if I was alright."

"They didn't look very friendly."

"Well, they want to be sure we are following the rules of the new government. Communists are very strict about their rules."

He started to get that far-off look in his eyes and abruptly changed the subject.

"What are you doing here, Chuong?"

"Mom sent me. She doesn't have any money."

Dad raised his eyebrows in muted surprise.

"She spent all of her coins?" he asked.

I nodded affirmatively.

"I told her she mustn't give people food on credit," he continued, "but she is too kind to say no. Is she upset?"

"Yes sir, she was crying when I left," I said.

He sighed.

"Very well, let's go get her and your siblings."

"Where are we going?" I asked.

"Here," he said. "It's about time I made a farmer out of you."

34

I became a man when I was twelve years old. I don't mean the pubescent transformation that begins about that age. I was still a scrawny boy physically, but my family's troubles matured me emotionally. Prior to Dad's prison term and Mom's business failure, I possessed a child's egocentric confidence that my parents were invincible, heaven-blessed and pre-ordained to brush aside any pathetic obstacles to the uninterrupted goodness I believed was our destiny. But then I witnessed the misfortune that struck them nearly simultaneously. I watched them both wince under life's cruel lash and I longed to protect them. Their fragility stirred fear and then responsibility within me. My eyes were opened to the capriciousness of fate and I began to grasp how little margin was built into our impoverished lives, how close we were at all times to disaster, and how little our new communist masters thought of us. I grew up quickly. I put away my pranking insouciance and bent myself to the service of my family.

Our new house along the canal matched the austerity of my new manner. The simplicity of the dwelling was monkish—four walls and a pitched roof without electricity or running water. The kitchen was a separate shed in the backyard, and the toilet was an outhouse built on top of two bamboo poles suspended over a pit. Walls of mud mixed with rice straw offered privacy and a roof of banana leaves provided some protection from the weather. I still remember the feeling of visiting the outhouse at night. If the moon was not shining, there was no ambient light to guide me through the consuming blackness, so I always carried a lantern and prayed the wind would not extinguish it. The lack of light coming from houses or towns also meant there was no light pollution to dilute the speckled brilliance of the starry sky. As I balanced on the poles and squatted to do my business, the stars hypnotized me and I wondered if they looked the same everywhere in the world. Did I see the same stars Americans on the other side of the world saw? Or were their stars bigger and brighter?

The inside of the main house was as spartan as the outside. Rooms were divided by sheets hung from the rafters. Mom and Dad had a bedroom for themselves, Thi Tuyen and Kim Tuyen shared a room, and the four boys crowded into a room. We each had a bed consisting of a wooden frame which was filled with rice straw. A fibrous, homemade mat served as a bedsheet. My pillow was a block of wood rolled up in a sedge mat. Mosquito netting was hung over each bed, but the enterprising blood-suckers always managed to get through. Itchy rashes caused by straw poking through the mat and welts from bites were each morning's record of overnight assault. Mosquitoes weren't the only wildlife with which we had to contend. Dad built the walls of the house with a small gap at the bottom and top to allow some air to flow through and relieve the stifling humidity. The downside of this architectural feature was that it gave unwanted guests like snakes, bugs, and rats easy access. The little gate-crashers helped themselves to our shelter without regard to the status of their invitation. I awakened to a pair of beady eyes staring at me from the edge of my bed frame more times than I could count.

The house sat on an embankment which was created by the initial dredging of the canal. Bamboo, papaya, and banana trees were scattered on the slope opposite the canal, and screened the low-lying rice paddies that stretched all the way to the next canal. The little artificial ridges raised on both sides of canals were the only elevation in an otherwise featureless swamp. Indeed, the Mekong Delta suffered a crisis of identity. Depending on the season, it manifested as either solid earth or liquid sea. Most of the region sat less than a meter above sea level and spent the diluvial months of the monsoon under water, and although we lived some 40 kilometers from the closest beaches at Rach Gia, the tide still swelled our inland waterways each day.

I made a personality switch from city boy to country boy in short order. Initially distraught to leave the quickened, entertaining pace of town life, I grew to appreciate, even revere, the simple grandeur of a life intimately connected to the earth. The marketplace of man dominated life in Thanh An with its maddeningly complex and contradictory interactions of competing human interests, and while this adversarial system may have expanded material options, the ugly side of human nature which was so often displayed contracted the unwitting soul. By contrast, a small life on the farm in Kinh D, paced by the unperturbed rhythms of earth, sun, and moon, was paradoxically expansive. There, far away from the hustling distractions of transactional humanity, earth and water spoke the truth of life with irresistible clarity. Elemental simplicity became profoundly spiritual. The common things held in contempt by city dwellers—rain, dirt, sun, and wind—grew sacred when imbibed without the chattering, striving arrogance of civilization. In a city, even a backwater town like Thanh

237

An, one could make their way through life lying to others. But not on the farm. One may as well lie to God as to lie to the earth. It was impenetrable to the forked tongue of a conniving man. Only great quantities of honest work unlocked its bounty.

Our world was utterly ruled by water, but one day each year, fire was given dominion over the land. At the height of the dry season in March, the farmers along Kinh D chose a day to burn their fields. The paddy was put to the torch to transform dead stalks into life-giving ash. Farmers stood guard with buckets of water in hand to douse sparks that threatened houses made of tinder. Smoke, the more vigorous visual cousin of fog, rose and tumbled in gray clouds as the fields turned black. The charred smell of burnt carbon inhabited our noses for days.

The sun baked and cleaved the ground with its scorching fingers. The cracked earth was not suitable for planting, so Dad hired a man who owned a tractor to plow the ground. Plowing had been done by water buffalo for millennia but it was a job the animal was inexorably losing to the great consuming maw of technology. The tractor was simply more efficient than the beast, but also more costly. We could only afford one pass of the machine and had to break up the leftover chunks by hand. With pitchforks, Mom, Thi Tuyen, and I stabbed and turned the earth. I possessed great amounts of energy for the task but little control of that energy. I hacked mercilessly at the ground. Clods of dirt flew in every direction. A tiny cloud of dust hung in the air like a force field around me. Thi Tuyen rolled her eyes at my grunting exertions until one day when the pitchfork glanced off a clump and dug into my ankle.

I screamed in pain as blood came to the gash squarely over my ankle bone. Upon closer inspection, I could see the white of bone through the oozing red. I howled in horror. Mom and Thi Tuyen ran to me as I writhed on the ground. Mom took a look at the wound and called over five-year-old Tien. I couldn't imagine what use he could possibly have at a moment like this.

"Tien, pee on Chuong's ankle."

"WHAT?" I protested.

She explained, "The cut is dirty. It needs to be cleaned. Urine is cleaner than water."

Tien fished out his little worm and gleefully pissed on me, giggling the whole time. When he finished, Mom examined it again.

"O.K., looks clean. Let's get you bandaged," she said.

She took me to the house and wrapped the cut in tobacco leaves. For days, I limped in pain as the deep cut healed. Every time Tien saw me hobbling along, he sweetly offered his specialized medical service. I respectfully declined.

When the field was prepared, we waited like tense soldiers on the eve of an attack. The four-fold dragon rose up from the sea, swollen with power and fury. Storms came in probing sorties, thrashing in a show of strength. But these showers were a feint, a ruse the dragon used to trick the foolish farmer. Often these big storms would be followed by days of dry weather. If the farmer scattered his seeds after the first rain, he risked losing them as they lay dormant on dry ground, an easy feast for hungry birds, mice, and insects. Mom and Dad were no fools. They waited and watched for the unmistakable beginning of the monsoon and they never, ever misjudged. This was astounding to me. At that age, I could not tell one type of rain from another, but I figured there must be some meteorological marker—a change in the wind perhaps, or a minute difference in humidity—that formed a scientific basis for their decision. I asked Dad how he timed it so perfectly, hoping to be inducted into that society of esoteric knowledge. He winked at me as he explained.

"My bones are made of rice. My eyes, ears, skin, and muscle, too. It is not the rain that tells me when to plant, but the seeds. They know when it is time to go to the ground and they sing out. Because we are made of the same stuff, I can hear their song with my rice ears and feel it with my rice skin."

"What does it sound like?" I asked.

"It sounds like life."

35

When the soaking rain came, Mom and Dad went into the field to spread the seeds. Thi Tuyen and I were not allowed to seed the paddy. It was exacting work and we did not yet possess the technique to evenly distribute the seeds. Thi Tuyen watched from the house while I peeled the bark off a bamboo pole.

"What are you doing, Chuong?"

It was Kim Tuyen.

"Making a crab trap," I said.

She admired the trap's pleasing conical symmetry for a moment.

"Who taught you how to do that?"

"Duy," I said.

Duy was our next-door neighbor. Two years older than me, he had lived his whole life on Kinh D and had become a savant in the ways of rural living. I was curious and impressionable, casting subconsciously for a mentor in the absence of my big brother Doat, who had been accepted to a school in Long Xuyen and spent most of his time there, learning mathematics, technology, and unsanctioned views about communism. Doat was disinterested in farm life and its back-breaking labor, and because he was the first-born male, he was given the honor and responsibility of carrying the family name beyond the bucolic boundaries of the rice paddy.

I was not so favored. Because of my birth order, the rice farm was my only destiny. I did not question this or rebel against my lot in life. In fact, I embraced it. I found enough rich, intellectual soil in the complex process of extracting sustenance from the land to supply a lifetime of mental stimulation. Duy must have recognized my enthusiasm and felt a surge of pride to be in a position of expertise, so he took me under his wing. He taught me how to strip bamboo bark without getting splinters. He showed me how to use a casting net, and the best places to catch crabs in the dry season. The amount of knowledge he possessed was astounding for a teenager and he shared it generously.

I began to feel comfortable in my skin as I gained competency. Farming and fishing suited me and I began to make a real contribution to my family, providing them with another pair of hands for farming, and protein from the fish and crabs I caught. My only disappointment at this time came from school. Dad held firm to his position regarding formal education, regardless of the greater value of the lessons I was learning at home, so each day, rain or shine, I made my barefoot way two kilometers along Kinh D to the far bank of Thanh An, boarded the dangerously overcrowded ferry, and crossed Kinh Cai San to town. The only thing I carried from home was a pair of rubber sandals. I didn't wear them on the walk from home because I didn't want them to get muddy. I put them on when I got to school and took them off when I left the building.

More often than not, I arrived at school soaking wet, as did many other children. Either the monsoon drenched me on my walk in or I jumped in the canal if a water buffalo was blocking my path, preferring to swim rather than taking a chance of getting trampled. Kim Tuyen howled with laughter each time she saw me plunge into the canal.

"Chuong, it's not going to hurt you. Quit being such a baby."

"Shut up, Tuyen, I don't like them."

"They're sweet. Watch me."

She strode confidently up to the buffalo and petted it while cooing soft words in its ear. She inherited Mom's easy connection to the beast and never missed a chance to pet one in my presence to mock my fear. Her silent shaming did not change my views on the subject. I never had any desire to test my opinion and maintained a healthy distance from every buffalo I encountered.

School was tedious and repetitive. Day after day, the teacher wrote the lesson on the chalkboard as students furiously copied the information. When the board was filled, the teacher erased every word and began writing again. If anyone was too slow at copying, that student was out of luck. The teacher did not stop, slow down, or repeat anything. He was not available after class, nor were we offered any type of tutoring. To make matters worse, ridicule was universally practiced by the faculty as a motivational tool. If a student failed to keep up or understand a lesson, the teacher would shame that student in front of the class. Sloppy handwriting often resulted in a ruler across the knuckles.

It was a miserable place. Thankfully it only lasted four hours a day and it gave me some time to visit with the friends I left behind when we moved to the farm. After school, we sifted through the wastebaskets in classrooms to find usable paper. Richer kids had crisp white sheets with blue rule lines. The paper gleamed in impossible, hypnotic whiteness to us poor kids, but seemed to hold little value to its owners who contemptuously threw it away without using it fully. Sometimes a sheet was found which had no more than a single written line. This was puzzling. I thought the benefits of wealth would be humbly respected and soberly conserved, yet, if notebook paper was any indication, it produced a wanton, undignified wastefulness. While poor kids were rifling through the trash for scraps of cheap brown rice paper, rich kids were flippantly discarding something worth ten times what we were afforded. If I took a moment to reflect on the situation, a seed of envy and resentment sprang up within me, but I tried not to dwell on it. In the end, it didn't really matter. All paper, white or brown, depreciated to equal valuation for its final use. When there was no more space for writing, sheets were taken home to be used as toilet tissue in the bamboo outhouse. As far as I could tell, white paper did no better job of wiping an ass than brown.

After pillaging trash cans, my buddies usually asked me to stay in town for a while to play soccer or swim, but most times I turned them down. I had to get back home to fish or help with gardening. The trek back home was just as arduous as the walk to town. Buffaloes had to be dodged and many farms kept mean dogs, or worse, ill-tempered geese as guards. Dogs were bad, but they at least had a capacity for reasonable judgment as to what was a threat and what was not. Plus, they could be bribed and turned from foe to friend with treats.

Geese, on the other hand, were insane. These hell-birds had no off switch and their integrity could not be compromised. Their loud honking was unsettling in itself, but they also charged at suspected intruders with unyielding aggression. Worse still, they had weapons one would not expect from such a mild looking package. Their wing elbows had hard knuckles that could break a human arm, and their beaks had sharp serrations. I had several pairs of shredded pants which attested to their potency and excessive zeal at protecting property. I hated them.

After running the afternoon farm animal gauntlet, I settled into my preferred method of spending time. I farmed, fished, or learned something from Duy. Sometimes, Thi Tuyen and I paddled our handmade canoe along the canal, selling rice. In the evenings, farm boys would meet at the monkey bridge to swim. *Monkey bridge* was a name American soldiers had given bamboo bridges or *cau tre*. The bridges were handmade, spindly structures made of tied bamboo poles. Poles were driven into the canal bed to act as support piers for the deck which was made of single poles tied end-to-end. The impossibly narrow walkway created a precarious surface for crossing, especially after a rain or if it was coated with slick moss. The whole thing had the appearance of a gigantic walking stick bug standing motionless in the water. Our bridge hovered about three meters over the surface of the canal and we took turns jumping from it into the water. The edges of the canal grew thick with silky water hyacinth under a canopy of papaya, banana, and bamboo trees.

The Mekong Delta was draped in layers of exuberant life. Trees, rivers, and land all burst with sustenance provided by the beneficent monsoon, and with Duy's tutelage, I learned how to recognize it and harvest what my family needed. I began to see myself as not merely a clever exploiter of the abundant natural resources, but as part of a mysterious whole. While the rest of humanity was rushing headlong into ever more complex systems of civilization and technology that separated and insulated them from the sometimes destructive whims of nature, I settled into the ancient rhythms of surrendering dependency on the earth.

And for a short time, I was happy and fulfilled.

36

All forms of tyranny are deplorable. That which comes cloaked in magnanimity is damnable. From Marx's dreary diagnoses to the sociopathic prescriptions of Lenin, Stalin, Mao, and Castro, communists blithely trod the primrose path, promising utopia while doggedly ignoring the most basic and immutable facets of human nature which make utopia unattainable. That which could no longer be ignored was violently suppressed, for they soon found that it was not enough to control the corporeal aspects of society. The mind and spirit remained the wellspring of human yearning even after physical property was confiscated, so the Marxists went about extinguishing the mind's property of conscience which drives action. The results were sadly predictable. Robbed of both property and their right to opinion, speech, and religion, production stagnated and tens of millions perished from starvation, imprisonment, execution, and disease. Millions more were shackled by poverty and despair.

Those who did not perish and were not ground into hopelessness dreamed of escape. People who were intimately connected to their countries, people whose ancestors had lived in the same place for hundreds, even thousands, of years were suddenly motivated to discard everything—possessions, history, language, culture—and take a desperate chance to find a life worth living. In post-World War II

Germany, 2.5 million citizens raced into the Allied controlled west before the Berlin Wall was erected. In China, some 2.6 million retreated to the island of Taiwan after Mao founded the People's Republic. In Cuba, hundreds of thousands sought the nearby haven of Florida aboard barely seaworthy rafts.

In Vietnam, the story was repeated once again. The victorious North began consolidating its power over the South and the ugly reality of collectivism revealed itself. Businesses and homes in Saigon were seized and their owners sent to farm the poor soil in mountainous areas. Meanwhile, the city's most valuable real estate was given to communist party members and Viet Cong fighters for their service. Farming was reorganized into a state-run cooperative. Farmers were forced to sell their produce to the government at artificially suppressed prices so the bureaucrats could redistribute it.

Unsurprisingly, food shortages appeared throughout the country almost immediately. In this lush paradise where food practically begged to be harvested, people suddenly found it a challenge to obtain it. There is a term in economics called the "invisible hand," in which an unintended social benefit results from self-interested production and trade. Free market economies unwittingly employ this powerful force to the great advantage of all its people, but the envious communist, fixated on insolvable inequality, erects byzantine equality schemes with the unassailable confidence only the truly ignorant possess. With disastrous hubris, the Marxist employs the "meddling hand" which is utterly overmatched by economic complexities and must then, in the interest of survival, ball itself into an iron fist. The iron fist, though, does not concern itself with the welfare of people, but merely the maintenance of its grip on power over the people.

All religions had to be registered and organized into government-controlled churches. Speech was monitored and infractions were punished. People who ran afoul of the speech police were designated as reactionaries and subject to harassment, loss of employment, or prison. Finally, there were the re-education camps like the one my father attended.

The sum of Vietnam's experiment in repudiation of natural law was misery. And though misery is surely a thing tasted by all who live, the promise of everlasting, generational misery was unbearable to those marked to suffer the most. Just as it was in the Soviet Union, China, and Cuba, people began to flee. Catholics, merchants, ethnic minority Hoas, Buddhists, and former soldiers of the ARVN all started looking for a way out.

But where to go? To the north, a thousand miles of mountains separated the southerner from the nearest border. Beyond that lay China and more communism, and beyond that, frozen Siberia and Russian communism stretched to the Arctic Circle. To the west, Cambodia had fallen to the genocidal Pol Pot, who was in the process of killing 2 million of his own people in an attempt to create an agrarian utopia. The people of Vietnam were surrounded and had only one way out.

As they had done 20 years earlier, they would take their chances on the South China Sea. But this time, there would be no navy ships to ferry them to safety. This time they would be on their own.

The size of this sea was unimaginable. More than 3 million square kilometers and countless billions of gallons of water lay between Vietnam's east coast and the islands of Indonesia and the Philippines. On the other side of the sea, those island nations, along with the peninsular nations of Malaysia and Thailand, formed the hazy outlines of a goal. Determined Vietnamese created hasty plans to sail to one of those safe havens and declare asylum. But they were unaware of the peril beyond land's end.

The first danger was the sea itself. The Vietnamese were not a seafaring people. They were people of the land, accustomed to great quantities of water from the ocean-born monsoon, but not the terrible mother of the monsoon. The home of the four-fold dragon was a stranger to them— vast, salty, and mysterious. They found abundance in rice cultivation and did not need to court danger in the great blue abyss, so when it came time to find deliverance on the ocean, they were utterly unprepared for the trial that awaited them. They crammed too many people into flat-bottomed river boats with too little food and water. Without navigational skills or an adequate boat motor they gave themselves to the mercy of the waves. Many thousands would pay for their ignorance with their lives.

The refugees had to traverse no less than 400 nautical miles of liquid desert to reach a friendly shore. Even in the most fortunate circumstances, it took days to cross the distance in an underpowered boat, which gave the capricious sea and its fickle partner, time, opportunities to create disaster. The unconscious, eternal sea remained indifferent to human suffering, offering beguiling calm or murderous fury in patterns that were indecipherable. Glassy stillness swelled into thrashing white mountains and swamped overloaded, unsuitable craft, drowning dozens within minutes. Overworked motors stalled, setting boats adrift for days and weeks. Food and water ran out. Dehydration and starvation withered passengers and the punishing sun baked their dry skin.

The second peril was human. Malaysian and Thai pirates, long the scourge of this vital waterway which carried one-third of the world's goods, found easy prey among the slow, overcrowded boats. Valuables were stolen at gunpoint, women were raped, and anyone who resisted was murdered. One group reported a hellish day in which they were boarded four times by pirates. Each of the four times, women aboard were raped. On two of the occasions, one passenger was kidnapped while another was shot and thrown overboard to drown.

If the refugees survived sea and pirate, a third cruelty threatened to undo the fruits of their bravery and luck. As the refugees swarmed the sanctuary beaches in growing numbers, host nations—poor themselves—began to turn away the boats, condemning the refugees to a sure death at sea or forced repatriation to Vietnam. A humanitarian crisis erupted as the death toll skyrocketed.

It must be said that I was not aware of any of this. The dissonance between my idyllic life and the nearby life-and-death struggle of my countrymen speaks to either a youthful naiveté or the sheltered isolation of Kinh D. Whatever the reason, the ghostly emigration took place without my awareness, yet right under my nose. Classmates began to disappear from school without a word, never mentioning their departure—one day they were at school, the next day gone, never to be seen again. At the time, I simply attributed their absence to a successful petition to drop out of school, which was the dream of most boys of that age. In fact, they were part of a silent exodus.

Though I could not perceive the events happening all around me, the world watched it unfold in grim detail and was moved by the plight of these strangers on the water, all thanks to a single man with a tiny camera and a mountain of courage.

Once again, Eddie Adams would change my life.

37

Eddie Adams hated the photo that made him famous. During the Tet Offensive in 1968, the photojournalist had captured a grainy snapshot of South Vietnam police chief General Nguyen Ngoc Loan executing a Viet Cong assassin on a Saigon street. Adams won a Pulitzer Prize for the photograph which caused anti-war sentiment to explode in America. It was soon called "The picture that lost the war."

Adams had been born in the coal and steel country of western Pennsylvania and was imprinted with the gritty ethos of the industrial working class. He got his start as a combat photographer in the Marine Corps and would go on to photograph 13 wars. Towering talent, endless ambition, and an inexhaustible work ethic won him access to the highest echelons of power and culture. He photographed presidents and celebrities, but easy access to others' fame coupled with his own did not fill a bottomless void within. It was in the photographs of the downtrodden that he found a semblance of meaning. The miner, the soldier, the refugee were the subjects he respected most and he returned to them throughout his career. His images are honest and raw, taken in the vicinity of death where life burns most brightly; when the hot emotions of pain and panic and exhaustion strip away the veneers of civilization and we see ourselves for what we truly are—fearful, fragile, and oh-so-temporary creatures. Yet through the pain and pathos etched in the faces captured by Adams, one can see the divine spark, invested in suffering as glimmers of irreducible perseverance, shine like diamonds reflecting a hard-earned virtue which could never be manufactured by a vapid, pampered movie star.

The fateful picture, called *Saigon Execution,* haunted its creator. After the war, General Loan settled in the U.S. where he was branded a war criminal by anti-war activists, spending many years defending himself against their smears and threats of deportation. Adams felt great guilt for the General's troubles and eventually went to a congressional hearing in defense of Loan, explaining the lack of context presented in the photo, recounting the horrible execution of a family the assassin had just committed. Then Adams testified about two killings that happened that day. "The General killed the Viet Cong assassin with his pistol and I killed the General with my camera." Loan's deportation was thwarted and the two men became friends, but Adams never forgave himself.

Adams got his shot at redemption as the Vietnamese refugee crisis exploded. He made his way to a Thailand port and waited for a boat to come in. On Thanksgiving Day, 1977, a small fishing boat overloaded with 50 people puttered into the harbor and docked. When the order came to turn them away and push them back out, Adams requested permission to go with them. He bought 100 gallons of gas and a sack of rice and joined the despondent passengers.

Regret soon set in as he realized the predicament his rash decision created.

What am I doing here? He asked himself.

The equatorial sun blazed mercilessly upon the still water. The boat made little progress under its extreme passenger load and no one knew where to go. There was nowhere for Adams to sit, so he did the only thing he knew. He snapped pictures furiously until Thai police realized they had stupidly let an American journalist board a refugee boat. The police sent a patrol after him and forced him at gunpoint to disembark. Adams left the boat to a fate that likely ended in the deaths of all aboard within a few days, but he was allowed to keep his camera.

Upon developing the photos, Adams noticed something odd. In all his years of photographing wars, he observed that children always smiled in the pictures he took. No matter how dire the circumstances—bullets flying, bombs exploding—a kid would reliably mug for the camera. But not these children. As he flipped through his negatives, Adams saw no smiles on the faces of the suffering children and knew he was dealing with something remarkable. He christened the collection *The Boat of No Smiles* and transmitted it to the United States.

Within days, the photographs made their way to the halls of the U.S. Congress where a response to the crisis was being debated. There was considerable resistance to renewed U.S. involvement in the affairs of Vietnam until Adams' pictures landed on desks. The images captured the urgency of the moment in painful, irresistible detail. Hopelessness dulled the eyes and slackened the muscles of those souls at the threshold of death. One woman's face was slashed with grief as she held the body of a lifeless child. Consuming despair hung in each photo like a pall draping a coffin.

The pictures had a shocking effect in Washington D.C., where officials accustomed to glacial deliberation moved swiftly to action. The

Americans promised to accept refugees, followed by Canada, Australia, and several countries in Western Europe. In turn, Malaysia, Thailand and the other countries where refugees landed begrudgingly agreed to temporarily shelter them. No one knew what happened to the passengers of the *Boat of No Smiles*, but because of them, thousands more would be saved.

And Eddie Adams, the mercurial perfectionist, the temperamental, daring artist who foolishly boarded a doomed vessel and was delivered from his own doom at the point of a gun, drew a cup of living water from that well of death. In it he found a refreshing moment of peace for himself. Years later, while being interviewed on camera for a documentary about his life, he commented on the time that his photos influenced his country to do the right thing, saying, "It was the only thing I did in my life that was good."

Then he smiled.

38

n the months following Eddie Adams' heroics, the number of people finding life and death on the open sea multiplied. Refugee camps were overwhelmed with lucky arrivals. Fatalities at sea climbed to astronomical levels, with estimates anywhere from one out of every five refugees to a shocking one in three. Despite the assurances of the western governments that they would resettle the Vietnamese, local authorities in Thailand and Malaysia continued to push boats back to sea, seeding a gruesome and shameful death toll.

While this drama played on the world's stage, just over the horizon, life on Kinh D remained unperturbed in its pre-industrialized state. We did not have television or newspapers to inform us of the refugee's struggle with the great watery dragon. I was busy doing my own dance with the dragon—less deadly, but urgent in its own way.

There was no time to waste when the rains came. We engaged in a race against time and water, which in the long scheme of things sounds like a fool's pursuit, but was crucial in the struggle for seasonal survival. The field was flattened and paddies were dammed on all sides to allow water to accumulate in the artificial basin and power the miraculous growth of *Oryza sativa*. Incidentally, rice doesn't have to be flooded to grow, but a submerged field deters weeds and vermin from the competition.

The only problem with the flooding method of cultivation was the flood itself. Nature does not comport herself to the preferences of man, rather choosing to dole out rainfall by unfathomable caprice. It was up to us to fit our designs into the day's gifts. This meant labor—hard physical exertion that drained muscles of every watt of energy they could produce. In the days after Mom and Dad seeded the field, the swirling water invariably washed the evenly distributed seeds into heaps, leaving bare spots. It was our job to fill the bare spots with seedlings.

In the evening hours, after sowing the field, Dad began a seedling bed behind the house. With that task completed, he left home to pursue his plan of becoming a saltwater fisherman at the seaside city called Rach Gia, about 40 kilometers to the west of our farm. He and Doat were both gone which left me, barely a teenager, the man of the house. The thought—premature as it was—of having the responsibility of passing on the family genes filled me with dread that I didn't yet understand. A sense of inadequacy to my temporary office made me anxious and pushed me to give effort that would bring honor to the family.

Within a few weeks, the plants in the bed were six inches tall and ready to be transplanted. Mom, Thi Tuyen, and I donned our *non la* and took the seedlings to their new home. The field looked like a brown cheek dotted by patchy green stubble. As instructed by the ancient Vietnamese proverb, *back to the sky, face to the earth,* the three of us strained for days to fill the spaces where the seeds did not take root. The procedure became robotic—bend over, dig a hole with a thumb, place the seedling in the hole, move forward, repeat. We had to work fast, for once the water rose halfway to our knees, it was too deep to plant. Every empty square meter of land was one that didn't feed us. I felt ashamed if we didn't fill the paddy.

Once the rice was planted, there was little else that could be done to it other than to pray God would bless the crop. During this time, I shifted my energies to gardening and fishing. Duy stopped teaching me because I had grown from eager student to competitive nuisance. It didn't matter. I had learned enough to catch something daily, becoming proficient at pole fishing, gill netting, net casting, and crabbing. Sometimes I caught a surplus that could be sold to families nearby. I was not about to let my family go hungry.

When I wasn't fishing or attending school, I worked in a small garden beside the house. I tended tomatoes, corn, cucumbers, squash, and okra. We had chickens and the occasional pig which I helped raise. We even grew tobacco for Dad's habit. Banana leaves were fashioned into seedling cups to start the growing process. From these, we selected exactly 100 of the best specimens to plant. A few months later, the plants began to turn yellow. I harvested them and stacked them under a blanket of rice straw to allow them to cure. When removed, the leaves were golden and beautiful. They were then bundled, shredded and dried. A sticky rice broth was sprayed over the leaves as a bonding agent and allowed to dry. Within a few days, Dad and his friends were smoking this tobacco from a hookah pipe.

In late fall, the rains let up, the fields drained, and it was harvest time in the rice paddy. The stalks had vibrated with ambition, straining against drowning water and chaining gravity to touch the sky and live forever. When it came time to die, they defiantly painted the earth in a burst of reproductive glory, exhausted themselves and expired. The land was transformed from monochromatic green into bright yellow squares bordered by unchanging green trees. Our field fluttered like a yellow flag in a breeze. The quiet was profound. More eloquent words about life and death in that simple sight could not have been written by all the poets who ever lived.

Gravity, eternal and unrelenting, pulled the stalks back to earth as the vigor drained from their veins. The intense, living yellow panicle faded into inert brown. The stalks lay in all directions like dead soldiers on a battlefield. Into the silent field we descended, herbivorous vultures to draw life from the strewn corpses.

With sickles in hand, Mom, Thi Tuyen, and I went about the harvest. Dad returned from his enterprise in Rach Gia to manage the proceedings. Day after day, we hacked at the stems, stacked and bundled the plants into bales and tied them with bamboo straps. Carrying the bales from field to house was the worst part of the procedure. I was too short to balance two bales at the ends of a pole sitting on my shoulders, so I had to carry one on my head. Mom and Thi Tuyen lifted and balanced the heavy bale on top of my head and sent me on my way. I took great care not to drop it because I could not pick it up again.

The task took on a Sisyphean character as we went back and forth from field to house. For three weeks, every day, from sunup to sundown, my family and I chopped and carried. At the end of each day my body ached all over, especially my skinny neck which was not designed for such loads. Bales were stacked in the front yard as tall as the house's roof, but the work wasn't finished.

Once the harvest was complete, the rice had to be hulled. Bales were unstacked one at a time and spread on the yard to dry. Panicles were then fed into the top of the concrete millstone. The power to drive the heavy, grinding stone came from the same motors which harvested and transported the rice. Usually, Mom was harnessed like a water buffalo to the stone which she dragged in around and around, separating the grain from the tough, protective hull. Thi Tuyen and I pushed from behind until Mom got tired and Thi Tuyen took her place. I was not allowed to pull the stone because it was an operation that required consistent application of power. Being a teenage boy, I was utterly bereft of any such regulating mechanism, or as Mom liked to put it, the destruction of rice in my wake looked like a "disaster strike."

From there, the rice we grew was divided into many uses. Some was eaten, some was stored as seed for the next season, and some was used to feed the pig and chickens. Byproducts were turned to compost which would fertilize the field. Nothing was wasted. If we had a surplus of rice, we sold much of the extra, but Dad insisted on saving enough to get us through a bad harvest. When he talked about saving, he always mentioned something about a famine in his youth, but I was a cynical, easily bored teen and disinterested in such ancient history.

The cycle ended with the Tet holiday and then it began again. It was simple and true. Muscles were stressed, but minds were not. It was beautiful. The rhythm was 10,000 years old and would go on 10,000 more. Here, I would stand and dance with the dragon. Here, I would spend my trips around the sun until I died. Then one day my bones would turn to dust and fertilize the field.

39

I t was late autumn, 1979, the Year of the Goat. The season had unfolded about the same as others in my memory. The monsoon came and burst swollen clouds over the paddy. The rice grew tall and luxuriant. Panicles painted the field yellow and the harvest was nearly upon us. Then something terrible happened.

It didn't stop raining.

Rain is the lifeblood of farming, but too much can kill a crop as surely as too little can. The Mekong Delta sits above sea level only in the most academic sense. Much of it is less than a meter higher than the South China Sea, which means it is functionally at sea level. Without gravity to give it purpose and speed its transit, delta water moves with lazy indifference, unconcerned with the anxiety of the farmer. Flooding is common.

The rain kept falling. It had nowhere to go but up. It crept up the stems of the rice until it touched the fair face of the panicles and then swallowed them. Thi Tuyen and I watched helplessly, sickened as our hard work disappeared under the brown surface. Mom and Dad were away from home and we didn't know what to do. The sound of voices coming from the front of the house roused us from our ruminations. My sister and I followed the voices until we saw Tam, Tien, and Kim Tuyen excitedly talking to their big brother. Doat had returned from school.

"Where are Mom and Dad?" Doat asked.

We shrugged our shoulders. Our parents never told us their business unless they wanted us to know.

"Chuong, drag the canoe around to the back. Thi Tuyen, get the sickles. I'll meet you there in a minute," he said.

In Doat's absence, the farming expertise Thi Tuyen and I had earned far outstripped Doat's knowledge about the subject. It seemed utterly foolish to attempt to harvest submerged rice, but being mindful of the hierarchy of age, we swallowed our pride and deferred to his orders. We met at the edge of the paddy. Doat waded in. We did not follow. He turned around and looked at us with disdain.

"Come on," he said.

"It's too deep and I can't swim," Thi Tuyen protested.

"It's not over your head. You won't have to swim," Doat promised.

"What about Chuong? It's definitely over his head," she said.

"Chuong is part fish, he will be fine."

We waded in as the rain pounded our bare heads. I pushed the canoe and held onto the side when the water got over my head. Despite our tropical latitude, the water was freezing. Doat gamely dived under and sawed off a few stalks. He surfaced with a measly handful and sloshed it into the canoe. He dived again. Thi Tuyen stood neck-deep and looked at me with terror in her eyes. I hung on to the side of the canoe and shivered. Doat came up again with a small load and shamed us.

"Come on you two, we've got to get this crop in if you're going to eat this year."

Thi Tuyen reached down and groped for a stem, desperate to keep her face above water. I let go of the canoe and dived. I had a flashback to the day I was pinned under the barge and almost drowned. With great difficulty, I harvested a single panicle. I surfaced and threw it into the canoe. I didn't go back under. Thi Tuyen continued to reach down and saw as her teeth chattered. Doat came back up, looking defeated.

"I can't do this anymore, it's too cold."

The three of us got out of the water and went into the house. Mom and Dad were there waiting on us. We stood just inside the doorway, three dripping, shivering rats, as our parents surveyed us. Doat spoke as I stared at my fingertips which had turned stark white and shriveled like raisins.

"I'm sorry. We tried to get the rice in. It was too cold. If we can warm up for a few minutes, we will go back out."

Thi Tuyen looked at him like he was crazy. Doat had not shared this plan with us before pledging our service. I had no intention of going back out, but remained quiet.

"No, you will not go back out," Dad said. "Go get some dry clothes."

None of us, even Doat, protested this order. We walked by our parents with heads bowed, ashamed that we had failed them so miserably. Mom and Dad looked at us as we disappeared into bedrooms and then looked at each other wistfully.

"We have good children," Mom said.

"Yes," Dad replied. "I just wish I could've given them a better life than this."

"You have provided well for all of us. We have a good life," Mom said.

265

Dad shook his head.

"Our kids are smart. They could do better if we lived in a country with opportunity," he said as he looked at the rising water. "But there is no time to talk of that now, we have to get ready."

"Ready for what?" Mom asked.

Dad motioned toward the door.

"The flood. The water will be in the house in a few hours."

The water kept coming and breached the front door. With our help, Dad raised all our beds on stilts. That night was surreal. I lay deathly still, afraid of dislodging my bed from its makeshift scaffolding and plunging into the black water below. Each minute move I made caused the whole contraption to shudder, giving me a sensation that I was floating in air on a flying bed. I couldn't see the water beneath my bed even if I could have summoned the courage to move enough to look. The house was without a scintilla of light, utterly and totally dark. I could hear the murmuring water stealing into our house like a burglar, lapping softly against solid walls and chairs as ripples spread across the room. Creatures swam into the house looking for high ground. Snakes slithered in and rafted themselves aboard floating household items while mice scratched along the rafters above. We had no recourse to evict the trespassers, for we were prisoners in our flying beds.

The flood waters receded within hours but left days of misery in their wake. A thick layer of fine silt was deposited everywhere the water stood. There was no escape from mud, even in the house. It penetrated everything—clothes, hair, even our bedding. There was no point in washing anything because it immediately became dirty again. We had no choice but to endure and wait for the mud to dry. When it dried, the floor of the house was a few centimeters higher than before.

With the harvest ruined, I spent more time fishing, which was fine with me. Harvest was punishing work, fishing was pleasant. One afternoon a couple weeks after the flood, I was in the front yard repairing a gill net. Doat came up to me.

"Hey Chuong, I'm leaving. I came to say goodbye."

"O.K. Doat, headed back to Long Xuyen?" I asked.

"Um, yeah, going back to school," he said.

"I guess we will see you in a few months," I said.

"Yeah, I hope so."

Doat walked down the path toward Thanh An and I went back to my net. A few houses down, he met Dad.

"Good luck, son."

"Thanks, Dad. It will be fine."

Dad nodded his head in forced agreement. It would be fine. It had to be fine. The alternative to fine was too painful to consider. He handed Doat a pouch that jingled softly in the exchange.

"Be sure to let us know when you get there," Dad said.

"I will. Bye, Dad."

Doat turned to walk toward town. When he got there, he didn't turn left to go to Long Xuyen. He went right, toward Rach Gia.

40

Rach Gia lies on the northwestern shore of the Ca Mau peninsula, the triangular piece of land at the extreme southern end of Vietnam. Protected by a large bay, the city developed a thriving fishing fleet and became a well-known market for honey, beeswax, and feathers of exotic birds. The port's distant-water fishing boats were solidly made from sturdy wood from Cambodian forests and had a distinctive shape, with unusually tall bows that swept dramatically to a low waist amidships before rising gently to a transom stern. Also, unlike other Vietnamese fishing boats of the Ca Mau which were uniformly painted blue, the fishing fleet of Rach Gia, influenced by Cambodian culture, sported a riot of colors—bright shades of red, green, and blue with contrasting white trim.

Beginning shortly after the fall of Saigon in 1975, Rach Gia developed another industry. As the closest port to the safe haven of Thailand, it became the primary departure point for refugees leaving Vietnam. Refugees swarmed the city and shoved off in any boat they could afford, usually dilapidated small craft designed for the more placid waters of the bay. Set against the backdrop of proud, seaworthy boats of the fishing fleet, the overcrowded, low-riding refugee boats looked bedraggled and pitiful.

A black market emerged and flourished, providing products and services to fleeing refugees. Boats, food, water, and temporary shelter were all sold at inflated prices. Even the well-to-do commercial fishermen found easy money transporting people and got in on the action. Scam artists and thieves filled in the underbelly of the enterprise, preying on unsophisticated farm folk who vacated their rice paddies, some for the first time.

When the refugees first began to leave the country, the government didn't try to stop them. In fact, they supported the idea of depopulation and profited from it in the form of exorbitant exit fees. But as the death toll reached crisis levels, the international community took notice and pressured the government in Hanoi to implement some level of control. Local police forces were ordered to stop the outflow. Soldiers were stationed at popular ports to crack down on the exodus. Those who were caught were turned back and had their boats confiscated. Those deemed reactionary could be sent to the reeducation camps. This added a cat-and-mouse element to an already dangerous endeavor.

Doat entered the teeming city and headed straight for the Catholic Church to meet his contact. The church was unique among the buildings of Rach Gia, and even among other Vietnamese Catholic churches, for it did not employ the eastern architectural style which was so heavily influenced by the sweeping, upturned, decorated roofs of pagodas. This church was thoroughly western, with the dour judgment and oppressive authority of a Baptist house of worship in the American south. Except for a few fanciful details in the façade, the blocky angles, joyless symmetry, and heaven-piercing dagger-like steeple could've weathered a fire and brimstone sermon in Vicksburg, Montgomery, or Augusta.

Doat had received his instructions from organizers in Long Xuyen. He was directed to look for a man wearing a *non la* sitting on the step at the front of the church. Doat walked slowly along the canal that fronted the church and spied the *non la* just as described. He kept his distance and observed the man and the surrounding plaza for authorities who might be lying in wait to trap an unsuspecting rube from the country. When he was satisfied, Doat approached the man and asked the prearranged question.

"Could you tell me where I could charter a fishing boat?"

"Ah, a fisherman, ay?" the man asked.

"Yes," Doat answered nervously.

"Boat leaves tomorrow morning at six from the city pier. Don't be late. Bring your money."

"Do you know where…"

"No questions," the man interrupted. "Leave now."

Doat felt a hot rush of embarrassment in his cheeks and turned away abruptly. He would have to figure out for himself where to spend the night. He made a half-hearted attempt to find lodging, but realized he was too nervous to concentrate on the task and likely too nervous to sleep. He gave up and walked to the pier. A few benches were scattered along the pier. He sat down and waited. He didn't sleep.

As the pre-dawn sky began to brighten, three small boats puttered up to the pier and docked. The boats looked about the same size as the packed refugee boats Doat had seen leaving the harbor the day before. The sight made his heart plunge. One of the boat captains saw him looking and walked over to him.

"You idiot farm boy. Can you be more obvious? Go away before you get arrested. Come back at six like you were told."

Doat stumbled backwards, turned, and almost broke into a run as he retreated from the pier. He ducked into the closest alley to catch his breath and calm himself. He peeked around the corner to see if he had attracted any attention. Only a few produce sellers were up at that hour and they were busy setting up their wares for the day's market.

He had no way of knowing the time, so he found a place where he could be concealed and watch the pier. As the departure time approached, refugees seemed to materialize on the pier. Doat bolted from his alley and walked briskly toward the man who chased him away earlier.

"Ah, you again?" the man said, "You are lucky you didn't get caught. You will lend us some of that luck, yes?"

The man smiled crookedly.

"Let me see your money."

Doat handed him the pouch and he peered inside.

"Alright, get in."

Within minutes, the three boats were full of people and headed out of the harbor. Doat had never been on the open water before, and had he not been petrified, he would've found the salty breeze exhilarating.

Seven other boats departed simultaneously from other points along the coast. All ten boats made a beeline for a vessel anchored in the bay, which was one of the town's uniquely-shaped fishing boats. It was a big boat— 80 feet long—and painted an electric shade of green with white trim and audacious red registration numbers on the looming bow.

The small boats buzzed around the larger one like flies on a piece of meat. One by one, the small boats transferred their passengers as the crew of the large boat shouted at them to move faster. Within 30 minutes, all 107 refugees were aboard and the anchor was raised. Crew members were harsh with the passengers, making them all sit huddled together on the small deck. No toilet was offered, no food was served.

Doat's good fortune held out. His assigned place to sit on the deck was next to a 10 liter water container with a cup. He served himself and those near him until the water ran out on the first day. The next thing that ran out was the boat's luck.

On the morning of the second day, a fast craft approached the fishing boat from behind. The boat came alongside and its crew, holding rifles pointed in the air, demanded they cut the motors. The captain of the green fishing boat complied and the men climbed aboard with their rifles slung across their shoulders.

"What's going on?" a simple-looking farmer whispered to Doat.

"Pirates," Doat said.

"What do we do?" the man asked.

"Whatever they tell us to do," Doat said.

The pirates went from person to person, demanding valuables. Rings, jewelry, and gold coins were confiscated. No one offered resistance and the pirates worked methodically, almost politely, through the crowd. When everyone had been relieved of their possessions, the pirates disappeared over the gunwale. Then one came back carrying a large canister of some sort. Was it a bomb meant to sink the ship and destroy evidence of their raid? Everyone held their breath, fearing the worst, as he walked through the crowd straight toward Doat. He stopped in front of the water container and removed the lid. He removed the lid of his canister and dumped its liquid contents into the empty water cooler.

Water. The pirate, in a gesture of very un-piratelike thoughtfulness, had given them fresh water. He capped his container and took it back to his boat. The pirates sped away, looking for more easy targets. Doat and the other refugees sat open-mouthed and paralyzed with astonishment for several minutes while they processed what had just happened. They had just been boarded by pirates and robbed at gunpoint, and yet somehow, smiles crept across their faces. Relief filled their lungs and broke into chuckles as the passengers relived the bizarre moment.

Ironically, the refugees probably made out better than the pirates from the exchange. The pirates didn't make a great haul from the poor passengers' valuables, but gave them priceless water in return. The fishing boat wouldn't make landfall for two more days and the passengers had no refuge from the relentless sun. The pirate water, while not nearly as much as they needed, preserved them from more serious dehydration.

On the third day, the hazy coast of Thailand came into view. The ship's crew, who had not interacted at all with the refugees for the entire trip, began scurrying about the deck in preparation. The captain directed the boat to an uninhabited beach area and pulled in close but did not touch shore. About ten meters from land, the helmsman turned the starboard side to face the beach. The crew ordered everyone up and over the side.

"Swim little fishes! Swim for your freedom!" the crew members jeered.

Almost everyone jumped in and swam. The few who protested they could not swim were put into a raft and ferried across. With the passengers ashore and the raft stowed back on deck, the boat unceremoniously turned and departed without giving the refugees instructions or even a farewell. The crew didn't give the soaked people on the beach a second look, but busied themselves with their tasks. The refugees, on the other hand, stood dumbfounded and dripping, staring at the boat as it got smaller and smaller.

A heavy realization burrowed deep in Doat's heart. He had done something big, something that could not be undone. Before the journey, he had convinced himself of the unshakable wisdom of his decision, but now that it was finished, he began to doubt, and even regret it a bit.

A tall, thickly-built man who fancied himself the leader of the group roused Doat from his ruminations with a loud call to move inland in the hopes of finding help. Nobody had a better suggestion or felt like contending with the thick man for leadership, so they began to trudge up the beach. They didn't get far.

As the group reached a small road behind the beach, a company of Thai soldiers drove up in their jeeps and surrounded the group. The thick man stepped forward to talk with the leader of the soldiers. After a few moments of conversation, the thick man announced to the group that they would be taken to a safe place to wait for the "refugee helpers." The group shuffled a few kilometers to a seaside village. An empty farmers' market with a high chain-link fence stood near the center of town. The refugees were taken to the market and ordered inside. The gate was closed and locked behind them. Soldiers stood guard to prevent escape. Doat was concerned but not frightened. Yet. When the soldiers brought them food and water, the mood lightened a great deal.

The group was kept locked in the farmers' market for a week. For seven days, they had to endure the elements unsheltered. At night, the mosquitoes ravaged them. Doat and the others scrounged for any kind of covering to give themselves some protection from the blood-suckers. The people were fed adequately but had no proper toilet, only a bucket they took turns emptying in a corner. They had enough water to drink, but not enough with which to clean themselves. When the thick man complained repeatedly of the abysmal conditions to the soldier in charge, he was told in broken Vietnamese, "help come soon."

Help eventually came. Representatives from the United Nations arrived and evacuated the group in buses to an established refugee camp. The camp, known as *Sikhiu Camp*, would not have been deemed luxurious by any reasonable standard, but it looked like the Ritz compared to the farmers' market. Real shelter, beds, running water, and bath houses seemed the height of decadence to the exhausted people. Doat and the others recuperated from their ordeal and began to look forward to their next chapter. An American volunteer befriended several of the refugees and began to teach them some English since it was likely that the refugees would be resettled in an English-speaking country.

Doat remembered his promise to our father. Through a translator he asked the American if he could send a letter to his parents. He was given paper and a pen. For hours, he struggled with words. He wanted to share all that he experienced in cathartic detail, but he was mindful of the trouble he might cause should the letter be intercepted by the government. Worried his family might become the target of recriminations and added surveillance, he kept his letter brief and vague.

Dear Dad
I made it to camp.
Your son,
Doat

A few weeks later, the letter arrived at our house. Dad received it and found a private place to read it. He read the words over and over, trying to extract more detail than the few words could give. The information given was maddeningly brief, but Dad understood why. When he could squeeze no more meaning from the letter, tears came to his eyes. As he cried, he prayed God would let him see his son again.

41

The fisherman named Nhon looked at the man before him with suspicion. The man had come to Nhon looking for work. The man was obviously a farmer from the Mekong Delta. His nervous eagerness betrayed much more information than he intended. And that accent. The man's ridiculous northern accent gave him away instantly.

"Probably a Christian who came down in '54 after the fall of Dien Bien Phu," Nhon thought. "Maybe a former soldier of the ARVN."

When asked for his name, the man said he was called Thanh Nguyen. Nhon snorted. Calling oneself Thanh Nguyen was the Vietnamese equivalent of "John Smith" in America. Surely a fake name, Nhon was convinced. But it didn't matter. The police had their hands full with hundreds of refugees coming and going each day. They wouldn't have time to dig too deeply into a mysterious stranger's identity. Besides, with help leaving on boats daily, Nhon couldn't be too picky about his hires.

Thanh Nguyen was a bit old to be starting a new career. Nhon guessed he was in his late 40s or early 50s. This gave Nhon some anxiety about the man's fitness to withstand the rigors of commercial fishing, but decided to give him a chance. His age soon became irrelevant. Thanh Nguyen won Nhon's admiration with his indefatigable stamina. He worked harder than any crew member Nhon had ever employed. No job was beneath him. He chopped and shoveled chum, cleaned fish, mended nets, and scrubbed the deck with focused resolve. Moreover, Thanh Nguyen had an insatiable inquisitive streak, soaking up every piece of information he could gather and asking endless questions. He asked about the tides, the construction of boats, the character of open water, storms, pirates, and more. He took a great interest in the comings and goings of boats in the harbor, especially the refugee boats which bounced precariously past Nhon's boat in an endless parade heading to the expanse of the gulf.

Despite Thanh Nguyen's curiosity, he didn't ask many questions about fishing and he didn't progress in competency. Nhon first judged him to be just an egghead more suited for theoretical understanding than action, but Thanh Nguyen's prodigious work ethic belied that easy judgement. Something else was going on. One evening the two men were finishing the catch. The golden sun turned orange as it approached the horizon behind them, throwing dancing sparks into the sea before retiring for the day. Nhon watched as Thanh Nguyen struggled with a trawling net and was moved to confront him.

"Thanh Nguyen, why are you here?" he asked.

Thanh Nguyen was caught off guard for the question and stiffened. He turned to deliver a hasty defense to Nhon.

"I want to be a fisherman," he squeaked.

There was little air behind his words and even less conviction.

"You are the hardest worker I have ever had and one of the smartest men I have ever met, yet you are a terrible fisherman," said

Nhon. "A man of your abilities couldn't help but be a good fisherman if he desired, which makes me think you are here for another reason."

Thanh Nguyen looked into Nhon's piercing eyes, gauging the extent to which he should commit to the lie he wanted to tell. The resolute gaze of his boss convinced him to give up the charade and come clean; but in exposing himself, he would become vulnerable. Nhon could report him to the authorities and wreck his dream. Thanh Nguyen weighed this possibility, but he had come to trust Nhon. He hoped his trust was not misplaced.

"I want to leave Vietnam," he blurted.

"Why?" asked Nhon.

"Only a rich person can make it in this country now—only a person who has connections and money to pay bribes. I have six children. I won't be able to afford all the bribes I will have to pay to get them established or buy them out of trouble. I want them to have a better life than the one that awaits them here. I want them to be able to live without the fear that hovers over me every day—the fear that the government is watching everything I do. I want them to be allowed to worship God."

"I see. Then why are you here? On *my* boat?" Nhon asked.

"I need to learn how to do...all of this."

He stretched his arms wide as if he were embracing the whole bay.

"I was born to the rice farm, not the sea. If I'm going to escape on the water, I thought I had better learn a few things about it.

Nhon nodded. He got very quiet as he processed the confession he just received. Thanh Nguyen grew more nervous with each silent moment. Finally, Nhon spoke.

"Well, you now know the basics of seamanship and how to handle a boat, but there is so much more."

Nhon warmed to the subject and fired objections like bullets.

"Where are you going to get a boat? How many people are you going to carry? Where are you going to dock? How are you going to get everyone aboard and shove off before the police catch you? And do you know how dangerous it is if you manage to make it to the gulf? The kind of boat you are going to be able to afford will hardly be seaworthy. Like those fools we see every day, going out in flimsy little skiffs. The people who leave here don't come back, but the stories do. Wreckage is strewn from here to Thailand. For every three boats we see leaving the harbor, one sinks or capsizes and everyone on board is lost. Are you sure you want to take that chance?"

"I must," Thanh Nguyen replied softly.

"Even if it means losing all your children?"

"My children are already lost if we stay," Thanh Nguyen said.

Nhon shook his head in disgust. He didn't fear the communists like so many did or understand what could drive someone to take such an extreme risk. His was the Rach Gia perspective. Port towns usually had a different personality from the interior. They took their culture like cargo from the ships which visited their harbors. Also, Rach Gia was farther from Hanoi than any city in the country and sheer distance attenuated much of the government's oppressive oversight. The Rach Gians danced to their own music and painted their boats any color they wanted. Their true loyalty was to the sea, not some distant capital and its self-aggrandizing proclamations.

"I think you're crazy," Nhon said, "but I may be able to help. I have an old boat that is used to deliver produce to floating markets along the bay. The man who worked it for me joined one of the refugee boats. I need someone to take over his deliveries. You can do that, and when you are finished with the day's work, you can use the boat to practice. Are you interested?"

"I hate to leave you alone out here," Thanh Nguyen offered.

Nhon smiled.

"That's all right. You aren't much good for catching fish anyway," Nhon said, showing his big teeth as he threw his head back in laughter.

Thanh Nguyen learned his delivery route quickly. Each morning he started before the sun rose, filling his boat with the day's produce. Several hours were then spent calling on customers to sell fruits, vegetables, and flowers. His attention to detail and punctuality endeared him to the vendors in the markets he served. In the afternoons, he drove the little boat out to the edge of the bay and imagined what it would be like on the day his whole family was with him. Even as foreboding waves beat their warning rhythm against the sides of the little boat, in moments of unblemished reverie he imagined a joyful adventure complete with mild sunlight and calm seas. He could see the smiles on the faces of his family.

A boat full of smiles.

The daydreams worked like a narcotic, filling his head with pleasant images while stealing his time. He fell into complacency, preferring the comfort of fantasy to the hard edges of reality. Only when his first target for a departure date slipped into history did he rouse himself. He decided to seek help.

Dong and Phat styled themselves as *departure consultants*. Brothers from the outskirts of town, they found an opportunity to part aspiring refugees from their money by providing advice. Thanh Nguyen was informed of the brothers' business and sought their help. On their first meeting, the brothers saw his boat and laughed.

"You're going in that?" Dong asked incredulously.

"It will be big enough for seven," said Thanh Nguyen.

"Yes, but will it be big enough to withstand the waves of the gulf?" asked Phat.

"It will have to be."

Skeptical as they were, the brothers met with Thanh Nguyen several times, doling out their wisdom miserly and making sure they were paid up front. They had a shady demeanor about them, which made Thanh Nguyen uneasy, and they never passed up an opportunity to tell him he would die on the too-small boat. The information they shared was mostly generic pap meant to impress a rube who was fresh off the farm, but they had a few nuggets worthy of remembering. They knew the docks and marinas least likely to be frequented by police patrols, the tide schedule, and they were well acquainted with the arrival times of cargo ships and the chain of activity and distractions they initiated.

Thanh Nguyen became disillusioned with the arrangement and began to think about finding a way out. He didn't trust the brothers to just agree to part ways. He was wary about what they would do to keep bilking him, up to and including violence. Luckily, money did all the negotiating as Thanh Nguyen's funds began to run low. On two consecutive days he was short on his payment to the brothers. On the third day they did not show up and he never saw them again. They must have figured this particular well was just about dry and moved on to more promising marks.

Disappointed and relieved at the same time, Thanh Nguyen decided to try again. He did not feel ready to make an attempt and wanted someone to teach him something valuable. He enlisted the help of his delivery clients. The name *Loc Trinh* was mentioned by several people. Many knew him personally and vouched for him. Thanh Nguyen searched for the man and eventually found him in a seedy bar in the warehouse district. The man sat halfway down the bar, hunched over a glass of brownish liquid. Thanh Nguyen walked up to the man, introduced himself and stated his business.

"Mr. Trinh, I hear you are in the export business."

Trinh didn't turn to look at the stranger.

"What are you exporting?" he asked.

"Something priceless to me. I need help arranging departure and I have heard that you have expertise in this field."

Trinh looked at the man.

Another farmer turned sailor turned food for fishes, he thought to himself.

He looked back at his drink, sighed heavily and spoke to the glass.

"Do you have a boat?"

"Yes," answered Thanh Nguyen.

"Do you have money?"

"How much?" asked Thanh Nguyen.

"Two *cay vang,*" said Trinh.

Thanh Nguyen did a quick calculation in his head. Two *cay vang* equaled 75 grams of gold. He sucked air through his teeth.

"That's a lot of money."

"It's a dangerous business," said Trinh as he slowly rotated his glass.

"I'll be back," Thanh Nguyen said.

Trinh didn't respond but cocked his head to watch the man walk out the door.

Two days later, Thanh Nguyen returned to the bar to find Loc Trinh sitting in the same place, wearing the same clothes, and spinning the same drink as if minutes, rather than days, had passed. Thanh Nguyen placed a tinkling pouch on the bar. Trinh opened the pouch, looked inside, and quickly pocketed it.

"There is a dock behind this building. Bring your boat and meet me there tomorrow morning."

Thanh Nguyen didn't wait till morning. He piloted the little boat to the place Trinh described and tied it off. As he did every night since obtaining the boat, Thanh Nguyen slept in the boat's small pilot house on a mattress stuffed with rice straw. Early the next morning, he heard footsteps on the creaky boards of the dock coming his way. He stepped out of the pilot house and saw Trinh, looking annoyed. Trinh saw Thanh Nguyen's face and stopped. A look of confusion crossed his face. He softened slightly and began walking again.

"I didn't expect you this early," Trinh said.

"Farmers' hours," Thanh Nguyen replied.

"This dock is going to have too much traffic this morning, we have to go to another place. Take your boat up the Kinh Long Xuyen. About two kilometers on the left, you will see a green house with a red roof. Beside it is a little inlet. Follow that inlet to the end and tie off at the pier there."

"Do you want to come with me?" Thanh Nguyen asked.

"No," said Trinh. "I have to pick up some supplies. I will meet you there."

Thanh Nguyen did as he was told and motored north to the mouth of the canal. He found the green house easily. The morning was bright and the air had not yet become laden with humidity. Thanh Nguyen felt a rush of optimism and was eager to begin his lessons. He tied the boat and stepped onto the dock. Two men seemed to materialize before him. He did not see them as he glided to the pier. He guessed they must have been hiding. In a moment, one was behind him and the other was in his face.

"Rach Gia Police, you are under arrest," said the man in Thanh Nguyen's face as he flashed his police identification.

"For what?" Thanh Nguyen stammered.

"Trying to exit Vietnam without authorization."

"I'm here to meet a man who is teaching me how to fish. I just bought this boat," Thanh Nguyen said.

"Stop talking, we know why you're here and we know who sent you. Give me your money."

"My money?" said Thanh Nguyen.

The policeman punched him in the gut. Thanh Nguyen doubled over in pain. The arrest was starting to feel more like a stickup. The man behind him stood Thanh Nguyen up straight and jammed his hands into the farmer's pockets. He pulled out a few coins and showed them to his partner.

"This is not enough to pay your fine. I guess we will have to confiscate your boat."

Thanh Nguyen didn't have the breath to reply and would've known better if he had been able to speak. The two policemen untied the boat, stepped in, and drove it toward the canal. As they turned the boat, the policeman who punched him shouted, "Go back to the farm!"

Thanh Nguyen sat on the pier and let the shock ebb from his body. When the last of the adrenaline in his bloodstream burned itself out, he took a deep breath and waited for Loc Trinh to arrive.

Trinh never showed. As Thanh Nguyen sat on the pier, he began to piece together what had just happened. Trinh had betrayed him. He and the police had an arrangement whereby he would send refugees to the trap and the policemen would pay him a bounty. In turn, they would sell the boats on the black market. Everybody made money except the poor refugees who were caught in the web.

Thanh Nguyen stood and started walking north along the dusty path that paralleled Kinh Long Xuyen, away from Rach Gia. Chastened. Wiser. Disheartened. Broke. He was going back to the farm.

42

D ad didn't tell us about Doat for many months. He didn't want the hassle of fielding dozens of questions he couldn't answer. He had a difficult enough time managing his own anxiety and didn't need intruding reminders from concerned family members. Nor did he want any attention from the authorities regarding his missing son. One stray word in the wrong person's ear could send an agent to the farm and trigger more supervision and harassment. As the months passed without a visit from Doat, however, our inquiries became more frequent and bothersome. Dad finally told us in his nonchalant way that Doat was in Thailand and warned us not to tell anyone.

Thailand? Though only a few hundred kilometers from our farm, Thailand might as well have been the moon. I had a foggy notion that we lived on the surface of a globe, but its size was incomprehensible to me. My grasp of the world was limited to the extent of my travels—in other words, it extended from our house to Thanh An, a distance of two kilometers. Nearby Long Xuyen and Rach Gia had the mysterious air of exotic foreign capitals one hears about in legends. I lived a life of granular exploration, discovering worlds contained in the art and science of fishing and farming.

News of Doat's escape triggered a complex brew of emotions. I mourned in the belief that I would never see my brother again. I was also genuinely happy for him. All those years at school in Long Xuyen would surely secure him a prestigious job wherever he landed. Finally, I was slightly jealous that while he was living an adventure, I would spend my days in the paddy, face to the earth and back to the sky.

Self-pity was a luxury a farmer could not afford to indulge. There was no time or energy to be spent moping. I was a farmer and always would be. I had to accept that. Doat would never be back to help and Dad was gone much of the time, so I had to become the de facto *Man of the House*. I didn't have time for such titles, either. Pride was another unaffordable luxury when hunger lurked in the shadows of a poor harvest. There was always work to be done and daylight was forever slipping away.

Refugees were assigned to host countries by a long list of criteria. The United States prioritized, among other things, service in the ARVN. Doat, being the son of an ARVN veteran, benefitted from this connection and was sent to a place called Martinsville, Virginia. I would've searched for Martinsville on a map or in a book, but there were no geography books to be found in Thanh An.

Doat found work in a textile factory as a loom operator and shared an apartment with other refugees. He sent letters with money enclosed to repay Grandmother for his passage to Thailand. The arrival of his letters always set off a frenzy of excitement in the house. When everyone finished their turn reading the letters, I peeled the stamps from the envelopes and began a collection. American stamps were so pretty and varied and exotic. They were my one and only connection to a world beyond the verdant sameness of the Mekong Delta.

America. *My brother is an American now, I thought.* It was strange, but true nonetheless.

I outworked the sun, beginning each day well before it turned the sky from black to blue and ending long after its orange head slipped beneath the covers of its celestial bed. In the dry season, when the sky was swept clean of the darkening blankets which delivered the monsoon, the moon and stars performed their silent pageant. Like diamonds set against black velvet, stars shimmered in ancient, inaccessible splendor. I regarded the icy twinkle simply as decoration. One could neither plant nor harvest by their weak light, so I categorized them with my stamp collection—pretty to look at but devoid of practical purpose.

In the dry season—late March or early April, I suppose— in the Year of the Dog, 1982, I was walking home from the monkey bridge where I had enjoyed a late afternoon swim with my friends. As the sun sped across the earth to tend to the other side of the planet, darkness gained a foothold in the waters of the canal and spread upward until the blackness of night filled the heavy air. I walked home by memory, as my eyes no longer served me. As I arrived at our house, I could see the fiery ember of a cigarette. Dad was outside smoking. I walked toward the front door without a thought of engaging him. Years of childhood in a Vietnamese family drilled certain cultural norms into my head, one of which was a "speak-only-when-spoken-to" deference to one's father.

"Chuong, come here a second," he said.

I obeyed, noting the odd warmth of his tone.

"Did you have a good swim?" he asked.

Again, more oddity. He never cared about that kind of frivolity before.

"Yes, Dad," I said in a respectful yet business-like response.

The cigarette cast a soft red glow against his features as he held it in his mouth. He looked upward.

"I was just looking at the stars. Did you know that some of them have names?"

"No sir, I did not," I said.

He pointed to the biggest, brightest star in the sky.

"That is the Southern Star. The French called it Sirius or the Dog Star."

He pointed out others and called their names.

"I didn't know this before, but the fisherman in Rach Gia taught me that sailors use the stars as a map and can find their way across the ocean with them."

I looked up. *A map?*

His impromptu lecture was interesting, but pointless. A map wasn't going to help me grow rice. I searched for a polite answer, but Dad switched gears and began again.

"I'm proud of you, Chuong. You have grown into a fine provider for our family. I will be leaving again tomorrow, but we will all be together soon. You will need to watch after your mother and brothers."

With that, he turned and went into the house.

Mother and brothers, I thought.

It was odd that he didn't mention my sisters. Maybe he was thinking they would be married within a few years and out of the house. I didn't spend a lot of time dwelling on the cryptic advice as I was too elated. In my mind, the conversation marked a change in my status. A promotion to adulthood. The talk had the tone of an exchange between colleagues. There was respect and admiration in his words. I had earned the approval of my father. Was there any more satisfying feeling than that?

I stayed outside for a long time, replaying our talk over and over, swelling with pride at each recollection of the words "I'm proud of you." I looked at the stars again. I had already forgotten the names Dad told me. Not that it mattered. When it came to growing rice, the rain mattered. The sun mattered. Seedlings mattered. Maintenance of the paddy mattered. Stars, as beautiful and awe-inspiring and comforting as they were, did not make any difference in the life of a farmer.

I was a farmer.

But not for long.

43

"Chuong, wake up."

It was my sister Thi Tuyen. She stood over me until she was sure my eyes were open, then she went to wake Tien and Tam. I was disoriented as I emerged from a deep sleep. Something was amiss, I never overslept and had never been awaked by my sister. The alarm caused by the strange situation brought consciousness rushing to my head, carried by a tide of fresh blood.

"What's going on?" I asked.

"I don't know, Mom said to wake you," she replied.

"What time is it?"

"Early," she said as she gently shook my younger brothers. "She woke me too."

The three of us boys staggered out of our rooms, each with a stand of thick black hair sticking up from our heads at random angles. When we got to the main room, large plates of food sat steaming at our places. Kim Tuyen was already there eating. I punched her playfully on the shoulder as I sat.

Despite our confusion about the situation, years of training in the observance of mealtime silence activated and we all started eating without question. I had so many questions. Why did my sister wake me? Why were we up so early? Why were we having this huge meal for breakfast? My routine, which was as consistent as the rising of the sun, was suddenly upended, but I said nothing. Deference to parents was absolute in our culture, so I shoveled food into my mouth and kept my thoughts to myself.

When breakfast was finished, Mom directed us to make our toilet and come straight back. We dutifully went to the bamboo outhouse and did our business. When we returned, Mom was standing by the door with a small bag slung over her shoulder.

"Let's go," she said.

We followed her down the dirt path that ran alongside the still water of Kinh D. It was the path I walked every day to go to school, but I got the feeling that Mom wasn't taking us to school. Ahead of us to the east, the approaching sun turned the underside of the gray clouds pink then orange. Dogs barked at us. Geese hissed their warnings. Duy, my mentor turned competitor, was heading to the canal with a pole in his hand.

"Hey Chuong, where are you going?" he asked.

"I don't know," I whispered with shrugged shoulders.

When we reached the end of Kinh D, the ferryman was just beginning his day. He ferried us across Kinh Cai San to Thanh An. The six of us were his only passengers. It was the first time I had been on the little boat when I didn't fear it capsizing from overcrowding.

In town, near the ferry, a short bus was idling at the bus stop. It was very crowded. Inside the bus, we saw a few people we knew including our cousins Minh and Kha. They were about Thi Tuyen's age and shouted for her to come with them. Mom looked at Thi Tuyen and told her to go ahead.

"But where are we going?" Thi Tuyen asked.

"Minh and Kha know, just follow them," Mom said. "We will catch the next bus."

I didn't see or hear the interaction between Mom and Thi Tuyen. I had busied myself playing with Kim Tuyen, Tien, and Tam in the street. It was just like old times when we lived in town. While we were playing, my aunt Lanh and her family came up to Mom and started talking to her. When Kim Tuyen saw her, she broke away from our game to greet our aunt. Kim Tuyen was Lanh's favorite and she treated my sister as her own child. My brothers and I continued playing until the next bus pulled up to the little bus stop.

"Chuong, Tien, Tam. Come on, it's time to go," Mom called.

We boarded the smelly, dirty bus but Kim Tuyen did not. The bus couldn't hold us all so she was told to wait with Aunt Lanh for the next bus. Kim Tuyen didn't mind. She smiled and waved at us as we pulled away. From my seat I could see the little block house and the produce stand where I had lived and worked. Then I saw the church where I had played my altar boy pranks.

As the bus bounced and creaked along the potholed road, I realized Thi Tuyen was missing.

"Mom, where is Thi Tuyen?" I asked.

"She went on the first bus with Minh and Kha."

"Where are we going?" I asked.

I could no longer stand the mystery and decided to chance an inquiry.

"We are going to the market in Thot Not," she said stiffly.

Thot Not? I had never heard of the place. Her chilly reaction prevented me from asking more questions. Then she turned to me.

"It will be big and crowded. Don't get distracted. Keep your brothers close and stay with me."

Her tone of voice alarmed me. It was so out of character for her to be so assertive. After an hour or so, the little bus stopped to let some passengers off and some on. Some street merchants walked up to the window of the bus and offered food for sale. Mom bought each of us a sweet rice cake and some fruit. The snack was delicious and comforting and made me forget about Mom's troubling mood. The bus rocked down the road, wind came through the windows, and for a few minutes the trip became an exciting adventure. I was in new places, seeing new sights, and though the scenes looked much like those in Thanh An, there was something fascinating about seeing a place—any place—for the first time. As we neared our stop, Mom turned to me once more.

"When we get off the bus, do not talk and make sure your brothers do not talk. Your northern accents will attract attention," she said.

I have an accent? I thought to myself.

I didn't know I had an accent. I thought I spoke the same as everyone else. In Thanh An, this was probably true since most of the settlers around Kinh Cai San came from the north. Now we were travelling outside our little cultural bubble and the confidence I had regarding my place in the world vanished. Suddenly I felt very small and vulnerable.

We got off the bus and waded into a throng of people as the smell of cooking meat filled our noses. After years on the quiet farm, the low roar of the crowd was frightening. I grabbed my brothers' hands and watched Mom with unwavering attention. The market was huge and stretched as far as I could see. The town of Thot Not sat on the southern bank of the Song Hau, one of the biggest branches of the Mekong Delta. The market filled the streets and spilled over into the river as some merchants sold directly from their boats. There was not enough docking space, so boats rafted together and created a floating market. Mom weaved through the crowd toward the river as I struggled to keep up. Tien and Tam held tight and we snaked through the crowd. We were too nervous to speak.

As we reached the river, a woman stepped out from an alley and addressed Mom. I hadn't caught up to her yet and didn't hear what the woman said, but she turned and walked out onto a pier. Mom followed her. Still clutching my brothers, I followed Mom. We passed many boats full of fruit, flowers, or sedge mats. There was a good bit of shopping traffic on the pier and we had to weave our way through the crowd. At the end of the pier, we came to a boat laden with sugarcane and coconuts. The woman began a distracted sales pitch while looking around nervously.

"These coconuts are fresh from the Dong Thap province. They are…nice to eat," she said.

As the woman staggered through her unrehearsed, awkward words, she made flourishing gestures toward the produce, as if to fortify her unconvincing presentation. She made her way slowly to the stern of the boat, pointing at almost every individual coconut. When we came to the end of the walkway, she turned to Mom and spoke.

"There are more things to see on the boat. Please join me. Bring your sons."

We climbed over the gunwale into the boat. At one time, the craft had been painted the traditional blue, but many years had passed since its last coat. Only flecks of paint still clung to the worn wood. The woman led us into the shabby pilot house. An opening had been cut into the front wall. Beyond the opening, a dark compartment lay hidden beneath the coconuts.

"Go in there, sit down, and be quiet. Don't come out," the woman said. Tien and Tam were scared, so I went first. The boys followed me and Mom came behind us. As my eyes adjusted to the dim light, I could see Thi Tuyen. She looked at me with wide, scared eyes. I crawled up to her.

"What's going on?" I whispered.

"We're leaving," she whispered back.

My mouth dropped.

"You mean like Doat?" I asked.

"Yes. Minh and Kha told me everything. They've been helping Dad get ready. That's why he stayed so long in Rach Gia. He wasn't fishing, he was trying to figure out how to get us all out, but something happened and he got caught. He decided it was too risky in Rach Gia, so he came here."

"Whose boat is this?" I asked.

Thi Tuyen shrugged.

"Where is Kim Tuyen?" she asked.

"She is coming on a later bus with Aunt Lanh."

More people crawled into the compartment. I didn't know them. Over the course of the afternoon, the darkened hold became crowded with people— some relatives, some strangers. We packed ourselves close to allow room for everyone. There was no room to stand, so we sat and drew our legs to our chests. The afternoon heat baked the closed air of the secret cargo hold. We began to suffer. The putrid air weighed heavily in our lungs and radiating body heat raised the temperature to unbearable levels. We sat drenched in sweat that wouldn't evaporate and thus gave no relief.

A sensation began to swell within my chest. Malevolent and hungry, it gnawed its way through the walls of my lungs and into my stomach, spilling acid and bile that ate its way up my body into my beleaguered brain. A dam made with layers of days and months and years had arrested the flow of memories of a black bunker in Saigon and the watery underside of a boat in Kinh Cai San, but the torrent of new stress breached the dam, and the trauma of those two events unleashed a black flood on my soul once again.

My insides were roiling but I remained motionless thanks to the example of those around me. I looked at Thi Tuyen. Suffering was written on her face but not panic. Similar expressions were worn by Mom and my brothers. I was ashamed. If women and children could suffer in silence, I had no excuse to let my anxiety control my actions. I was a man. Honor dictated I act like one. I sat still and waited.

The afternoon passed though I was convinced time had stopped to cruelly prolong the agony. Dad stuck his head in to take a headcount from time to time. When he noticed Kim Tuyen missing, he spoke briefly to Mom to find out what happened. People eventually stopped crawling into the hold. Kim Tuyen didn't show up. I would've worried more about her had I not been consumed with my own misery. The noise of shoppers on the pier died slowly and was eventually replaced all together by the sound of whining boat motors. The merchants were leaving. I could hear the happy sellers retelling the stories of the day as they readied their boats for the return trip to their homes. I wondered what their lives were like, where they lived, and what my own life would look like on the other side of this day.

The sound of the last boat drifted into nothing and all I could hear was the water slapping the boat. Another low sound began in the distance and grew in volume. It was two men talking, accompanied by percussive footsteps on the boards of the dock. The men stopped walking when they reached our boat but didn't stop talking. I could recognize the voice of my father but not the other. They were having a disagreement.

"Dinh, we have to go now, it's 5:00 p.m." the other man said.

"We can wait a few minutes for them," Dad said.

"It's not safe to stay. The other boats are gone. The police will notice a boat staying late."

"I'm not leaving without my daughter."

"You are putting everyone in this boat in danger. Even if we don't get caught, we will never make it out once the tide starts coming in. We have to leave now," the man said.

"Just a few more minutes," Dad said.

The man sighed heavily and walked away from Dad. I could hear him untying ropes and throwing them onto the coconuts. I looked at Mom. She had instinctively grabbed Tien and Tam and pulled them close. Thi Tuyen and I looked at each other with silent panic.

Surely we would not leave Kim Tuyen behind. Surely she would come running across the dock at any second.

She didn't come.

The other man told Dad they were out of time. They had to leave or cancel the whole thing. Silence fell between the two men, then I could feel the boat sway as they climbed aboard without speaking. The motor was brought to life and the sensation of motion vibrated through the keel as the boat struggled to push us into the current of the Song Hau.

It was 5:05p.m. The date was May 24, 1982.

44

May 24, 1982

The boat puttered down the muddy Song Hau with its secret cargo, 57 souls hiding under the coconuts. Along with Dad and the unknown man from the dock, a grand total of 59 people were wedged in the 10 meter craft.

We stayed hidden, buried alive in the mass grave until it was dark. When nightfall shrouded the river, Dad started throwing coconuts overboard. From our darkened quarters we could hear the plop of each one as it was dropped. The sugarcane was jettisoned with a rustling whoosh. When the final pieces of the platform were removed, Dad warned everyone not to stand up at once or the boat might capsize. One by one, passengers stood and breathed and stretched. Some were so frightened by Dad's warning they stayed glued to the bottom of the boat.

The Song Hau was large, much wider than the Kinh Cai San which I knew so intimately. Twinkling lanterns dotted the distant black banks that held the moon-glowing river. A shudder radiated through me. I had never been on water this big and it terrified me.

The squeezing claustrophobia of the past few hours had crowded all other concerns from my mind. When the hypoxia of the coconut tomb was finally relieved by the expansive view and cooling breeze, thoughts of my sister came rushing into the void. One panic was replaced with another.

Kim Tuyen, where are you?

Frustration from confinement aboard the tiny boat flamed from the waning embers of claustrophobia. My sister was somewhere over there in the folds of the black bank and I couldn't get to her. Surely we would turn around. Surely Dad would order the other man to go back.

Our course didn't change. We kept going. The lights of Thot Not dwindled and disappeared.

I wanted to scream her name, swim to the riverbank, or walk upon the water like Jesus to rescue her, but nothing could be done. She was lost. I could see the white-hot desperation on Thi Tuyen's face as well and then turned to look at Mom who was slouched against the side of the boat. Her eyes were closed and her mouth was slack and her face had drained to a ghostly white. She could've been mistaken for a corpse except for the cold tears running down her cheeks. Tien and Tam sat with her and wrapped their arms around her. Dad stood motionless at the rail, gazing at the bank, lost in regret and despair.

It was at that moment I felt certain I would never see Kim Tuyen again. Hollow nausea threatened to throw my heart up into my hands. I cried and reached to hold Thi Tuyen. We sobbed on each other's shoulders. Our sister was gone.

The little boat hummed softly through the silver water. Its destiny, and ours, would be met without the presence of two members of our family. First Doat, now Kim Tuyen.

45

May 25, 1982

The night turned cloudy and the guiding moonlight was lost. The flickering lanterns on either side of us diminished as the night progressed, until finally, the riverbanks slept in darkness. The unknown man from the dock, who turned out to be a river pilot hired by Dad, steered the boat from memory and breaks in the cloud cover which gave the faintest glimpses of our course. At some point in the deep night, the black riverbanks grew wider and smaller until they merged behind us into a single dark line separating water and sky. We were in the South China Sea.

The place where a great river empties into the sea is one of unremitting violence. The forces that propel millions upon millions of liters of river water do not resign themselves so timidly into assimilation in the measureless ocean. The land-born brown and the briny blue clash like ancient gods at the place where they meet, each invested with unspeakable power. The river's mouth is a battlefield of silt and waves. Currents slash like swords under the surface. Sandy monsters mound up as if by a magic spell and lurk beneath the waves to wreck hapless boats, only to disappear and materialize in another part of the channel. It is the arena of titans. It is no place for man.

But man—cunning, voracious, and equally full of hubris and ignorance—enters valiantly, foolishly, into worlds he did not inherit. Human history is littered with tales of those who put their trust in brains and bravery to overcome unconscious, omnipotent nature. River, lake, and ocean bottoms are littered with wrecks of those who chanced environments where lesser, wiser animals dared not tread.

The little boat entered this alien place and bobbed like a cork as giants fought below. Black waves rose from the depths to slap the sides tauntingly. The poor flatwater craft struggled to stay afloat while the weight of the 59 pushed it to find the bottom. The motor, a small two-stroke engine, turned a tiny propeller made for the languid waters of the delta. It was vastly overmatched against the power of the raw sea, but it pushed faithfully and we moved further and further from our home.

Until we stopped.

The boat jerked to a halt and its passengers were thrown forward. We had run aground. But how? In the moments I could catch a glimpse of the land we left behind, it was barely visible. We were far out to sea. The little engine whined in high-pitched protest. Dad reversed the motor but the boat didn't move. He shut off the motor and silence rushed in to fill the newly created void. Waves irregularly smacked the boat, rocking it from side to side. It reminded me of a cat toying with a mouse before killing it. The pilot spoke.

"Sandbar. Very bad. With this much weight, waves will push us right over."

Dad wasted no time.

"Minh, Kha, Chuong," he snapped, "get out there and push us off."

Out there? In the middle of the black ocean?

Of course, I didn't actually say that. Before my brain could register the protest, my subconscious commandeered my muscles and threw me overboard. I landed with a splash and a thud as my feet found thick sand. The water was about waist deep. Minh and Kha joined me and we instinctively began searching for the edge. Once the closest ledge was found we relayed the position to Dad. He told us to push the boat toward it. He started the motor once more and reversed the blades. The propeller was attached to a two-meter shaft. The motor was mounted on a ball and could be raised, lowered, and rotated 180 degrees, acting as both propulsion and tiller. The contraption was called a long-tail or beavertail motor and excelled in the shallow flatwater of the delta.

I pressed my body into the bow. In front of my face was the faded registration number of the boat, HG-1102. HG stood for *Hau Giang*, the province in which it was registered.

"Come on, *Hau Giang*, MOVE!" I grunted.

As we pushed, Dad swung the beavertail back and forth, trying to find a spot where the propeller could dig into the water. We barely moved. More men jumped in the water and began to help. Whether by their added efforts or by lightening the load, the boat moved. We pushed it to deeper water. Extricated from the sand, *Hau Giang* bobbed naturally, if sluggishly. Those of us who had jumped onto the sandbar now had to swim across open water to return to the boat. Terrified of the creatures that might have been lurking below, I hesitated. An unseen wave sprang up and filled my mouth with salty water. I swam. There was no safety here. Anywhere. There were only degrees of safety, and at the moment the pathetic boat was the safest place available to me. I climbed aboard with the others and we moved on.

The taste of salt lingered in my mouth. It was my first experience with seawater. As I was dwelling on the strange sensation of my mouth drying and drawing inwards, the sky began to brighten ever so slightly to the east. An orange glow leaked through a ripped seam between sky and sea and the black canopy of stars was rolled back to reveal promising blue. We had survived the night.

As the sun began to rouse the earth from sleep with its warm hands, so too was the wind stirred to begin its day of wandering. Vigorous gusts raked the water of the South China Sea, churning it into infinite peaks and valleys. The waves reached the boat and breached the low-riding gunwales with explosions of shimmering, hissing white water. *Hau Giang* was pitched high and low as the pilot struggled to steer it into the kindest angle over the swells. Dad grabbed the tiller as well and the two wrestled the overmatched vessel as it tried to succumb to hopelessness and dive into each watery grave that opened up on the other side of each crested wave.

We waited in unbearable suspense for the plunge that would sink the boat; for the cold wet cocoon which would shock our senses and wrap our bodies in an instant and fill our lungs with doom. Unearthly moaning erupted from the petrified passengers. Screams rose and fell with the waves. In the midst of the noise, I heard my mother's voice. Distressed but clear, she began to pray the rosary. She had seen so much death and devastation in her years. Twelve hours before, she had lost a child to an unknown fate. Yet through all the suffering that her heart had absorbed and the horrifying fate that could consume her at any moment, she held onto the promise of a reward purchased for her and redeemable on the other side of imminent destiny.

I joined in and so did Thi Tuyen. We prayed and sang hymns. People drew close to their families and held one another. I glanced to the stern where Dad and the pilot were fighting the tiller. The pilot, the only experienced seaman on board, was white with fear. The rough seas continued throughout the morning and the prayers and songs became punctuated by the sound of vomiting. One by one, seasickness visited the passengers. Thankfully, Dad had packed several buckets to serve as toilets. The buckets were passed and filled with foulness. Whether from motion sickness or the smell, nearly every person vomited when the bucket came to them. When it reached the back of the boat, its contents were poured into the sea and the circuit began again. Some couldn't wait for the bucket to reach them and threw up on themselves and in the bottom of the boat. As the morning sun climbed to its invisible peak, it grew strong and baked the vomit and sweat into a putrid concoction which only added to the misery.

The day had dawned murderously and progressed with cruel sluggishness. It raged with pitiless, inescapable heat and innumerable sickening waves, but finally spent its energy and settled into a tranquil evening. Exhausted from fear and nausea, everyone on board collapsed into fitful sleep. I climbed to the roof of the pilot house and surveyed my surroundings for the first time. Water stretched to an infinite horizon on all sides. We were a speck of life on a lifeless plain. Above, black sky unfurled its starry map and I recalled the curious conversation I had with Dad back on the farm. The seeming irrelevance of his words now made sense. In his mind, he was already on the sea, trying to find his way safely to the other side.

"Dad," I called.

He raised his head to look at me.

"Sirius. The Dog Star," I said as I pointed toward the brightest star.

"You remembered," he said with a sad smile.

I think I saw regret in that smile.

When we last spoke of the stars, his head was full of plans and possibilities. Now the voyage in his imagination had come to pass and it had brought 59 people to the threshold of death. I felt bad for him. I doubt he would have put his family and the others in such grave danger if he had been able to foresee the hellish day we had experienced, but it didn't matter now. We were there in the great blue nothing with only two possibilities—escape or death. There was no way out of our predicament but to go through it. Still, the past beckoned with its siren song of what-ifs. Twenty-four hours earlier, I felt exceedingly sorry for Kim Tuyen. After our first day on the sea, I would've given anything to have been wherever she was, orphaned but at least on solid ground.

46

May 26, 1982

The second day dawned like the first with a strong breeze racing the eastern sun, pushing water into waves that made *Hau Giang* buck and dive like a young goat with a heart full of springtime. Weary passengers felt the heaviness return to their stomachs and the vomiting started again. No one had eaten since the previous day's bout of seasickness, so the only thing that returned was acidic saliva.

Nobody was hungry, but everyone was thirsty. Dad began dispensing rations of water. Each passenger received one scoop of water in the morning and one in the afternoon. One woman from Saigon took her scoop of water into her mouth, swished it back and forth, and spit it into the bottom of the boat. Scorn rained on her.

"You idiot! What do you think you're doing?"

"Stupid city girl. Do you think water comes out of a tap?"

On and on the insults came until the Saigon woman began to cry.

"That's enough!" came a voice from the stern.

It was Dad. Everyone stopped. The only noise, besides the sea and motor, was the woman sobbing. Eventually, the prayers and songs started again.

I noticed Dad's authority. He was the unquestioned captain of the vessel and master of the voyage. Even the pilot, who had vastly more boating expertise, deferred to Dad's orders. Minh and Kha, whom I learned had assisted Dad in preparation and often accompanied him on scouting missions, were chief mates. I was assigned the disgusting task of emptying and rinsing the vomit/toilet buckets, so I estimated my rank in the crew to be somewhere near the bottom.

Dad began to rotate the people in and out of the shade of the pilot house to give some relief from the scorching sun. As pale, sick faces shuffled to and fro, I learned more of their stories and how they came to be included in this miserable, perilous venture. Dad, of course, was the architect of the whole thing. After his arrest at Rach Gia (Kha told me the story of Dad assuming a fake name and getting his boat stolen by the police), he began again at Thot Not. He realized the boat he had at Rach Gia was too small, so he shopped for a bigger boat. Bigger boats cost more money, so he secretly enlisted investors. Most were extended family—about half by my estimates. The rest were the families of trusted friends from his army days. They secured their place with money, an ironclad oath of secrecy, obedience, and an agreement to hold him blameless in the event of any passenger's death.

As the long day dragged on, the wind-driven waves diminished but the swells grew large, which meant we were free from the shallow, tangled currents of the dying Mekong. We were truly at sea. Gliding swells looked like the backs of sea monsters breaching the surface, hinting at their deadly strength. I sat on the gunwale with my legs dangling over the cobalt abyss, hypnotized by the infinity that surrounded me on all sides. Emptiness filled and dissolved me. My eyes were drawn from my head to bathe in eternal nothingness, for what use are eyes in the ocean? There were no landmarks by which to navigate, no variety, or shades of colors with which to affix perception. Nothing but endless, unconscious blue.

The boat sat low in the water and my feet churned the blue into a white wake. I saw a fin emerge from the surface. It was large, much larger than those of the tuna I had seen in the market. A great arching back was attached to the fin, catching and scattering glittering droplets of gray light as the water skidded from the slick body.

A shark! I thought in terror.

I pulled my feet up and hid behind the safety of the wooden wall but kept my eyes locked on the shifting position where the fin disappeared. Thi Tuyen saw my abrupt movement and called over to me.

"What is it?"

"A shark! Right there!" I said as I pointed.

Thi Tuyen didn't stir from her misery or even acknowledge my fear. She closed her eyes and leaned her head against the wall of the pilot house.

Another fin slid out of the water to the right, then another to the left. I counted eight distinct fins. I recalled that last night I swam in the same dark water that contained these beasts. I shuddered. Ignorance was replaced with terrifying knowledge.

My ignorance was largely intact, for it wasn't shark fins I saw, but porpoise. In my situation, however, that was a small distinction. For the first time, I had seen creatures in the sea—big, lurking creatures which were hidden in the silent depths. The sea had previously seemed an impersonal force, capable of killing with endless strength but no animosity. Now it was invested with ambitious teeth and ravenous malice. It teemed with large, motivated life forms which could rip and devour my flesh if they so desired. I hoped we would not hit another sandbar, for if we did, I would be put in the uncomfortable position of disobeying an order from my captain to get in the menacing water.

47

May 27, 1982

The third night descended. Darkness absorbed the earth and it shrunk existence to the quantity of stimuli received, such as the people and items lit by a single weak lantern. I could feel the rough, old wood of *Hau Giang* beneath me, thus confirming its existence. I could hear the sea splashing gently against the boat, therefore it existed, diminished by muted perception yet still full of terrible potential.

Nighttime drew the energy of the sun-stirred earth into its dark void. Hot, angry air of daytime dissolved into pleasant coolness. Wind grew quiet and waited for the sun. The sea paused its itinerant restlessness and slept. It was a moment of tranquility, but not for us. Night made us hostages of our fears.

Jesus warned us about the fruitlessness of worry. In supernatural eloquence He tried to drive understanding into our murky brains, telling us plainly that worry, anxiety, and fear do not add to our days. It is a hard lesson which we so easily forget when night falls. Darkness robs us of sight and anxiety fills the emptiness. Instead of the calming words of Jesus, we invest energy into worry. And so, the passengers aboard

Hau Giang did not rest easy like the world around them, but allowed fear to invent destruction in chambers of tormented imagination.

"Chuong," Thi Tuyen whispered.

Her tone was without energy or emotion, but she spoke of the one feeling she had left.

"I'm so scared, but I can't pray anymore. I'm too tired. When is this going to end?"

"I don't know," I said.

I wanted to encourage her, but didn't have the strength to put words together. We sat together in silence.

Daylight eventually crept across the globe. At the horizon, the gray underside of predawn clouds became bruised with red sunlight and slowly turned puffy white. The spirits of the people on *Hau Giang* rose with the sun until the sea was awakened and threw waves at the boat. It looked like a repeat of the last two days, marked by long hours of oppressive sun and seasickness. The prayers and songs began and the bucket was passed.

Something was not the same. The eastern sky fairly sang with heaven's streaming rays and freshening breezes, but to the south, darkness held on. Blue sky and bright sea could not penetrate, but weakly illuminated a wall of moody gray clouds which hung down and smothered the surface of the water. The wall of clouds flashed a predatory warning and an extended bass rumble rolled ominously over our ears.

The monsoon was coming.

It was the end of May. It was time. For the past few days, I had been so occupied by exhausting seasickness and terrifying thoughts of drowning, I had forgotten the defining days of a rice farmer's year were at hand. But the moment I saw the sinister clouds crouching with endless stored energy, I knew exactly what I was looking at. I glanced to see if Dad's expression confirmed my hypothesis. His face had drained to white as he, too, realized what was happening.

The clouds gathered the strength of the sea in their folds and marched across the surface like a conquering army. This however was just an opening sortie—a temporary, probing attack that presaged the main body that would come later. What the early rain lacked in volume and duration was compensated in fury. It was the wild terrorist, the unhinged and unpredictable squall that carried the accumulated rage of the dry months.

The storm spread right and left and loomed higher as it approached, blotting out the blue sky. Flashes of lightning grew brighter and thunder boomed louder. Dad ordered everyone to get as low as possible in the boat. Everyone complied except a Saigon man who insisted on staying on the pilot house roof. Dad cursed the man.

"You fool, get down, do you see that storm?"

"I will be fine here," the man said.

"The waves are going to be worse than any we've seen. Get down now!"

The man mulishly refused. Dad hurled a few more warnings and orders to him, and finally shrugged his shoulders and went back to the tiller as the wind began a mournful howl. I suddenly became worried about my brother Tien. I found him in the pilot house and knelt down to whisper in his ear.

"If the boat starts to sink, grab one of the empty gas cans at the back of the boat. It will keep you afloat until you are rescued."

"Are we going to sink?" he asked.

As I looked at the growing fear in his face, I realized I had said too much.

"No, we will be fine. Just remember that if something happens."

Tien nodded robotically but had a look on his face that suggested his pounding heart drowned out the sound of my voice. I patted his shoulder and went to sit with Thi Tuyen. Her face stretched in terror as she shared her deep fear which I already knew.

"Chuong, I can't swim."

I didn't have a calming rebuttal and was too scared to think of one, so I slid my arm inside hers and pulled her close.

"I won't let you go," I said.

Our tiny boat entered the mouth of the four-fold dragon. Day became night as we were consumed into the dark belly of the beast.

Dad quickly learned the little motor was useless against the storm and turned it off. We drifted inconsequentially as rain blew sideways across us. We were all drenched within seconds and the hurricane-strength winds chilled our bones. Lightning cracked the air with so much force that I was sure it had struck and opened a hole in the earth. Everyone covered their ears at the shattering sound and squeezed eyes shut against the blinding flashes.

Waves became mountains towering three times higher than the boat. Wispy white foam was blown from the top of the giants and carried on the wind like snow from a Himalayan peak. The water smashed into *Hau Giang* and threw it high over the crests. On the back sides of the waves, we dropped into dark valleys lit only by crooked fingers of lightning that streaked and disappeared overhead. The boat descended each watery slope with such speed that it seemed we would keep diving once we reached the bottom, punching a hole in the water and disappearing forever.

The loud, moaning wind was joined by the mournful prayers of the passengers, creating an unearthly sound. The ghostly wailing rose to a crescendo with the apex of each wave and then became a collective shriek as the boat fell to the bottom. The cacophony of wind and voices continued until they were interrupted by another sound. Faint, yet distinct shouting was coming from the back of the boat.

A wave had slammed into the boat and dislodged the stupid Saigon man from his perch on the pilot house roof. He bounced off the gunwale and had been thrown into the sea. Dad, Minh, and Kha sprang into action. Dad and Minh started the motor while Kha tied a rope onto the handle of an empty gas can. The little motor struggled to turn *Hau Giang* against the infinitely more powerful wind, but we managed to come alongside the splashing figure. Kha threw the can but the wind carried it too far. He pulled the can in and tried again. His second throw was on target and the man grabbed the can. Kha and Minh began to reel him in, but the man lost his grip on the slippery wet can and went under for a moment. A third throw was made and the man latched on again. Dad shouted for him to grab the rope instead of the can, but his voice could not overcome the howling storm. More men shouted the same and someone pantomimed hands grabbing the rope. The stupid man got the message and shimmied himself across the can. With a secure grip on the rope, he was pulled to safety.

Once aboard, Dad unleashed his fury on the man. His words didn't carry against the wind but the message was clear to everyone who saw his frustration. Once he finished his harangue, Dad pointed to the pilot house and the man slunk inside.

Only God knows how long the storm lasted, but to me it seemed a lifetime. Each wave, each soaking spray across the bow, and each thunderbolt used up a year's worth of emotional energy. The only positive thing I could say about it was that it moved quickly. A storm is a restless thing, eager to visit its terrors on as much of the earth as it can before its rage is spent and it dissipates back into the calmness from whence it came. Our storm tired of torturing us and moved on to the north where eager farmers would rejoice at the beginning of a monsoon that would bend trees and fill rice paddies.

Hau Giang did a heroic job of not sinking. The little delta boat was not meant for such tests, but it miraculously kept us alive. It survived with no visible damage, except several inches of rainwater pooled in the bottom. Dad resumed steering the boat and fumed at the stupid man who could've gotten us all killed. Thi Tuyen and I released our hold on each other. I could see relief on her face but she didn't smile. Nobody did. We had become just like the people on Eddie Adams' *Boat of No Smiles.*

48

May 28, 1982

We weren't supposed to be on the water more than three days by Dad's optimistic estimates. I don't know by what calculus he came to embrace this belief, but on the fourth day, land was still nowhere in sight. Neither Dad nor the pilot had any clue where we were. Two navigational aids had been brought on the journey— a compass and a pair of binoculars. The pilot supplied the compass which had an unfortunate tendency to suggest that sunrise came from the north. Dad heaped scorn on the pilot for that worthless contribution. The binoculars worked as advertised, but only magnified the endless nothing that surrounded us.

The other passengers looked and smelled like they had been on a week-long bender. I imagine I looked much the same. Hair and clothes were matted, crumpled, and dirty. Dried vomit stained some of the slack faces. The rotten stench of body odor and hot vomit hung in the air. Modesty disintegrated as exhaustion displaced delicacy. Men urinated over the side without shame. When bowels needed to be moved, the bucket was summoned and the business was completed within arm's reach of five or six people. Nobody cared. Everyone was too tired and too sick to observe traditional courtesies. Layers of civilization eroded with each day. Eventually, we would've become little more than talking animals.

Most of us began to regain our appetites as nausea waned. Dad had packed a single 50 kilo bag of rice for the journey. Because he thought it would be a short trip, Dad had not bothered to include cooking equipment. If we wanted to eat, we would have to eat the grains raw. A handful of rice was given with the water ration twice daily. Almost everyone took some that morning. Many threw it up again within a few hours.

Amidst the vomiting, praying, and singing, a gossip network sprang up. There was little else to do, so news of the passengers was passed around the boat. Most of it related to loved ones left behind. The limits of space on the boat meant families had to choose who would go and who would stay. Many parents sent two children—the second oldest and the youngest. The oldest had to stay behind to carry on the family name. I tried to imagine the heartbreaking decisions and tear-filled goodbyes those poor families had to suffer, then my thoughts turned to our own broken family and our lost Kim Tuyen. I wondered where she was. Surely she was not still looking for us in Thot Not. Surely she had gone home with Aunt Lanh and would begin building her life without the rest of us. I wondered what that life would look like as I mourned her absence. I looked over at Mom. Her face reflected the grief that had not abated since we pushed off without her daughter. I turned to my sister.

"Do you think we will see Kim Tuyen again?"

"I don't know," Thi Tuyen said. "I was just thinking about Muc."

Muc was our family dog. His name was the Vietnamese word for ink. He was as black as night and a good boy. It made me feel slightly better that at least Kim Tuyen and Muc would be reunited.

The only scandalous news in the gossip chain concerned the pilot. He had abandoned his wife and children at home and brought his mistress and her son instead. The Catholics shook their heads and tsk-tsked the rakish pilot for breaking the seventh Commandment. Buddhists raised their eyebrows and predicted the pilot would suffer for breaking Buddha's third Precept. The shared distaste for the pilot forged an ecumenical solidarity between adherents of the two religions. The pilot and his Jezebel stayed near the back of the boat and kept to themselves.

The Buddhists were a decided minority and showed a great deal of deference to the Christian majority. Rather than chant their own mantras or meditate quietly, they learned the words of the Catholic prayers and songs and joined in.

Lamb of God, who takest away the sins of the world, spare us O Lord
Lamb of God, who takest away the sins of the world, have mercy on
us

Adaptation is perhaps the greatest human strength. The Buddhists adapted to their new religious environment, just as we all were adapting to life on this alien surface. Days before, no one except Dad and the pilot had had a moment's experience on the open water, yet there we were, surviving in the harsh environment. A distinction has to be made between surviving and thriving. We were barely making it. Only by the grace of God were we not drowned in the thrashing sea. Waves sickened our stomachs and attacked our will to endure. Darkness preyed on our fear and then sunlight baked our skin in its inescapable white oven. We were weakening by the hour as our twice-daily ration of water could not keep pace with our bodies' demands. If it hadn't been so miserable, it would have been a curious sensation to be so isolated. On Kinh D, fruit, fish, nuts, rice, eggs, and water were spread across the land like buffet tables in an unending feast. Though dirt-poor, I had never known hunger or thirst. Yet there I was, confined to a bobbing prison cell in a liquid desert, withering fast with no relief in sight.

Relief winked at us with a glowing eye as the sun ebbed below the western horizon. A light, uncontrasted and invisible amongst the dominating rays of daytime, became visible when cast against the bluing backdrop of evening. It was far in the east and grew in both luminosity and allure as both sky and sea turned black. Dad turned *Hau Giang* toward the light. For the first time since I had entered the wretched boat and drank from its deep well of misery and hopelessness, I was unafraid. Hope spread through my battered body and made me forget my thirst and clawing hunger. Prayers were infused with new enthusiasm. Songs were lifted with expectation as we crawled toward the light.

49

May 29, 1982

Hau Giang moved, but its progress was excruciatingly slow. The beckoning light had a mysterious quality—glowing orange, pulsing like a star. Excited conversations dissected the possibilities.

"It's the Philippines," said one passenger.

"Maybe it's Malaysia," said another.

"No, there would be other lights on the land," said another. "It must be a small island."

It was decided the emitted energy was too strong to be a lantern.

"Maybe it's a lighthouse," the city dwellers from Saigon opined, since it was too big to be a streetlamp.

It had the visual texture of a fire, yet didn't grow or fade. It was a constant dancing ball. When all known possibilities of the light's origin had been exhausted, everyone stared in transfixed silence, entranced by mystery, bursting with insatiable curiosity.

The featureless sea played tricks with our estimation of distance. Because we saw the light, we assumed it could be reached quickly. But we were using perspectives honed on land. Here there were no trees or rivers or houses to lend visual depth, so every view was maddeningly two-dimensional.

Nighttime covered the earth with its thick, starry blanket. There was still death in the darkness. Sharks still swam below us in hungry circles. There was enough water to drown us until doomsday. However, the light had a salubrious effect on our collective psyche. We weren't forever adrift on a watery planet. There would be an end to what had seemed endless. More than that, there was *someone* out there. A human being had to create a light that consistent. We weren't alone. Something that felt like hope kindled in my chest. *If we could only get to it.*

So far. So very far away.

We didn't seem to be getting any closer. The motor was running. The propeller was spinning. I could feel the boat vibrate as it slid through the water and the wind as it blew across my hair. We were moving but got no closer to the light. I fell asleep looking at it.

I awakened as the first streaks of white lit the horizon. Our beacon was still there and had grown. We were getting closer. At the back of the boat, Dad was looking at it through his binoculars. I tiptoed around sleeping bodies to get to him. He handed me the glasses and I saw it in confusing detail.

It was a fire. Orange and yellow streaks grew pointed ends and knifed the sky. Darkness concealed the land that held the fire, but I could make out a long vertical tube from which the flames shot. I thought it was some kind of building but no land seemed to surround it. Then it hit me.

"It's a ship!" I said to Dad. "I can see the hull sticking out of the water."

"No," he said, "it's an oil rig."

"What's that?"

"It drills into the seabed, pumps out oil, and ships it back to land for processing."

"Are there people on it?" I asked.

"Yes. Men live and work on it for months at a time," he said.

"So they can rescue us?"

"We're about to find out," Dad said.

The rig became huge as we approached. Four massive trussed legs shot out of the water to a height of 15 or 20 meters. Perched on the legs was a thick platform festooned with smaller buildings and a rat's nest of twisting tubes. A tall derrick crowned the center of the platform, soaring some 40 meters above the surface of the sea. At the very top, our guiding flame erupted steadily, a serene king's eye surveying its vast watery domain.

As the sun rose, the full majesty of the structure became visible. I had never seen anything that large, and could hardly believe that such a behemoth could be man-made, much less sitting in the middle of the ocean. The other passengers began to wake up and gasped at the sight. Nervous whispers rippled across the boat. We got close enough to make out human figures standing on the platform. They wore white hard hats and gathered along the railing to look at us. Several of our passengers waved to the men, put their hands together in prayer and lifted them in desperate petition. An excited panic nearly capsized *Hau Giang* as too many of us stood up to cry out for salvation. The workers waved back, but their wave looked more like they were pushing open an invisible door. More men came to the railing and did the same. They were telling us to go away. While they waved, another group of workers carried a large hose to the railing. Six or seven men picked up the hose and the one at the front opened a valve. Water shot forcefully from the hose and peppered *Hau Giang* with angry spray. Pleading cries became screams of pain as the hard water strafed the passengers. I felt the sting of the stream as it passed back and forth.

Dad had no choice. He turned *Hau Giang* away from the rig and the spray stopped. Fury erupted as our people protested the unprovoked attack with curses and empty threats. Dad shook his fist at the workers and shouted at them.

"You have sentenced us to die, you bastards! Our deaths will be on your hands!"

We turned our eyes away from the rig as our anger subsided into sullen depression. We didn't see the rig's crane lowering a boat into the water. No one noticed the boat rapidly gaining on us until the soft whine of a motor became increasingly audible. As the rig's boat overtook the plodding *Hau Giang*, one of its sailors motioned for Dad to cut the motor. Dad complied and we drifted to a halt. The other boat came alongside but did not get within five meters of us. One of the men called out in English, which meant the workers were most likely Malaysian, since the country had once been a British colony. We were lucky to have an English-speaking teacher aboard who translated for us.

"We are sorry for spraying you. You were in danger. A wave could've pushed you against the support and snapped your boat in two.

We have supplies for you but you must not try to board us or we will shoot you. Do you understand?"

The two other men held up shotguns to prove they weren't bluffing.

Dad agreed to the terms and the boat came in close. The man who had done the talking passed bread and a few liters of water to Minh and Kha while the other two held their guns at the ready and stared at us suspiciously. When the transfer was complete, the man pointed across his portside bow and spoke once more.

"Malaysia is that way, about a day's journey from here. Good luck."

The boat turned and bounced quickly across the waves back to the rig.

Malaysia is that way. Dad turned *Hau Giang* to the south and we went that way, eating our gifted bread. It wasn't enough to make a dent in our five-day hunger, but it tasted better than anything I had ever eaten.

The sun scorched us again that afternoon and the bread expanded in our stomachs, feeling foreign and heavy. A fresh phalanx of waves rose up to batter *Hau Giang* and make us sick again. Worst of all, the water Dad brought from Thot Not was gone. The only thing we had left was the small supply the oilmen gave us and the filthy pooled water in the bottom of the boat.

"*About a day's journey,*" the man had said. I hoped he was right. Neither the boat nor its passengers had much more than a day left.

50

May 30, 1982

On the seventh day, the dawning sun oozed into view, spilling lazy splotches of color across the horizon. Waves of transparent heat blurred the orange ball as it drifted into the sky. The beautiful morning went unappreciated by the suffering passengers aboard *Hau Giang*. At that point, we wanted only one of two things from the new day—the salvation of land or eternal sleep among the fishes. Either would have been infinitely preferable to another day of living damnation in that hell of heat and thirst.

The water the oil workers had given us did not last through the end of the previous day. Dehydration which had been stalking our bodies for the previous few days attacked with undisguised fury. My head pounded as my shrinking brain pulled away from the skull's moorings. Eyes scraped against dry sockets. Lips and skin opened in painful cracks. Blood thickened into sludge, creating a crippling fatigue. I, along with everyone else, existed in a semi-conscious state, deeply tired but racked with pain that denied the deep rest we needed. Somehow, Dad, Minh, Kha, and the pilot found strength and motivation to keep the boat moving south. The sun rose to its midday peak and still no land was in sight.

Lack of potable water was the most immediate of our problems, but other variables turned against us one by one. Our boat was beginning to fail. Brave *Hau Giang* was not designed to cross the ocean, yet it served us heroically in the pitiless environment. Alas, nature was pounding it into submission with each pummeling wave. Boards loosened and creaked. The poor little motor faltered, overheating and seizing at shortening intervals. Each time the motor stalled, the crew worked feverishly to get it running again. The prospect of being adrift was a terror second only to sinking.

The ancient forces of sun, wind, and sea were so powerful they became gods to primitive man. Tamed by technology, they had been stripped of their awful power of life and death, demoted to serve as a romantic backdrop for summer dreamers. But without our protective inventions, we experienced the deities in their original majesty, as they reclaimed their lordship and exercised disinterested tyranny. We stood before their thrones, naked of our clever defenses, cut off from the artifacts of cunning. Inadequacy became our identity. Shelter, clothing, water, food, locomotion—all inadequate. The god we called science, elevated from secrets which had been untangled and harnessed over thousands of years, proved impotent against the eternal forces which wrapped the earth long before the ambitious eyes of man beheld and coveted it, and would remain long after he vanished as a result of weakness or hubris.

In creation, light came first, the genesis and sustainer of all living things. Balm for our first fear. With the light came caressing warmth. But in God's wisdom, He made the line between enough and too much painfully thin. In undiluted form, the sun's rays cook skin. Delicious warmth can turn murderously hot, pulling the water out of a living body one bead of sweat at a time.

Breezes fill our lungs and give us a voice to sing and pray. They cool and comfort us on a hot afternoon. Yet, these same winds can become immoderate, spinning into typhoons and tornadoes which rip and shred whole towns, or blowing straight and hard, pushing over flimsy boats which have been foolishly chosen and overloaded.

And the sea, the upside-down world where life thrives below yet perishes in lonely isolation on top, remains an incomprehensible and terrifying mystery. Life's first home is a bountiful provider to land-dwelling creatures, but it remains undiminished in its godlike countenance—foreign, aloof, and infinite. It could have ended our journey with a rogue wave, a thunderstorm, or even the slow stress of constant battering eventually breaching the hull. That we should enter endless heaven by first passing through endless water seemed poetic; born from water to die in water.

Stripped of pride, humbled by raw power, and subjugated by deities of antiquity, I relinquished my weak grip on hope and let it fall into the oil-streaked slurry of water and filth at the bottom of the boat. I was sure I would die in the next few hours along with most of my family. I had spent so many hours over the past few days pitying Kim Tuyen, now it seemed she would end up being the lucky one. Thi Tuyen and I were too tired and wracked with pain to speak to each other. The prayers and songs dwindled to silence. One voice remained.

Mom prayed the Hail Mary as the sun descended behind the stilling sea. Her voice was calm. She changed a word in the last line which usually said "...pray for us sinners, now *and* at the hour of our death."

This time she left out the 'and' to reflect the fact that we were almost out of time.

"Holy Mary, Mother of God, pray for us sinners, now *at* the hour of our death."

The last night fell upon us. We sat quietly and waited for the end.

51

May 31, 1982

Stars glittered their lonely lights across a billion kilometers of black space, too weak to illuminate anything but an appreciation of stark, sad beauty. Waves lapped softly against the sides of *Hau Giang* as its motor hummed through the planks. It was a lovely night, incongruous with the suffering we were experiencing.

The pain of dehydration was compounded by our close quarters. Packed like sardines, we began to feel the effects of confinement as sharp points of bone crushed strained skin against the wooden floor. Exhaustion and pain fought for control of my consciousness. I slept in short snatches when the pain was momentarily overwhelmed, but not even sleep provided a temporary escape from the mental torture. I dreamed of sharks, and sinking boats, and swimming in black water. Panic often jolted me awake.

I glanced at Thi Tuyen sitting beside me. Her eyes were closed and her breathing labored. She was my mother's child—calm, spiritual, nurturing. She had spent her childhood training to serve as a wife and mother; a calling which I was now sure she would be denied. Nor would she get a chance to learn to swim.

My brothers Tien and Tam were snuggled on either side of Mom. Their resting faces looked serene in the flickering lamp light. I wondered if Tien would manage to find a gas can when *Hau Giang* took its plunge. I wondered if it would matter if he did. Maybe it would only be delaying the inevitable.

Mom's lips moved in prayer and her fingers shuffled instinctively among the beads. I guessed that she was thinking about Kim Tuyen as she prayed. Her faith astounded me. She had lost so much and was about to lose everything, yet she persisted in her petitions. Surely God wouldn't forsake one as faithful as this. Surely Mother Mary would recognize another mother's suffering and be moved to intercede. Her fortitude shamed me and I resolved not to despair as long as she prayed.

Dad, the stoic captain, remained at the helm and steered. This disaster was his idea, but I could not bring myself to fault him. In desperation he acted. For most of his life he had been resisting the inhumanity of communism and it kept catching up to him. Ho Chi Minh had finally won and Vietnam had been lost. In one final gamble, Dad had played all the cards he had left to create a new destiny for his family; a destiny free of famine, confiscation, war, corruption, persecution, and poverty. His fatal flaw had been underestimating the size and strength of the South China Sea, but who in his position could have done any better? Who, but a seasoned mariner, could even begin to comprehend the immensity of the deity that carried forever in its blue breast?

Though we were on the precipice of tragedy, with the bow peeking over the edge, Dad had not failed yet. Though he regretted undertaking the journey and lamented his ignorance, he vowed to persist until the motor could not be restarted, until he lacked the strength to hold the tiller, or until *Hau Giang* took a deep dive in a valley between waves.

A new star came out a few hours before dawn. It sat low in the sky as if it had just been born from the watery womb of the sea. It had a peculiar twinkle that was interrupted for unusually long milliseconds, as if some obstructive meteor weaved in and out of the light's long path. I noticed the star as I was jarred from a fitful sleep by an outsized wave. Waves began to slap louder and more frequently and the boat pitched in response. I sat up and craned my neck to look around. The low star was eye-catchingly big. I looked to see if Dad noticed it. He and the pilot were both pointing at it and talking in hushed voices I couldn't hear.

"Another!" the pilot exclaimed loudly.

The shout was enough to stir many of the passengers from their stillness. I looked at the star and sure enough, a second appeared beside it. It had the same texture and size as the first. I figured we had crossed the equator and were seeing southern hemisphere stars, but Dad's conversation with the pilot took on more urgency and volume. The waves slammed bigger and harder and reminded me of the day we left land behind.

Land!

I jerked my head back around to look at the stars. More appeared as I stared. Five, six, seven—and all in a horizontal row. They weren't stars, they were lanterns.

"Land!" I shouted.

The word spread like wildfire across the ears of the semi-conscious passengers. Everyone bolted upright and looked. The speeding sun lit the eastern sky. Refracted rays bounced across the sea and illuminated a black strip that divided water and sky. The black divider contained all the new stars which were multiplying by the second.

Land. No sweeter word existed. Extinguished hope flamed anew from buried embers presumed gray and cold. Dying bodies manufactured new strength. Everyone looked longingly at the now illuminated coastline. It beckoned us to come and stand on solid ground again. Prayers and songs were enthusiastically lifted with tones that were more expectant than panicked.

We might yet live.

We still had a long way to go and our success was far from assured. Waves rose chaotically in the shallower water. *Hau Giang* was thrown harder against the surface than she had been when we exited the Mekong Delta. Prayers became pleading wails. The cacophony of voices sounded like a riot. We were at the end of our ropes. This was it. It was time to reach land or be dashed to pieces and sunk. We prayed for salvation, but the prayers had a desperate edge, as if we were saying, "Save us or destroy us, Lord, but do *something* with us."

The motor died again. The crew rushed to restart it. A big wave knocked Minh backwards into the steaming engine and he cried out in agony. His calf was burned badly. Mom dropped her rosary and leapt to his aid. She poured cool seawater on the wound and bandaged it with a ripped shirt.

The land in front of us grew bigger, but slowly. Morning passed into afternoon. The sun stabbed at us with pitchfork rays, and the sea seemed to grab the boat like two hands wringing a dishcloth. Nausea returned to churn our stomachs, but no one was deterred from focusing on the goal ahead.

Hau Giang's motor quit over and over. It, too, was almost dead, but it was resuscitated each time to push us a little closer. When we came within a few hundred meters, I was convinced I could swim the rest of the way if I had to, but how would I get Thi Tuyen to shore? The thought of her drowning and me surviving was unbearable. My brothers could swim, but maybe not that far. I wasn't sure about Mom. Dad could do everything else, so I was sure he could swim too. I locked my sister into focus. If we went into the water, I would get her to shore somehow.

The motor stopped for the last time just as waves formed themselves into a marching line of breakers. *Hau Giang* was carried a few meters at a time. Unfortunately, without a motor we had no steering. Each wave twisted the boat a little to the left until it was parallel to the beach. Curling white water crashed over the boat and lifted it onto its side. People spilled into the surf, including me and Thi Tuyen. Water filled *Hau Giang* and pinned it to the sand. The surf thundered around us. Thi Tuyen and I stood up in waist-deep water and began to slosh toward the shore. Then I heard Dad call to me.

"Chuong, help these people get off the boat."

I looked back. Nearly a dozen people were clinging to any part of the boat that was above water. Some had been injured in the crash and needed assistance. I went back and helped the injured to shore and returned to coax the ones who were petrified. Within minutes, everyone had gotten off the boat and onto the beach. Dad did a headcount to make sure no one had been swept away by a current. All 59 were present and very much alive. Wailing prayers of thanksgiving erupted.

We hugged each other and cried joyful tears, but our ordeal was not quite over.

Two dozen men armed with bamboo poles and solid wooden clubs formed a mob and stomped down the beach. Someone must have seen our approach and warned the locals. When we realized they were coming for us, the celebration ended abruptly.

"What are they going to do to us?" Thi Tuyen whispered to me.

"I don't know. Why do they look so threatening?" I said.

Dad already knew the answer to that question. Years earlier, Malaysian Prime Minister Mahathir Mohamad had declared they had reached their limit of hospitality toward refugees from Vietnam and threatened to push boats back to sea if they tried to land on Malaysian soil. As the mob moved closer to us, Dad took Minh and Kha aside.

"Go back to the boat. Get hammers, pry bars, anything you can find. Smash holes in the bottom of the boat."

The two looked puzzled. Dad preemptively cut off their questions.

"No time to explain, just go. Make sure that boat never floats again."

The two splashed out to *Hau Giang* and began maiming it. As the mob arrived, Dad instructed us to sit facing the men with our hands visible. We did as we were told. The men spread out and blocked any path of escape. Their leader spoke to Dad in a language none of us understood. Dad shrugged his shoulders and said "I don't understand" in Vietnamese. The man turned to his associates to see if anyone spoke our language. None did.

Something of a standoff ensued as neither party could understand the other. Minh and Kha finished their demolition and rejoined the group, making an exaggerated show of throwing away their tools so the mob did not think they were secreting weapons into our ranks.

Finally, an official-looking man strode across the beach with two assistants. He spoke first to the mob's leader and then addressed our group in French.

"Parlez-vous Francais?"

Luckily, our teacher who spoke English also spoke passable French.

"Are you Vietnamese refugees?" he asked.

The teacher said yes.

"Are you seeking asylum?"

Again he nodded. The official looked beyond us to the boat. Each crashing wave spit water through the holes made by Minh and Kha.

"Well, it looks like you won't be doing any more sailing today, so welcome to Malaysia."

He smiled. We couldn't understand what he was saying, so nobody smiled back. We just looked at him blankly. The teacher translated for us. Dad smiled back and replied in our language.

"*Cam on ong.*"

"Thank you."

Epilogue

Our adventure didn't end on the beach that day. It was only the beginning. We were treated for dehydration at a field hospital and sent to the infamous refugee camp at Pulau Bidong a week later. The hardship we endured there for three months—overcrowding, inadequate shelter, unsanitary conditions, and perpetual dampness from the constant rain—would have horrified the average person, but I never went hungry, never went thirsty, and was never seasick or scared for my life. It was at Pulau Bidong, baptized in my final monsoon, where I had an epiphany that has guided me all my life. Everything would be measured against the eight days I spent on the South China Sea. Any situation I found myself in which was less dangerous, terrifying, or miserable would be respected and appreciated for its relative ease.

After three months, we were moved to another refugee camp on the mainland for another few months, and then a final camp in the Philippines while we waited to be assigned a host country. The people who sailed with us on *Hau Giang* were sent to countries throughout the world like Germany, Australia, Canada, and France. We, on the other hand, would be assigned to the United States. Doat's presence in

Virginia, plus Dad's service in the ARVN, put us on the inside track to be sent to America. The Catholic Church in Doat's new hometown, Martinsville, sponsored us and all that was left to do was wait. I took as many English lessons as I could.

Less than a week after we arrived in Virginia, Dad was working as a janitor at a Bassett-Walker textile factory. The choir director from Luong Dien wouldn't take government assistance even though he qualified for it. He said he would rather scrub floors than take a check he didn't earn. It wasn't long before the bosses at the factory noticed the talents and work ethic of the little Vietnamese man who didn't speak a word of English and promoted him. He retired from the factory after working many years as a mechanic. Today, he is nearly 90 years old and lives with his second wife back in Vietnam, not far from our old farm on Kinh D. He is my everlasting hero.

Mom, the unassuming buffalo caretaker who lived through famine, survived 30 years of war, twice became a refugee, owned a business, toiled on a rice farm, and emigrated to a new country all while having children and raising them, finally found peace and quiet in a manufacturing town half a world from the rice paddy, the *non la*, and the monsoon. She remained a prayerful, devoted Catholic until her death in 2014.

The children of Dinh and Dung did pretty well. Doat, Tien, and Tam all became computer programmers. Doat is also an electrical engineer. Tien and Tam own small businesses. Thi Tuyen fulfilled her calling to become a mother and also worked to put her husband through college.

Kim Tuyen's bus broke down that day we left Vietnam, delaying her for several hours. She was stranded in the country for 10 long years. I have often thought about that day and how things would've turned out had her group been on time. Instead of 59 people aboard, we would've had 64. The water would have run out faster, the boat would have moved slower, the motor would have died sooner, and the extra weight might have been just enough to sink us under one of those waves. As horrific as it was to be left behind, Kim Tuyen's inadvertent sacrifice may have been the thing that saved us all. The day she joined us in America was one of the happiest days of my life. Kim Tuyen has made up for lost time. She owns her own business and her own home. In fact, all of my siblings own their homes outright. In less than one generation, they have all achieved the American Dream.

A little over a year after we settled in Martinsville, I was accepted at Virginia Tech. When I stepped on the campus at Blacksburg, it was the first time I had ever been by myself. Though there was no physical pain or raw fear like there was on *Hau Giang*, the loneliness and difficulty adjusting to a new culture produced its own brand of suffering. I battled depression for years. I missed my simple farm life, but there was no going back. I had to become an American. Thankfully America gives the opportunity to do just that to anyone who is willing to put in the work. Work was something I knew I could do.

I put in the work. Hours and days and months of it. My life on a rice farm prepared my body, and, in a roundabout way, my mind for the rigors I endured. When I wasn't in class, I worked any job I could find. When I wasn't working, I studied. Sleeping and eating were crammed into the margins.

Like my siblings, I, too, made it. I graduated from Virginia Tech with degrees in computer science and mathematics. When I was in school,

STRANGERS ON THE WATER

it was my dream to work for either IBM or NASA. Over the years, I have worked for both, and both turned out to be the privilege and honor I imagined them to be. I have travelled the world, and even returned to visit Vietnam. I found the love of my life in my life partner, Luke. We have been together 27 years and look forward to many more.

I'm very American now, but buried deep within me the Vietnamese farm boy persists. His history, fears, joys, and hopes inform everything I do. His voice still resonates in my thick accent. It reminds me with every word I utter where I came from and who I am. I have taken the American name, John, but I will always be Chuong.

Each May, I grow nostalgic for Chuong. I remember the mischievous altar boy who swam the canals. I remember being a rice farmer, face to the earth and back to the sky. I remember crawling under the coconuts of *Hau Giang* and enduring that terrifying trip. And I remember May 19, 1983, a day that arrived nearly a year after we boarded the boat in Thot Not. That was the day we boarded a Pan-Am 747 bound for America and a new life. I remember sitting in the very last row of the jet, looking out the rain streaked window and feeling wistful about the season that was at hand.

The monsoon was coming.

The End

Made in United States
North Haven, CT
21 October 2021